Modem Handbook for the Communications Professional

Cass Lewart
Project Engineer
Unisys Corporation

Elsevier Science Publishing Co., Inc.
Intertext Publications, Inc.

For Ruth

Library of Congress Catalog Card Number 87-61306

10 9 8 7 6 5 4 3 2 1

ISBN 0-444-01279-6

Intertext Publications
Multiscience Press, Inc.
One Lincoln Plaza
New York, NY 10023

Elsevier Science Publishing Co., Inc.
52 Vanderbilt Avenue
New York, NY 10017

Figures 1.5, 2.2, 2.3, 13.4, 13.5 were reprinted by permission of Codex Corporation.
Figures 1.6, 4.1, 14.11, 15.1, 15.5, 15.6 and Tables 2.1, 6.2, 6.3 were reprinted by permission of Hewlett-Packard Co.
Figures 4.11, 10.1 through 10.12 were reprinted by permission of Rockwell International Corporation.
Table 6.4 was reprinted by permission of Black Box, Inc.
Figures 7.1, 7.2 were reprinted by permission of Novation, Inc.
Table 11.7 was reprinted by permission of Universal Data Systems, Inc.
Figures 12.2, 12.3, 12.4, 12.6 were reprinted by permission of Sygnetics Corporation.
Figure 12.7 was reprinted by permission of Adaptive Networks, Inc.
Figures 13.1, 13.2, 13.4 were reprinted by permission of Fairchild Data Corporation.
The "Voice Grade DDD Modems" table was reprinted by permission of *Mini-Micro Systems*.

Contents

Preface vii

Introduction 1

Part One: Modems and Data Communications 5

1. Introduction to Data Communications 7
- Data Communications Terms 7
- Transmission of Digital Information 12
- Public Telephone Network 15
- OSI Model of the Data Network 20

2. Private Lines and Equalization 27
- Voice-Band Transmission Facilities 29
- Switched Wideband Digital Service 33
- Line Equalization 35
- Variation Between Calls on the Switched Network 36
- Signaling and Battery Options 40
- Eye Patterns 41

3. Transmission Bandwidth: Bits, Bytes, and Baud 45
- Maximum Transmission Speed of a Voice-Band Channel 45
- Relations Between Various Measures of Transmission Speed 48

4. Modulation Techniques 51
- AM Modulation 52
- Frequency Modulation 53
- Constellation Diagrams 54
- Differential Phase Modulation 57
- Combined Phase/Amplitude Modulation (QAM) 58

Trellis Modulation 59
Modulation Method Versus Susceptibility
Impairments 62
Bit Error Rate 63

5. Asynchronous and Synchronous Transmission 67
Synchronous Transmission Protocols 70
Hardware Considerations 72

6. The Serial Interface 75
RS-232-C Serial Interface 76
Computer-to-Computer Communication via Null Modem 82
Connecting a Serial Port to a Modem 85
Non RS-232-C Serial Interfaces 87
Interface Converters 90

Part Two: Modems for the Personal Computer User 95

7. Modems for Personal Computers 97
Modem Standards for Personal Computers 98
Built-In and External Modems 99
Initial Settings 105
Modem Incompatibilities 106
Optional Modem Features 108
Information Services 115
FCC and Telephone Company Requirements 116

8. Hayes Modem Standards 119
AT Command Structure 120
S-Registers 124
Modes of Operation 128
Weakness of the Current Standard and Possible
Improvements 131

9. Communications Software 133
Basic Software Features 134
Terminal Emulation 135
Menu-Driven Versus Command-Driven Programs 135
Basic Communications Package Commands 137

Command and Scirpt Files 139
A Session with a Commercial Bulletin Board 141
Electonic Mail 144
Error Checking 147
Data Compression 152
Effective Speed of File Transfer 152

10. Modem on a Chip 155
Individual Modem Building Blocks 159
Complete Modem 168

Part Three: Modems for the Commercial Market 173

11. Commercial Voice-Band Modems 175
Features and Protocols 176
Birth of a Standard 177
Transmission Speed Versus Cost of Operation 178
Bell and CCITT Modem Standards 181
Setting of Modem Options 191
Software for Commercial Modems 194
Examples of Voice-Band Commercial Modems 194
Low-Speed Modems 195
Medium-Speed Modems 197
High-Speed Modems 200
Proprietary High-Speed Modems 202
Facsimile Modems 203

12. Limited Distance Modems 207
Limited Distance Modems Using AC Power Lines 214

13. Specialized Modem Applications 217
Wideband Modems 217
Acoustic Modems 220
Security Modems 223
Multiplexing Modems 224

Part Four: Diagnostics and Testing 229

14. Testing Modems and Interfaces 231
Indicator Lights 233
Self-Test Features 236
Modem Noise Sensitivity Testing 243
Tests of the RS-232-C Interface Signals 244

15. Transmission Facility Testing 251
Attenuation Distortion Measurements 252
Delay Distortion Measurements 254
Noise Measurements 256
Phase Jitter Measurements 258
Specialized Data Transmission Impairment Tester 258
Transmission Impairment Measuring Sets 259
Bit Error Rate Test Sets 260

Conclusion: What the Future Will Bring 263

Appendices *265*

Glossary 267

Directory of Manufacturers 277

List of CCITT V. Recommendations 285

Standards Organizations 291

ASCII Codes 293

Voice Grade DDD Modems 295

Bibliography 301

Index 305

Preface

As an electrical engineer active for over 30 years in the telecommunications field I have always found data transmission, and specifically modems, to be a fascinating subject. There is more to a modem than just a name for a device that lets one computer talk to another computer over a telephone line. Modem technology combines various disciplines of electrical engineering and computer software such as circuit design, Large Scale Integration, use of microprocessors, switching, data transmission, and programming. My interest in this field and conversations with my coworkers and publisher convinced me of the need for a book dealing with modems as related to data communications.

The need for books describing data communications in practical rather than in abstract terms has been generated largely by the deregulation of the telephone industry in the United States. Deregulation gave the telecommunication manager more challenges, opportunities, and choices than ever before. Selection of a modem, this most important component of a data communications network, used to involve just a quick check for agreement with the applicable standards. In fact, the selection was frequently suggested and performed by a representative of the common carrier, the local telephone company. Now the decision has to be made based on the desirability of options, "smartness" of the modem, software availability, and other criteria determined by specific applications.

Without a thorough understanding of the various available modem features, their relative importance, and how they interact with each other, costly mistakes can easily be made. Sometimes a standard solution, connecting two computers equipped with modems via a telephone line, may be the least desirable. Use of less common modem types, such as short-haul modems, can result in substantial savings.

I wrote this book primarily for the communications professional (manager, supervisor, member of technical staff), who has been working in the field for several years dealing with common carriers and with equipment suppliers. I assume that this person would like to get a better understanding of various elements of the data communications networks which he or she designs in order to make cost-effective specification and planning decisions in modem acquisition.

The book is also written for the electrical engineer, not necessarily active in the data communications field, who would like to expand his or her knowledge of the latest developments in modem technology, relating to both hardware and software.

Finally, the book is written for the personal computer user who would like to select a proper modem to communicate with other computers and to learn about the available options and choices.

At this point I would like to acknowledge help from a number of individuals who helped me in understanding certain arcane areas of data communications and of modem design. I would like to thank in particular Dr. Adam Lender, the scientific consultant to the Lockheed Corporation, Mitch Baker, the field applications engineer at Rockwell International, and Jack Douglas, senior manager of technical services at the Universal Data Corporation. I would also like to thank the Hewlett-Packard Company for letting me use some of their data communications training material. Final thanks go to my wife Ruth for coming up with many new ideas for the book and to my son Dan for general and technical editing.

If the reader, after finishing the last chapter, improves his or her understanding of the data communications field in general and of modem technology in particular, then the purpose of this book will be fulfilled.

Cass Lewart
Holmdel, N.J.

Introduction

WHAT IS A MODEM?

The need for exchange of digital information between computers over analog transmission facilities, in particular over the telephone network, led to the development of modems. A modem performs the digital-to-analog (D/A) conversion between the computer and the analog transmission facility and it also performs the analog-to-digital (A/D) conversion between the analog transmission facility and the computer. The D/A conversion is performed by modulating the digital information on a ''carrier'' signal; the A/D conversion is performed by demodulating or extracting the digital information from analog signals carried on the analog transmission facility. The combination of the two words modulator and demodulator formed the word ''modem.'' Modems are always in pairs and perform both a transmitting and a receiving function. The user has to ascertain that the receiving and the transmitting modems use the same protocols, procedures describing the data formats, modulation schemes, etc., in order to carry information.

The rest of this book will explain in considerable depth choices and options of today's modem market, which is currently booming thanks to technological advances and competition caused by the deregulation of the United States telephone industry. The next paragraphs will describe the effects of this deregulation on the communication industry in general and on modems in particular. The following chapters will then give a review of data communications with emphasis on modems, which will be followed by a closer look at personal computer and commercial modem markets. The final chapters will go into testing and diagnostics of modems, transmission facilities, and other parts of the data channel. In conclusion we will look into the data communications crystal ball to see what developments are to be expected in the next few years.

DEREGULATION OF THE U.S. TELEPHONE INDUSTRY

Prior to 1975, common carriers, AT&T and independent telephone companies in the United States and government-operated Post, Telegraph and Telephone organizations (PTTs) in most other countries owned and maintained all communication equipment attached to the public telephone network. The rationale for it was protection of the fragile telephone network and its users from interfering "foreign" equipment. To show the need for such protection, one can consider a frequency multiplexed carrier system, which in its first stage "stacks" twelve voice channels into a so-called channel bank. The assumptions used in the design and operation of a carrier system are that frequency adjacent channels will not interfere with each other, as long as their bandwidth and power are limited. Due to nonlinearity of modulators and demodulators, a signal more powerful than average could easily generate modulation products falling into other channels, resulting in crosstalk and distortion in the unprotected system.

Before the deregulation of the U.S. telephone industry all common carrier and PTT equipment was thoroughly tested, before being put into service, thus assuring proper operation of the network. Because the equipment was leased, rather than sold, and the cost of maintenance was included in the monthly lease, the equipment was conservatively designed, and was thus highly reliable and expensive. A typical charge for a low-speed modem leased from a telephone company was around $50 per month.

The path to proliferation of communication equipment was opened in the United States with the famous 1968 Carterphone decision. The Federal Communication Commission decided then that the communication user has the right to own and maintain equipment, as long as it does not interfere with the public network. The first approach of the Common Carriers to assure that no interference would be caused by such equipment was to lease to the end users, for a fee of around $7 per month, the so-called Data Access Arrangement devices (DAA). The DAA was an amplitude and frequency limiter to protect the telephone network. The economical problem DAA created was that the monthly fee for users with private modems and other attached devices, such as answering machines and memory dialers, was not required on equipment leased from Common Carriers. The Common Carriers claimed that their equipment had been thoroughly tested and would not require the protection provided by the FCC. This created a considerable advantage to Common Carriers and was strongly opposed by equipment manufacturers selling to the private market.

The next step in the deregulation process was the decision by the FCC to let the equipment vendors build the protective circuitry into their equipment and not require a separate DAA box to be supplied by the common carriers. This decision was made effective in June 1977 after several appeals by AT&T and by the communication equipment manufacturers. From then on only "type" certification of the equipment would be required, in addition to individual registration of the equipment by the user with the local telephone company. These two measures are supposed to protect the public telephone network. The policy is apparently working well as the privately owned communication equipment has been operating now for several years in the public telephone network environment without any ill effects.

The subsequent breakup of the Bell System in the early 1980s and the competition of Far East equipment makers lowered modem prices and introduced a large variety of equipment available to the data communications user. Large Scale Integration (LSI) made manufacturing of high volume items, such as modems, more of an assembly than an engineering and development enterprise. This is particularly true for 300 bits per second (bps), 1200 bps, and 2400 bps modems, where a handful of chip makers, like Fairchild, Rockwell, and RCA, make modem chips used by dozens of manufacturers. Changing a mask during the chip fabrication or changing a few strap settings can give an individuality to a particular modem to differentiate it from similar products.

Part One
Modems and Data Communications

While reading the first part of this book the reader should become familiar with the basics of data communications. By doing this the terms and concepts found in the remainder of the book, even for a person not familiar with the subject, should start making some sense. If the reader has worked for a while in the data communications field, then I would suggest just paging through the first part of this book and treating it as a refresher course in data communications.

In the first chapter I explain the principal terms of data communications, and describe the basic transmission parameters, such as attenuation and delay distortion. I also explain how these parameters affect the transmitted data signal as it is being carried over the Public Telephone Network. A discussion of the Public Telephone Network, the backbone of most voice and data communications and of the OSI model of the data network, concludes the first chapter. In Chapter 2, I describe leased and private lines used to a large extent for commercial data transmission. Chapter 3 deals with transmission speed and bandwidth as related to the transmission facility. Then comes the fourth chapter, in which the reader will find out about the modulation methods used by modems at various transmission speeds and about assorted modem standards. Chapters 5 and 6 cover the asynchronous and synchronous transmission and various ways in which a modem can be interfaced to a computer.

1. INTRODUCTION TO DATA COMMUNICATIONS

This chapter will provide a short overview of the relevant aspects of data transmission, and of some of the terms used in the rest of this book, which will be required for a better understanding of applications and technology of modems. We will start with short definitions of a few important data transmission terms, which will be explained in more detail in the following chapters. This will be then followed with a description of the Public Telephone Network and the Open System Interconnect (OSI) model of the data network.

DATA COMMUNICATIONS TERMS

Voice Band

The French physicist Fourier was the first to recognize that even the most complex time-varying analog signals can be decomposed into separate frequency components, each one a simple sinusoid of a different frequency. Though the human ear recognizes sound frequencies between 50 and 20,000

Hz, most intelligible speech is concentrated between approximately 300 and 3000 Hz. To satisfy a voice subscriber, a standard telephone channel therefore has a bandwidth, the range of frequencies which it can accommodate, of approximately 300 to 3200 Hz. Such a channel is usually referred to as the voice-band channel, because it can pass a range of the most important frequencies associated with the human voice.

Transmission Medium

An electrical transmission medium, which can carry analog or digital information, can be anything from a pair of wires to a satellite link. In general we will not concern ourselves with the physical aspects of a transmission medium, but rather with its transmission parameters, like bandwidth, circuit loss, and various forms of electrical distortion associated with transmission of information.

Two- and Four-Wire Transmission

The local telephone loop, the pair of wires connecting the local telephone subscriber to the local telephone office, consists of two copper wires. Because both directions of transmission using the loop share the same physical medium, they may interfere with each other. The two-wire transmission is adequate for voice and certain types of data on short connections. However, four-wire transmission, where each direction of transmission is carried on a separate pair of wires, is frequently required for high-speed data transmission. Four-wire transmission is also used by the telephone company for their long distance transmission between toll offices. An analogy would be a divided highway versus a country road. An example of two-wire and of four-wire telephone connection is shown in Figures 1.1 and 1.2.

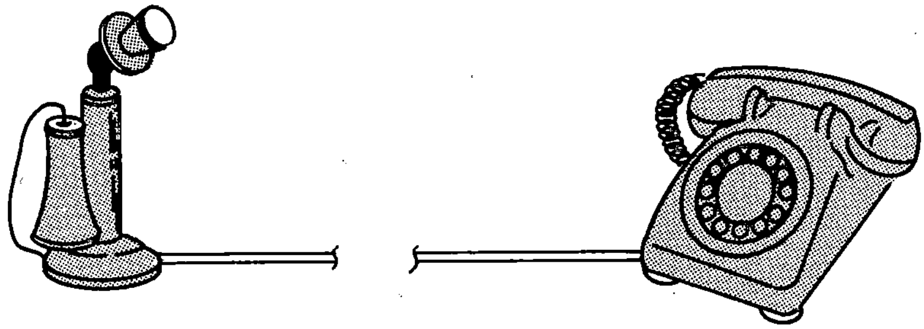

Figure 1-1 **Two-Wire Telephone Connection**

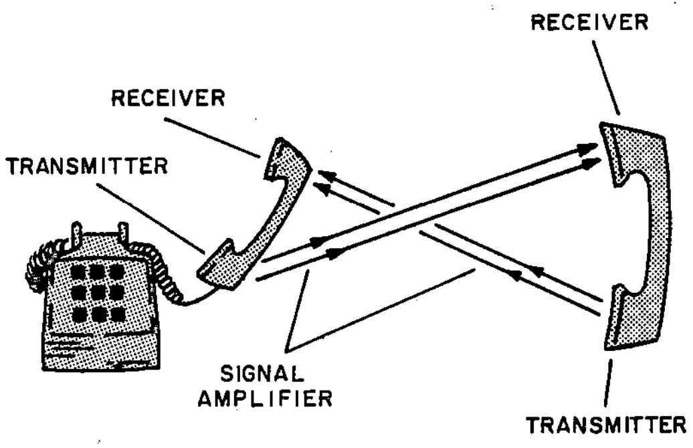

Figure 1.2 **Four-Wire Telephone Connection**

Asynchronous and Synchronous Operation

When transmitting data, there is always a need for synchronization between the transmitting and the receiving modem. As each character consists of several bits, typically 7 or 8, the receiving modem and its associated computer or data terminal have to know exactly where each character begins and where it terminates. This knowledge is extracted in a slightly different way in the asynchronous and in the synchronous operation methods.

The asynchronous method is used mostly for personal modem communication, where individual bits in a character are not synchronized with each other, but each character starts its own synchronization process. The asynchronous transmission is a succession of a start bit, 7 or 8 data bits corresponding to the American Standard Code for Information Interchange (ASCII) representation of each character, 1 or 2 stop bits and a parity bit used for error detection, all depending on the agreed upon protocol. ASCII equivalents of characters and symbols are shown in the Appendix.

The synchronous operation method, in which a continuous stream of data bits is being transmitted, is used mostly for commercial data exchange. Synchronization is performed for larger blocks of data, rather than for each character.

Transmission Impairments

An analog signal traveling through an analog transmission medium, such as a telephone line, is affected by a number of distortion parameters associated with the type of medium, the length of the transmission line, and the environment. The major parameters affecting data transmission are attenuation, delay distortion, phase jitter, and electrical noise. Attenuation distortion is the variation in gain or loss of a transmission medium as a function of frequency. The delay distortion is the difference in velocity, at which various frequency components of a signal travel along a transmission line. Phase jitter is a fast change in phase of the received signal as compared to the transmitted signal. Finally, electrical noise is a collection of random pulses and of periodic power line interference, superimposed on the signal. Each of these parameters, and even more, their combination, may make the signal at its destination unrecognizable to the receiver — a binary "0" may be interpreted as a "1" or vice versa. An example of a data signal distorted after

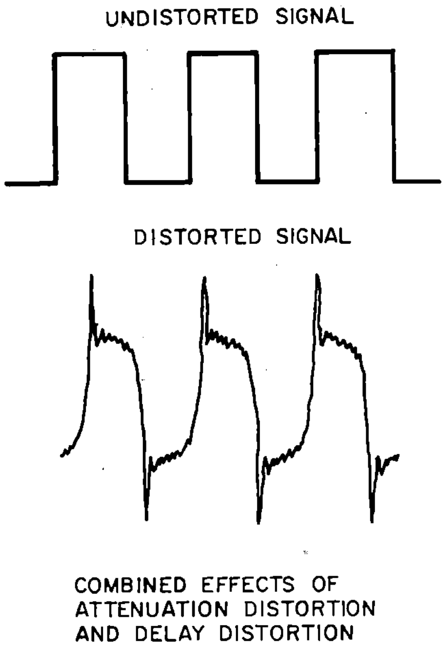

Figure 1.3 **Effects of Transmission Distortion on Data Signals**

passing over a transmission facility is shown in Figure 1.3. Notice that the effect of delay distortion is often more severe than that of the amplitude or attenuation distortion. The purpose of a modem is to translate the binary digital signals into analog electrical or light signals in a form least affected by the distortion introduced by the transmission medium. As we will see in the following chapters the modem, when properly selected, will satisfy these requirements, while being transparent to the data user.

Full-Duplex, Half-Duplex, and Simplex Operation

A modem can operate in a two-way connection, where data can be passed in both directions simultaneously, which is called full-duplex, it can operate in a half-duplex mode, where only one direction of transmission is active at a

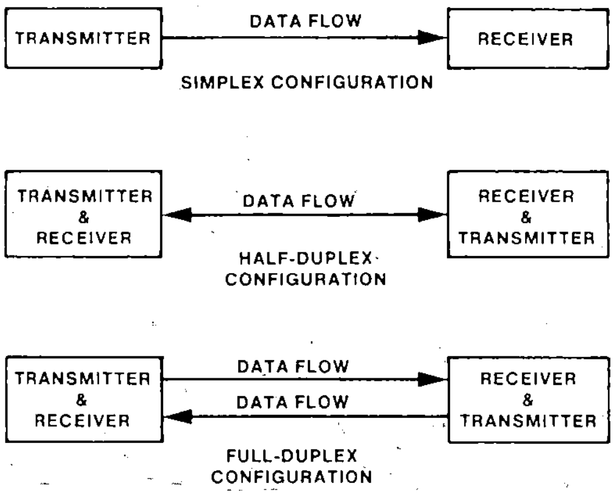

Figure 1.4 **Simplex, Half, and Full-Duplex Transmission**

time, or it can operate in one direction only, in the simplex mode. The three modes of operation are shown in Figure 1.4. All personal computer modems and many commercial modems use the full-duplex mode of operation. However, there are a number of commercial half-duplex modems which trade the full-duplex operation for higher transmission speed. Various schemes are then used to reverse the direction of transmission, when required. There may be a separate low-speed "attention" reverse channel, a separate circuit to activate transmission reversal, or the modem may reverse the direction of transmission automatically upon detection of carrier loss. The simplex mode is less common; it may be used for polling of sensors.

After explaining these basic terms of data transmission, we can start describing how data is actually sent from the transmitting to the receiving modem.

TRANSMISSION OF DIGITAL INFORMATION

To transmit digital information, the binary stream of 0's and 1's generated by a computer or a data terminal, one needs a transmitter, a transmission medium, and a receiver, as shown in Figure 1.5. Both the transmitter and the receiver are part of the modem. The function of a transmitter is to convert the digital signals into analog voltage, current, or light levels appropriate to the transmission medium; the function of the receiver is to convert the analog signals back into a digital form acceptable to the computer or to the data terminal. Depending on the properties of the transmission medium, for example, a pair of copper wires, a telephone line, or optic fibers, a different type of conversion will be appropriate.

A generalized form of a combined transmitter and receiver for two-way communication is called a Modem, short for MOdulator (transmitter) and DEModulator (receiver). The term Modulator has long been associated in carrier telephony with a device converting the low frequency voice signals into higher frequencies suitable for long haul transmission and for "stacking" of multiple voice frequency channels. The voice channels are "stacked" into groups of 12 channels, supergroups of 60 channels, etc., in the Frequency Division Multiplex (FDM) scheme used by the telephone companies. Frequency assignments used in the FDM scheme at the group level are shown in Figure 1.6. Notice the many filters, modulators, and demodulators involved in the frequency translation, each introducing attenuation and delay distortion to the voice or data signal. Similarly, in data transmission, a modem converts a digital string of 0's and 1's into an analog form by modulating frequencies suitable for the transmission medium. For example, a Bell 103A type modem would convert a binary 0 into a frequency of 1070 Hz or 2025 Hz and a binary 1 into 1270 Hz or 2225 Hz, depending on whether the modem is in the Originating or in the Answer mode. These four frequencies are all well within the passband frequency spectrum of a telephone line (300 — 3200 Hz).

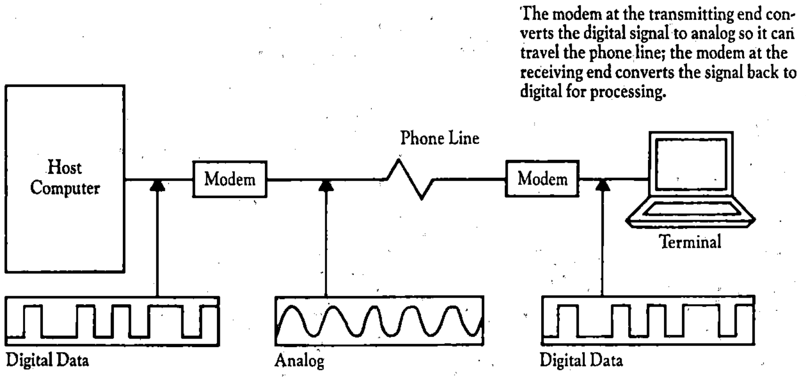
The modem at the transmitting end converts the digital signal to analog so it can travel the phone line; the modem at the receiving end converts the signal back to digital for processing.
Host Computer
Modem
Phone Line
Modem
Terminal
Digital Data
Analog
Digital Data

Figure 1.5 **Digital Transmission over Analog Transmission Lines**

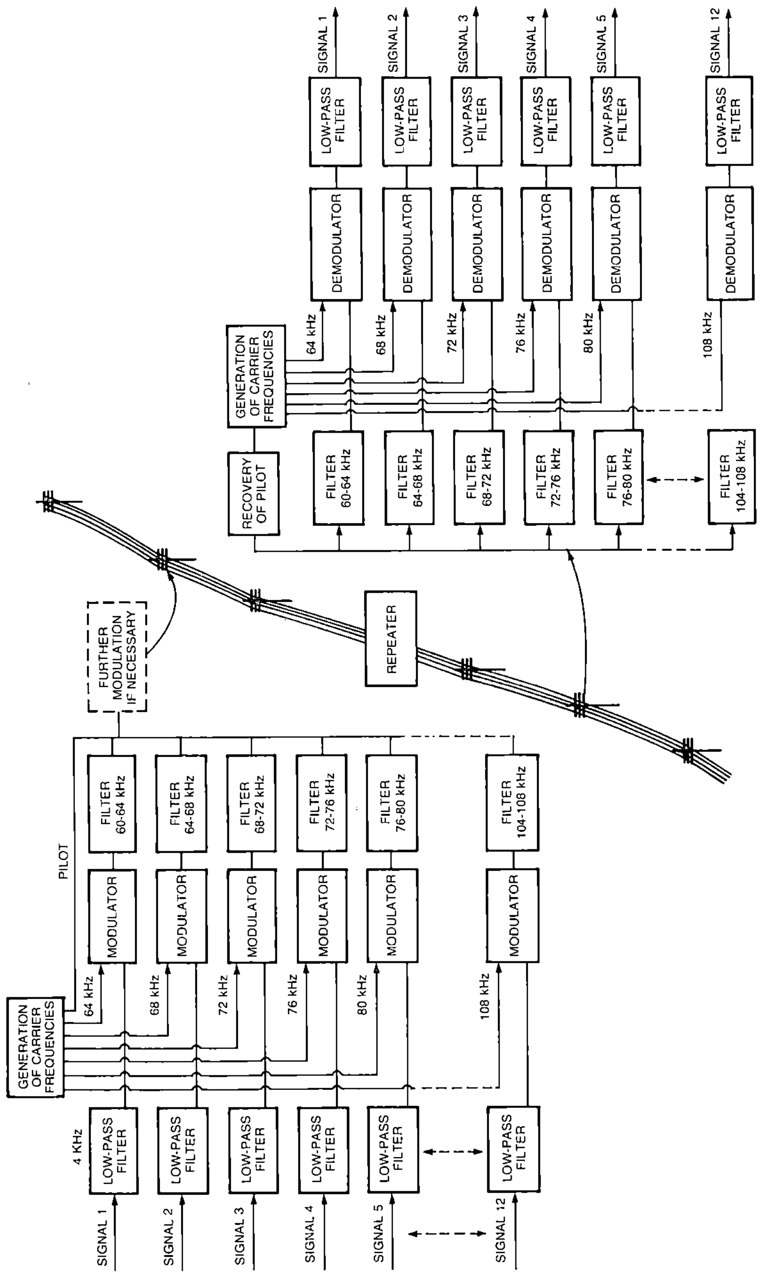

Figure 1.6 **Frequency Division Multiplex**

If an ideal transmission medium would exist, one which would accurately pass the digital signals to their destination, there would be no need for modems. The receiver and transmitter shown in Figure 1.5 would consist of a pair of wires, the received pulse would be identical to the transmitted pulse, and the life of a communication consultant would be very simple. There is a condition which is close to this ideal situation and it is called end-to-end digital transmission. Unfortunately for the data transmission, over 85% of the telephone network is still based on analog transmission and the gradual change to digital transmission takes place mostly between switching centers. The final links between the end telephone office and the customer remain analog and will probably remain so for the foreseeable future. Though a sprinkling of end-to-end digital 56-kbps offerings is made by the local telephone companies and the long-distance communication providers, it is difficult and sometimes impossible to connect these digital channels to those offered by another common carrier because of lack of common standards.

PUBLIC TELEPHONE NETWORK

The Public Telephone Network, which is the backbone of most data communications, was originally developed for voice and not for data transmission. It is optimized for a satisfactory voice communication between telephone subscribers. As most of the voice energy is concentrated between 300 Hz and 2500 Hz, the bandwidth of a telephone circuit is approximately between 300 Hz and 3200 Hz in order to satisfy the average telephone voice subscriber.

Telephone subscribers are connected to the local office, also called a Class 5 office, with a pair of copper wires, called the local loop. If the calling and the called subscribers are connected to the same local office, then to establish a connection, the call will be switched in the local office. If the call is destined for a distant city, then the local loop will be switched first to a toll connecting trunk, which is another pair of wires, or to a multiplexed carrier system. The toll connecting trunk from the local Class 5 office terminates in the toll office, the gate to the worldwide telephone network. From then on, the call will be carried on intertoll trunks, four-wire facilities which provide a separate path for each direction of transmission. Depending on traffic conditions, the call can be routed via switched transmission facilities through various hierarchical levels of the telephone network.

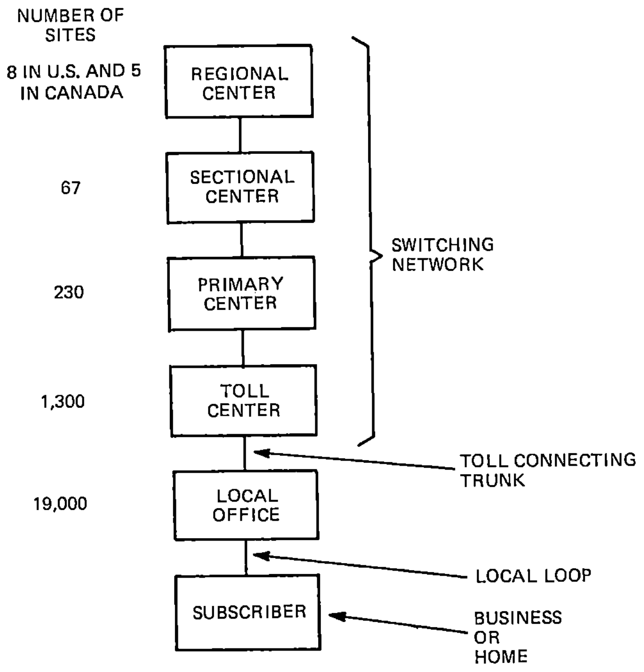

Figure 1.7 **Hierarchical Structure of the US Telephone Network**

The hierarchy of the Public Telephone Network implemented by the local telephone companies and AT&T, the long distance carrier, is shown in Figure 1.7. On top of the hierarchy are Class 1 Regional offices, of which there are eight in the United States and five in Canada; then come Class 2 Sectional offices, Class 3 Primary offices, Class 4 Toll offices, and Class 5 Local or End offices. Calls either follow the hierarchical ladder up and down or are shunted by means of high usage trunks. While traveling from switch to switch, the call is combined with other voice circuits traveling to the same intermediate destinations. At each switching point the signals are combined with other signals (multiplexed) or separated from other signals (demultiplexed). Each of these operations introduces additional transmission impairments, which though hardly noticeable on a voice connection are highly deleterious to the data signal.

Local Loop

The local loop is the pair of copper wires which connect the subscriber to the local telephone office. The built-in electrical capacitance of the telephone cable makes the transmission loss increase with frequency. To improve voice transmission, the telephone company inserts so-called loading coils in long local loops. The inductance of the coils combines with the capacitance of the cable, resulting in fairly flat attenuation up to about 2500 Hz and then a steep rise in attenuation at higher frequencies. Frequency responses of a "loaded" and of a "nonloaded" loop are shown in Figure 1.8. Because a modulated data stream carries energy at frequencies spread over the entire bandwidth of the voice channel up to 3000 Hz, loading coils should be removed from a loop used for data transmission. This will result in expanding the bandwidth and improving the data transmission at the expense of attenuation distortion and of inadequate voice transmission.

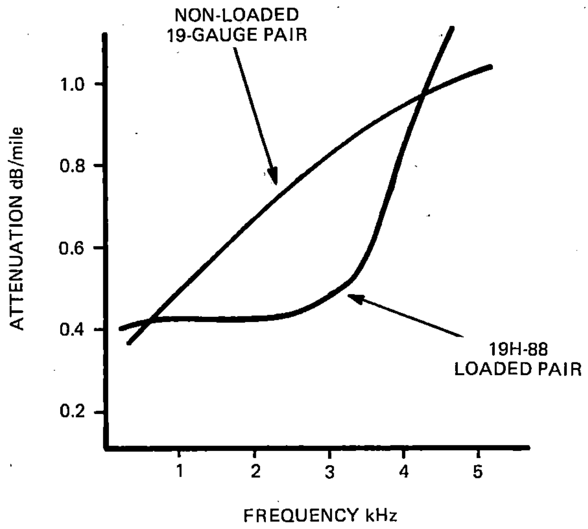

Figure 1.8 **Effect of Line "Loading"**

Hybrids and Echo

Since there is only a single pair of wires in the local loop and the loop carries two-way simultaneous communication, it is referred to as two-wire full-duplex transmission path. The toll network between Class 4 and higher offices, on the other hand, is full-duplex, four-wire. The question arises then, of how the transfer from a two-wire to a four-wire facility takes place. The answer lies in the circuit called a hybrid, which terminates each local loop in the local telephone office. The quality of the hybrid is measured in terms of the return loss, which is equal to the attenuation of the reflected signal. A higher return loss means a lower reflected energy. The hybrid circuit shown in Figure 1.9 is somewhat similar to a Wheatstone bridge, except that it uses special transformers instead of discrete resistors, capacitors, and coils.

The most important part of the hybrid, similarly to any other electric bridge circuit, is the impedance matching network, Z_b in Figure 1.9. The impedance of the matching network approximates roughly the complex impedance of the local loop terminated by the telephone set over the usable frequency band. The better the approximation, the higher will be the return loss. Because of the cost involved, the actual impedance matching network is a simple compromise circuit consisting of only a resistor and a capacitor. The mismatch caused by the compromise network returns some of the voice or data energy back to the source instead of the destination.

The energy reflected at the local hybrid is called the near-end echo; the energy reflected by the hybrid near the destination is called the far-end echo. The near-end echo is hardly noticed by the voice talker, but it affects data transmission because of its strong signal power. The far-end echo affects data to a limited degree, because of circuit loss along the transmission line, but it is very objectionable to the voice talker because of the associated delay. The annoying effect of the far-end echo in a voice conversation increases with the round-trip delay and decreases with the attenuation of the reflected signal. The way the telephone network protects its voice subscribers from far-end echo is by introducing extra circuit loss, making it proportional to the length of the connection and thus to the time delay of the reflected signal. This approach to echo/loss compensation is called the Via Net Loss (VNL) method. The extra loss introduced in a telephone connection affects echo more than it affects speech, because echo makes a round-trip on the network and is thus attenuated twice. The annoying effect of the increasing delay, approximately 20 ms per 1000 km (625 miles), is compensated by this extra circuit loss.

On calls exceeding 2400 km (1500 miles) in length the delay amounts to

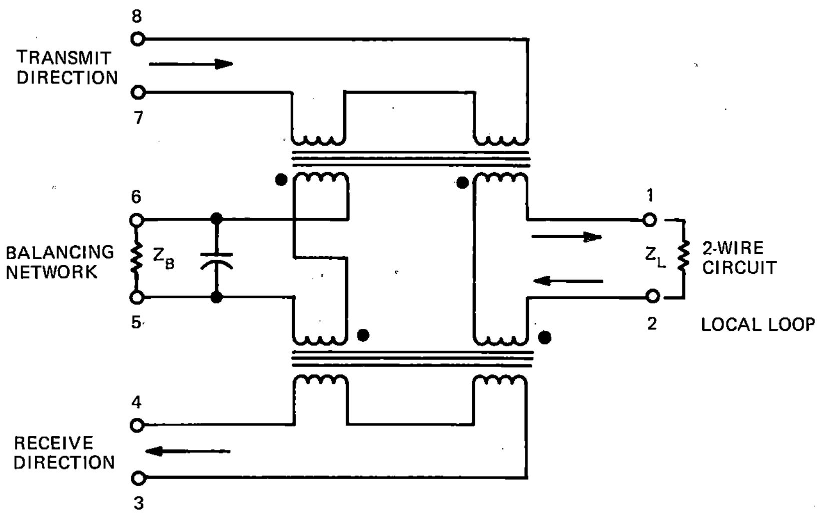

Figure 1.9 **Telephone Hybrid Circuit**

approximately 45 msec, and the extra loss introduced to fight the far-end echo would impair the telephone connection and would no longer be acceptable. Therefore, instead of increasing the circuit loss, the telephone company on such long circuits provides so-called echo suppressors, which are shown in Figure 1.10. An echo suppressor puts a high loss in the nonactive direction of transmission by constantly monitoring energy in both directions of an active circuit. Instead of a full-duplex circuit we now have a half-duplex circuit, which reverses its direction as each party starts talking. In a voice connection echo suppressors, being the least evil, are tolerated. On a full-duplex data connection, however, they cannot be accepted, because they would not allow for two-way communication. In addition, the far-end echo, though objectionable in a voice conversation, will hardly affect a data connection, just slightly decreasing the signal-to-noise ratio of the circuit. The telephone company recognizes this problem and gives to the data subscriber means to disable echo suppressors on a telephone circuit by allowing the subscriber to send a tone of 2100 Hz on the United States telephone network and of 1800 Hz on the European telephone networks. Modems frequently send such tones, called the

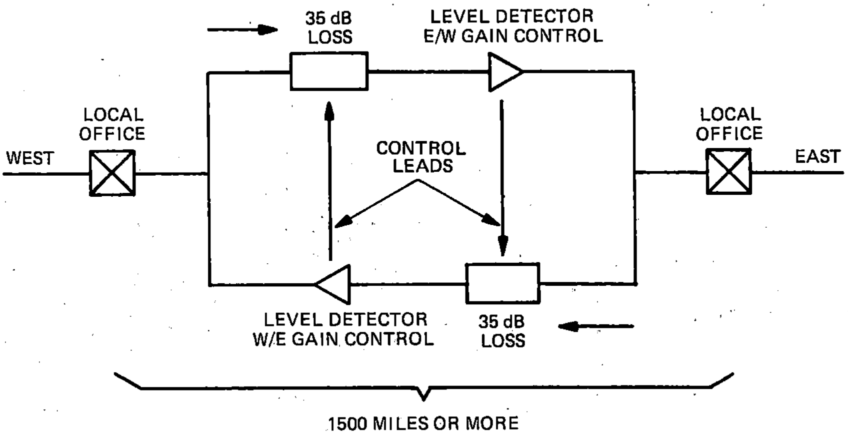

Figure 1.10 **Echo Suppressors**

"guard" tones, during the initial handshake sequence, which always precedes exchange of data.

OSI MODEL OF THE DATA NETWORK

To be able to exchange data between different computers located in different cities, countries, or continents there is a need for standardization. This standardization occurs in a piecemeal way; there are modulation standards for specific modem types, there are standards for computer-to-modem interfaces, there are also various error protocol standards. To make development of standards more consistent and uniform an international standard for data communications was adopted in 1983. The standard developed by the International Standards Organization (ISO) defines the by now famous conceptual seven-layer model of an international data network, the so-called Open Systems Interconnect (OSI) model. The "openness" of the standard means that each layer of the model is open to any process or communication following such a standard. A diagram of the ISO model is shown in Figure 1.11. By adopting this model, standards can be developed for the clearly delineated layers, and an assurance exists that, if layer standards agree with each other, data will successfully pass between the layers. We will now describe the seven layers of the OSI model in some detail and give an example of a data communications passing through the individual layers. In general, however, the modem user will only deal with Layer 1 (Physical Layer) and with Layer 2 (Data Link Layer). Still, understanding of the higher layers of the OSI model may sometimes help in diagnosing problems related to data transmission.

OSI Layer 1 - Physical Layer

The Physical Layer consists of the hardware interface between the computer, modem, and the telephone line. The layer standards include functional, electrical, and physical specifications described in RS-232-C, V.24, X.21, and other interface recommendations. Other standards for this layer are the Local Area Network (LAN) standards being developed by the IEEE 802 committee. These LAN recommendations should follow the OSI model.

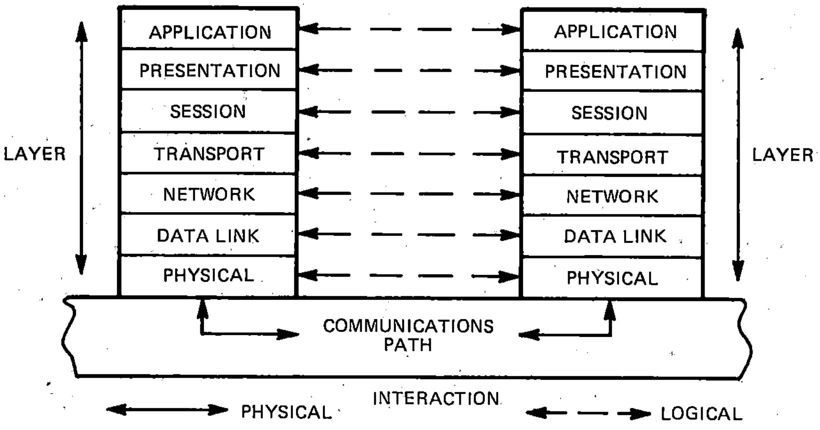

Figure 1.11 **ISO Model of a Communication Network**

OSI Layer 2 - Data Link Layer

The second layer is primarily responsible for error detection and correction. The later described MNP error correcting protocol works at this level. Data transmission protocols used at this level are SDLC, HDLC, and others, which will be discussed in later chapters. The protocols take care of data block framing and of synchronization, error control, and recovery, message sequence control, link initialization, connection, disconnection, and addressing.

OSI Layer 3 - Network Layer

The third layer provides means to transmit data through the network from the originator to the receiver. It provides the mechanism to establish, maintain, and terminate data connections between separate computer networks. The CCITT X.25 Packet Switching protocol is an example of the Network Layer standard. The standard describes how a ''packet'' of data is to be assembled, framed, and addressed.

OSI Layer 4 - Transport Layer

The fourth layer allows end users to communicate independently of network constraints imposed by Layers 1-3. The appropriate standards specify priority levels, security, response time expectations, error rates, and recovery strategies. The layer takes data from the higher layer (layer 5), splits it into smaller units if necessary, passes the units to the Network Layer, and ensures that they reach their destinations. The Transport Layer also provides guidelines for data flow management.

OSI Layer 5 - Session Layer

The fifth layer is the true user's interface to the data network. It handles the log-on and log-off procedures and user's authentication including password verification. This layer may also handle communications parameters to other local devices, e.g., choice of local disk storage units. It also handles recovery from unreliable Transport Layer connections.

OSI Layer 6 - Presentation Layer

The sixth layer is approaching the user's programs. It handles display of data, file formatting, code encryption and decryption, data compression, and data expansion. The layer also ensures that the syntax of the originator is understood by the receiver. If the originator uses ASCII and the receiver uses EBCDIC, then a translation procedure would be provided by this layer.

OSI Layer 7 - Application Layer

The seventh layer contains recommendations for user's programs. Some of the recommendations for this layer are suggested standards for electronic funds transfer, point of sale terminals, automated teller machines, airline reservation systems, and other large scale applications.

Application of the OSI Model to a Data Call

Layers 2 through 6 of the OSI model affect the data by adding successive headers to the blocks of data originated by the user in Layer 7. Each header adds some additional control bytes so that the network may successfully transmit the data from source to destination. For most users, Layers 2 through 7 are purely conceptual and are part of the user's computer and its associated software. However, we will assume in the following example, taken from the Hewlett Packard Data Communications Tutorial, that the OSI model is fully implemented, and that a data call is made between two locations using the OSI model network.

Let us examine in detail how end-to-end application data communications might take place. Our Los Angeles computer, in running its application program, needs to communicate to a database in New York. Assume that the communications link is established, and that a file transfer is about to take place. The data to be transferred may look like this:

<Region Sales = 50% of Quota>

The New York application process has pulled this data from a file and passes it into our model. We are now into Layer 6. The presentation layer adds some overhead to the message it received from the file. Does our system operate in ASCII-8 (8 bits per character)? Do we use text compression? Do we utilize encryption? This information is attached to the head of the message, perhaps in the form of "ASC8" and "NTC" (No Text Compression), so that the resultant information appears as:

<ASC8 NTC> <Region Sales = 50% of Quota>

Each angular bracket delimits a subblock of data, which can be recognized by the equipment. The composite message is passed on to Layer 5, which treats the data as a complete message. Here is one of the most important concepts in OSI: The information passed from layer to layer is treated by any one layer as user information, which is not to be perturbed in any way. So, the session layer takes our composite message from the presentation layer and adds to it the session layer header. The important information here is that the LA/NY link is established, perhaps with some session keyword that validates the session in progress. The resultant package of information passes to the next lower layer looking like:

<LA NY KEY> <ASC8 NTC> <Region Sales = 50% of Quota>

The transport layer adds whatever information is important to its peer. In this case, it may be only the network number through which communication is established. It thus adds that identifier to the growing information frame,resulting in:

<NET1><LA NY KEY> <ASC8 NTC> <Region Sales = 50% of Quota>

The network layer recognizes what it receives from above as data, and prefaces to that data the information important to its peer on the receiving end. In this case, it merely parrots back to the network the Virtual Circuit Number it was assigned when communication was established. The frame that gets passed to Layer 2 then appears as:

<VCN> <NET1> <LA NY KEY> <ASC8 NTC> <Region Sales = 50% of Quota>

The data link layer recognizes this as user data and frames it as such, conveying to the local network node, to which it is physically connected, the address and control information, as well as a Frame Check Sequence. Our frame now looks like:

<FCS> <VCN> <NET1> <LA NY KEY> <ASC8 NTC> <Region Sales = 50% of Quota>

This outgoing frame is passed to the physical link layer, which converts all the data to a bit stream going across the RS-232-C interface to a modem, or whatever device is connected to the transmission medium.

An important point to recognize is that only at the physical link layer can a protocol analyzer, like the one discussed in Chapter 14, actually "see" the data. A protocol analyzer must then juxtapose all these bits back into the appropriate protocol level of interest.

Current Status of the OSI Model

Three of the OSI lower layers are currently implemented in the X.25 standard and work continues in various international committees on development of standards for the remaining layers. The International Standards Organization and the CCITT have several study groups defining these standards. Still, the OSI model is more a template for future developments than a set of currently existing standards. It is an important step, which had to be taken to achieve more consistent standards for data transmission in the future.

In the future, Application Layer standards for specific areas of industry, such as banking, retailing, manufacturing, medicine, education, and government will be available in addition to "generic" Application Layer standards used across all industries. Still, progress in this area is rather slow as most large applications use proprietary software and protocols.

An organization called Omnicon Information Service (see the Appendix) keeps track of new developments in the area of international standards and recommendations and publishes a monthly newsletter for interested parties.

2. Private Lines and Equalization

There are three types of communication services which one can obtain from the Common Carrier, the local telephone company, or the long distance provider. These three basic services are shown in Figure 2.1 and are part of the Public Telephone Network. The first type of service is a switched or a dial-up connection, where charges are computed by the telephone company depending on the time of day, distance, and duration of the call. The second type of service is the one made over a leased nonswitched circuit between two or more fixed locations. The nonswitched circuit could also be privately owned, in particular if it covers only a short distance, for example, a span between two buildings. The third type of service is the hybrid service, which consists of a switched circuit leading to a node, which is then connected through leased lines to a second node. An alternate type of hybrid service would be a leased, conditioned circuit leading from the customer's premises to a local telephone office, the so-called Data Access Line, from where the call would access the Public Telephone Network. I will limit myself in this chapter to the discussion of switched and leased voice and broadband circuits, both analog and digital. These are the most common transmission facilities which connect computers or data terminals equipped with modems.

A dial-up connection made over the switched Public Telephone Network, the separately billed call, using Direct Distance Dialing (DDD), or the bulk billed call using Wide Area Telecommunications Service (WATS), has the enormous advantage of flexibility and reliability. One can call any other telephone subscriber in the world and, if a section of the telephone network breaks down, there is enough redundancy in the system to quickly reroute the

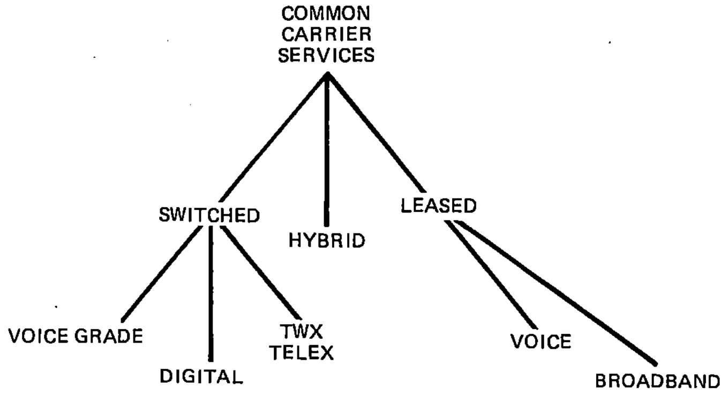

Figure 2.1 **Common Carrier Services**

call. The disadvantage, especially on a data call, is the unpredictability of the transmission quality. All the Common Carrier, the telephone company, or the long distance provider will guarantee on a dialed connection is that the two parties can communicate freely by talking to each other, and that the subjectively perceived quality of the connection will be satisfactory. There is no specific quantitative assurance of limits on attenuation or delay distortion, or freedom from noise bursts caused by fading of microwave links, or by switching transients.

Attaching a transmission measuring set to a switched telephone line used for data communications will show a wide distribution of noise and distortion even on calls dialed between the same two locations at different times. The variability is caused by different routing of calls, depending on traffic conditions, at the time the call is being made. Other disadvantages of switched service for data communications is the long time to connect, typically 10 seconds, and network signals present during the connection. In particular, in Europe there are periodic beeps indicating charging units, which may interfere with data transmission. Also, only two-wire connections are available on the switched public network. Still, for many purposes a dialed connection is the least expensive and is still a satisfactory solution for data communications.

If a corporation has a number of fixed field locations, between which frequent data calls are being made, then use of privately owned or leased transmission facilities should be considered. Leased line services are available from local telephone companies and from long distance carriers, including AT&T, MCI, and others. Leased lines consist of local loops, connecting the subscriber to the central office and of interexchange channels, which connect central offices. The advantage of a privately owned or a leased point-to-point or multiple-point circuit is its complete predictability. Because of lack of switching the call is always routed over the same facilities. In addition, the user can select from a number of Common Carrier offerings, which under tariffed schedules guarantee specific transmission parameter values. If the user, after installing a leased transmission link, finds that it does not meet the published specifications, then he/she can complain to the Common Carrier and the facility will be brought up to the guaranteed standards. The main disadvantage of a leased or a private line are the high initial costs. These initial costs will, however, be quickly amortized for high usage links. Other disadvantages are lack of flexibility, and a significant time to repair in case of trouble. In applications where reliability is of utmost importance the user may want to lease two circuits, rather than a single circuit, and switch automatically to the alternate circuit in case of trouble.

The following is a list of the principal types of leased or privately owned line facilities used for data communications:

Leased voice grade lines with or without conditioning — used for two- and four-wire modems, typical transmission speed up to 2400 bps asynchronous and 9600 bps synchronous.

Wideband analog lines — used for telephone channel multiplexing, one of these offerings is called Telpac. These lines find only limited application for data transmission.

Digital switched service — typically used for 56-kbps transmission and for multiplexing of several lower speed modems.

Fiber optic links — used for computer-to-computer and other high-speed applications.

VOICE-BAND TRANSMISSION FACILITIES

Table 2.1 shows leased voice-band transmission facilities currently offered by Common Carriers under applicable tariffs. The lowest priced offering is the so-called 3002 channel, which has characteristics similar to an average dialed connection. The higher priced offerings are called C1, C2, C4, and D1. The guaranteed characteristics are obtained by the Common Carriers by

Table 2.1 Leased Voice-band Transmission Facilities

	Non-Conditioned 3002 Channel		With C1 Conditioning		With C2 Conditioning		With C4 Conditioning		With D Conditioning
Frequency Range in Hertz (Hz)	300-3000		300-3000		300-3000		300-3200		
Attenuation Distortion (Net Loss at 1000 Hz)	Frequency Range	Decibel Variation	Frequency Response	Decibel Variation	Frequency Response	Decibel Variation	Frequency Response	Decibel Variation	
	300-3000	−3 to +12	300-2700	−2 to +6	300-3000	−2 to +6	300-3200	−2 to +6	
	500-2500	−2 to +8	1000-2400	−1 to +3	500-2800	−1 to +3	500-3000	−2 to +3	
			300-3000	−3 to +12					
Delay Distortion in Microseconds (μs)	Less than 1750 μs from 800 to 2600 Hz		Less than 1000 μs from 1000 to 2400 Hz Less than 1750 μs from 800 to 2600 Hz		Less than 500 μs from 1000 to 2600 Hz Less than 1500 μs from 600 to 2600 Hz Less than 3000 μs from 500 to 2800 Hz		Less than 300 μs from 1000 to 2600 Hz Less than 500 μs from 800 to 2800 Hz Less than 1500 μs from 600 to 3000 Hz Less than 3000 μs from 500 to 3000 Hz		
Signal to Noise (dB)	24		24		24		24		28
Non-Linear Distortion Signal to 2nd Harmonic (dB)	25		25		25		25		35
Signal to 3rd Harmonic (dB)	30		30		30		30		40
Maximum Impulse Noise	15 counts in 15 minutes								
Type of Service	Point-to-Point (two points) or Multipoint						Point-to-Point (two or three points)		
Channel Mode	Half of Full Duplex								
Local Loop Termination	Two or Four Wire								
Maximum Frequency Error	±5 Hz								
Maximum Bit Error	Approximately 1 bit error per 100,000 bits transmitted								

means of line conditioning, which consists of inserting fixed attenuation and delay equalizers selected after measuring the nonequalized line. The telephone company engineers have at their disposal computer programs, which will select the best possible combination of fixed equalizers to compensate for the measured delay and attenuation distortion of a telephone circuit and to satisfy a given tariff. In cases where a transmission facility cannot be equalized to the tariffed requirements, the Common Carrier will select for the customer a different facility. It should be noted that leased circuits are, in general, a part of the switched Public Telephone Network. The circuits are just patched through in various telephone offices instead of going through switching machines. Thus leased circuits are subject to the same amplitude and frequency restrictions, which are listed in AT&T Publication 43401, as other network users. The purpose of these restrictions is to protect users of the Public Telephone Network from mutual interference.

It is interesting to compare the guaranteed parameter values in Table 2.1 with the typical expected values of transmit and receive levels, line losses, signal-to-noise ratios and with the threshold range of signal-to-noise required by various types of modems for error-free operation. Table 2.2 shows the typical parameter values to be found on voice grade lines.

John H. Humphrey and Gary S. Smock of the Tele-Quality Associates reported in a recent study the minimum signal-to-noise ratios for various modems. The general measuring setup for this kind of test is shown in Chapter 14. The authors of the study found, similar to a PC magazine survey, that modems based on specialized chip sets performed better, and required lower minimum S/N ratios, than those using discrete components. The range of acceptable S/N ratios for various 1200 bps and 2400 bps modems was found to be between 20 and 25 db. The authors of the report also noticed considerable variations in the signal-to-noise ratio, of up to 10 dB, between various modem

Table 2.2 **Typical Transmission Parameters on a Voice Grade Facility**

	Leased DDD	Local DDD	Long Distance DDD
Transmit Level	OdBm	-10 dBm	-10 dBm
Receive Level	-15 dBm	-25 dBm	-27 dBm
Line Loss	15 dB	15 dB	20 dB
S/N Ratio	35 dB	34 dB	27 dB

types. Thus it may be worthwhile, before committing oneself to a specific modem, to try it out in the actual working environment.

To get some idea of costs of leased facilities, Table 2.3 shows the current AT&T pricing per month for a voice-grade leased 3002 circuit between Los Angeles and New York. The charges consist of fixed charges and of mileage-dependent charges, reflecting the cost of fixed equipment installed by the

Table 2.3 **Pricing of a Typical Leased Line Facility (1986)**

Interoffice channel line charge	$ 324
2443 miles @ 32 cents per mile	$ 782
Bell local connection charges	$ 195
AT&T connection charges	$ 52
Total monthly charge	$1353

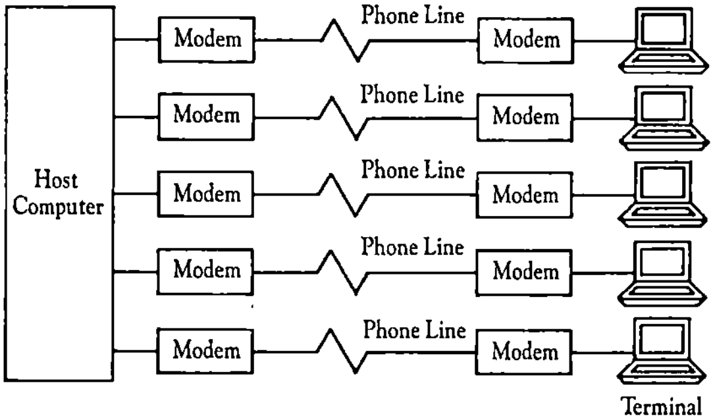

A series of point-to-point networks where each terminal is linked to the host computer by its own phone line can be very expensive.

Figure 2.2 **Point-to-Point Network**

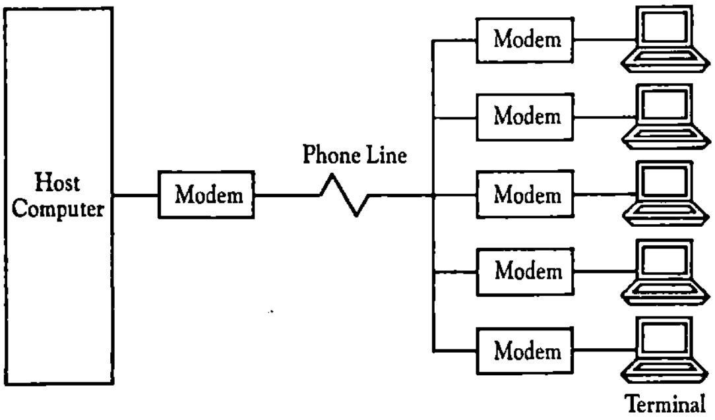

One solution for reducing line and modem costs is a multipoint network where several terminals share the same phone line. In this case, a multipoint configuration eliminates four phone lines and four modems.

Figure 2.3 **Multi-Point Network**

Common Carrier at the customer's premises and at the local and toll central offices, and of the usage dependent cost of the transmission facility. In addition there would be a one-time installation charge of several hundred dollars.

The leased circuits are connected either on a point-to-point basis or are part of a multipoint network. The two methods of operation are shown in Figures 2.2 and 2.3.

SWITCHED WIDEBAND DIGITAL SERVICE

In addition to analog transmission facilities one can also lease in selected areas of the country, digital circuits from either the local telephone company or from a long distance carrier. Unlike a leased analog transmission line, which is basically transparent to the user, and can carry voice, synchronous or asynchronous data traffic at various transmission speeds, a digital transmission facility can only carry synchronous data at prescribed transmission speeds. In February 1985, AT&T filed a tariff for a switched digital service called Accunet between 32 cities; it is capable of operating at 56 kbps. The tariff was approved by the FCC in May 1985. The service is now (1987) being expanded to 64 cities. In addition, many of the Bell operating companies filed their own tariffs for similar services. In theory, the Accunet service should provide the best of both worlds, flexibility and reliability of a switched network, and high transmission quality of a digital end-to-end connection. Each Accunet customer was assigned a 700 number and was able to dial any other Accunet customer. However, as of now, the service reaches only 2% of its predicted number of customers, a few hundred at best. The problem is similar to any other new offering; until a critical number of subscribers can be reached on the network, there is nobody to call.

The operating telephone companies are also offering digital services on their own, which unfortunately are not compatible with Accunet. For example, NYNEX offers a digital service called Switchway, which is not compatible with Accunet, requires different equipment, and can only be used within New York State. Pacific Bell also offers a digital service, but it is limited to a small area around Los Angeles. Thus, to be able to communicate with other cities, one has to obtain a leased wideband circuit from the local telephone company to be able to reach the AT&T Accunet switch. To make things even more complicated, the Accunet service is currently offered at only one transmission speed, namely 56 kbps, no slower and no faster, making it useless for the popular DEC VT-100 terminals. The service was specifically offered to facsimile users, but very few facsimile machines operate at 56 kbps.

Many of the problems which the digital switched service is currently encountering were caused by the breakup of the Bell System and lack of coordination between long distance and local telephone companies. Since the service has lots of promise, it may evolve in the future into desirable and useful offerings. In particular, it would be an ideal means of connecting multiplexers, each combining data streams of several lower speed modems.

When connecting a computer to a digital service, one uses a special kind of modem, called Data Service Unit (DSU). The DSU is a short-haul synchronous line driver, which converts the bipolar pulses used on the digital access lines to the standard RS-232-C or V.35 levels used by the computer. Another piece of equipment required for connection of computer equipment to a digital access line is the Channel Service Unit (CSU). The CSU may be a separate device, or it may be included in the DSU. Separate DSU and CSU devices are required, either where the Common Carrier insists on supplying the CSU or in older installations. The primary function of the CSU is to recover, amplify, and equalize the bipolar pulses from the Common Carrier and then provide an acceptable signal to the DSU. The CSU also provides transient protection, electric isolation, and loop equalization, functions normally associated with the Data Access Arrangement (DAA) device. An additional function of the CSU is to respond to testing commands from the Common Carrier's test center by providing loopback capabilities for testing. The function of the CSU and of the DSU is thus very similar to that of a modem, except that no analog-to-digital or digital-to-analog conversion has to be performed.

A phone line is normally connected to the CSU or the combined CSU/DSU through a four-wire terminal strip. The connection between the computer and the DSU/CSU is via a 15-pin jack.

LINE EQUALIZATION

As mentioned in the previous paragraphs the Common Carrier guarantees certain transmission parameter values on conditioned leased transmission facilities. The need for equalization arises from the fact that when a voice or a data signal is sent over a transmission facility, such as a telephone line, it is subject to several types of electric distortion. The distortion is caused by imperfections in the transmission facilities selected between the transmitting and the receiving computer. The imperfections of transmission facilities will affect all parameters of the transmitted signal, specifically its amplitude and the relative phase of its various frequency components. Some types of distortion caused by the transmission facility, in particular the attenuation and the delay distortion, which is related to phase changes, are time invariant and do not change for the duration of a call; others, such as noise and phase jitter, vary with time, even on the same call.

Attenuation distortion leads to a change in the shape of transmitted signals. Attenuation at low frequencies (high-pass effect) affects the top of a data pulse; attenuation at high frequencies (low-pass effect) affects the slopes of a data pulse. Delay distortion distorts the shape and stretches a data signal so that it interferes with the adjacent signals. Noise bursts change the signal amplitude, and phase jitter interferes with detection of relative phase in the phase and frequency modulated signals. All these effects are cumulative and they make it difficult, if not impossible, for the receiving circuit to decide whether a "1" or a "0" has been originally sent by the transmitting computer. Figure 2.4 shows how the various types of distortion affect a rectangular pulse representing a data signal.

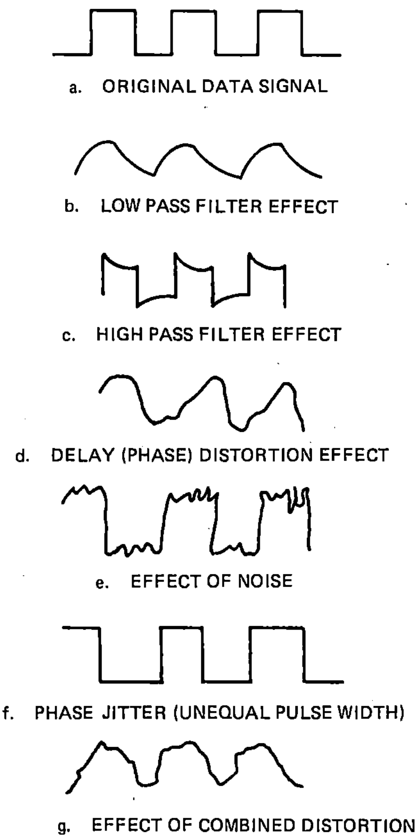

Figure 2.4 **Effects of Various Transmission Distortion Parameters on Data Signal**

VARIATION BETWEEN CALLS ON THE SWITCHED NETWORK

Though the attenuation and delay distortion are fixed for the duration of a specific call, they will differ from call to call on the switched Public Telephone Network, depending on the selected trunks. The reason for these variations is that on a dialed-up connection, even between the same two cities, two successive phone calls can be routed over different transmission facilities. A call between New York and Chicago can be routed, for example, over Atlanta and Dallas, if the direct trunks between New York and Chicago are busy due to traffic congestion. If the call is made over analog carrier trunks, the voice channel will be modulated into carrier frequencies and back again at each switching point, such as New York, Atlanta, Dallas, and Chicago. This is shown in Figure 2.5.

The modulation and demodulation step required at each switching center, as the signal traverses the Public Telephone Network, requires that the signal pass through narrow frequency limiting bandpass filters, in order not to interfere with adjacent voice channels transmitted over the same carrier circuit. Each filter and the associated circuitry add attenuation and delay distortion to the transmitted signal. Thus a call routed over Atlanta and Dallas will have more attenuation and delay distortion then a direct call between New York and Chicago because it will pass through more switching centers. The way to compensate for the attenuation and delay distortion picked up by the data signal between the originating computer and the destination computer is to add additional circuits, the so-called distortion equalizers, to the communications channel.

There are three types of distortion equalizers, which can help in reducing

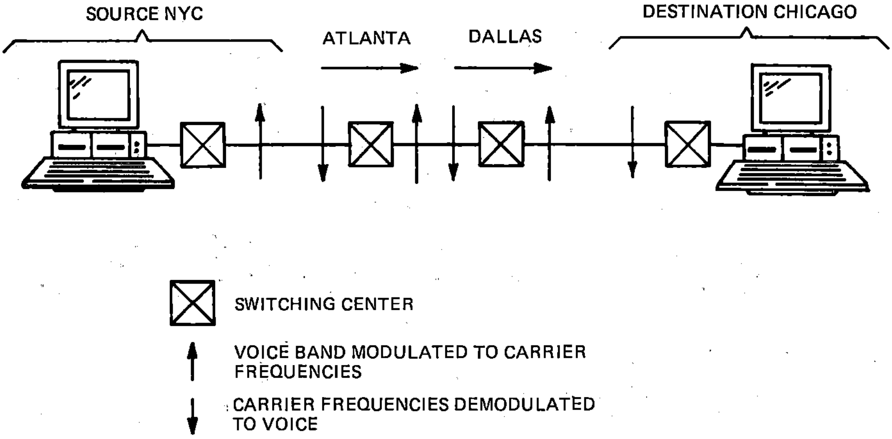

Figure 2.5 **Switched Telephone Connection**

attenuation and delay distortion on a data connection. Each of these equalizers presents the approximate mirror image of the facility distortion and, when connected between the transmission facility and equipment, compensates for the distortion. The first type is the compromise fixed equalizer, which compensates for the average distortion expected on a switched call. The second type is the specific fixed equalizer used on leased lines and tailored to the specific line distortion and to tariffed requirements. The third type is the self-adjustable adaptive equalizer, normally located in the receiving communications equipment, which equalizes instantly each call depending on the actually encountered residual distortion remaining after application of fixed compromise equalizers.

Examples of private line transmission facilities, as measured by this author before and after equalization with fixed attenuation and delay equalizers, are shown in Figures 2.6 and 2.7. The measurements were taken in a telephone office, where each circuit can be accessed at the so-called Voice Frequency Patch Bay. Use of compromise equalizers, which are normally included in the transmitting and the receiving section of a modem, and which compensate for the average distortion of an end-to-end switched connection, is generally sufficient

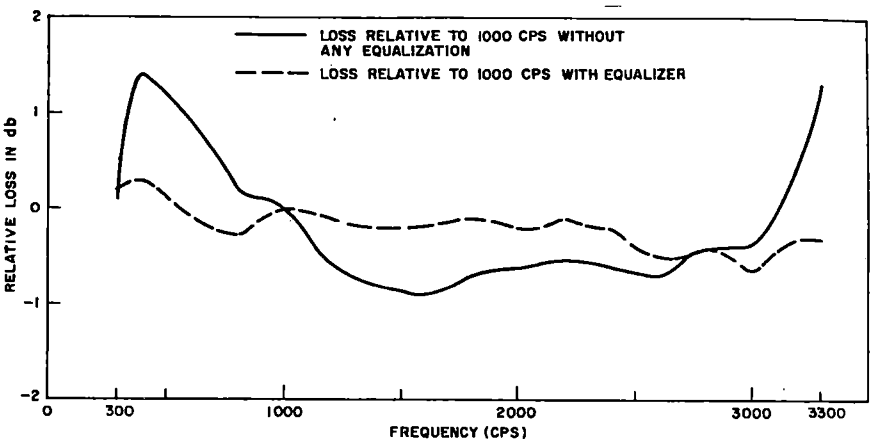

LOSS OF A TYPICAL L MULTIPLEX CIRCUIT CONSISTING OF TWO PAIRS OF TYPE A CHANNEL BANKS. (51R/54R WP2-BUFF CH. 2/8)

Figure 2.6 **Voice-Band Circuit Attenuation Before and After Equalization**

for low speed 300 bps and even for medium speed 1200 bps modems. These equalizers compensate for the average attenuation and delay distortion expected on a dialed-up telephone connection. With compromise equalizers one-half of the calls will be underequalized and the other half will be overequalized. This approach is not good enough for higher speed modems. Such modems require a more elaborate equalization technique, namely self-adjustable adaptive equalizers — equalization to order. Such equalizers are discussed in more detail in Chapter 10. Self-adjustable equalizers compensate for transmission distortion associated with a specific call, and not just with an average call. They are absolutely necessary for transmission rates above 1200 bps and will result in an additional 3 to 4 dB signal-to-noise immunity.

Various equalization, echo cancellation, and error correcting techniques will permit modem operation on the switched Public Telephone Network at transmission speeds of up to 9600 bps in full-duplex mode. Though 9600 bps

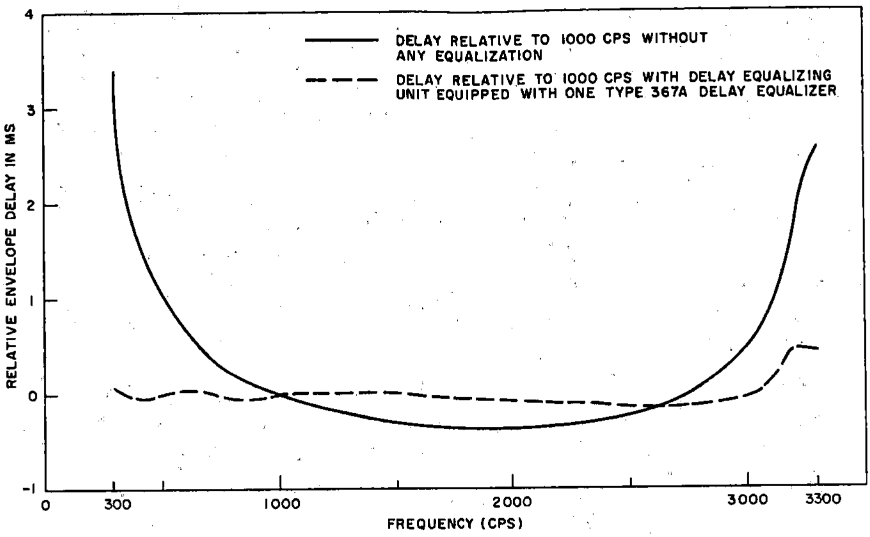

RELATIVE ENVELOPE DELAY OF A TYPICAL L MULTIPLEX CIRCUIT CONSISTING OF TWO PAIRS OF TYPE A CHANNEL BANKS. (51R/54R WP2-BUFF CH 2/8)

Figure 2.7 **Voice-Band Envelope Delay Before and After Equalization**

transmission on a dialed-up connection is possible, it is not always reliable and error correction schemes relying on block retransmission may slow the effective transmission rate considerably. The only solution then is to either lower the transmission speed, use a better modem, or to use a nonswitched private or leased conditioned line, as previously discussed. The Common Carrier achieves the tariffed limits on a conditioned line by equipping it with fixed attenuation and delay equalizers tailored to a specific transmission facility.

SIGNALING AND BATTERY OPTIONS

A circuit on the switched Public Telephone Network, in addition to being able to carry voice or data information, also accepts and carries signaling information, provides current from the central office battery, and sends ringing current, when the subscriber is being called. All these functions may or may not be provided on a leased transmission facility and have to be requested at the time that the circuit is set up. The simplest leased line circuit is the so-called 10 dB line, which provides 10 dB of loss between both ends and does not provide battery current or signaling option. The battery current is required for a regular telephone set to operate the carbon microphone, for a pulse dialer and for some line powered modems, but would not be necessary for a modem-to-modem connection. Ringing current and signaling capabilities may or may not be required, depending on the particular setup.

When setting up a private network using leased line transmission facilities one should always consider how the connection between modems will be established. The problem does not arise in the personal computer/modem field, where a modem behaves like a regular telephone set, and the user can dial the remote terminal from his or her computer and establish a connection. Many commercial modems used on leased circuits do not have dialing capabilities or cannot automatically answer a call from a remote modem. A separate dialing unit may then be required. Another option, which may be required for certain applications, typically limited modem or test circuits, is a metallic connection, which assures DC continuity. Such circuits can frequently be leased from the Common Carrier within the same telephone exchange.

EYE PATTERNS

The combined cumulative effect of various kinds of distortion and noise are best seen in the so-called eye pattern. The test setup to measure and display the eye pattern is shown in Figure 2.8. The setup consists of a pseudorandom bit generator and of an oscilloscope. The oscilloscope derives its synchronization from the generator, so that the scope trace starts at the beginning of each pulse. The eye pattern shows a superposition of random data pulses as they are seen by the receiving modem. Examples of observed eye patterns for two- and four-level modulation and for different amounts of phase jitter are shown in Figure 2.9. The reason for the "smeared" look of the patterns is that, due mainly to delay distortion, each data pulse leaves behind a decaying tail which interferes with the successive data pulses. The height of this tail depends on the value of previous pulses. Thus a sequence 01010 will add a different tail to a subsequent pulse than a sequence 11110. A pseudo-random sequence of bits, which approximates the real world transmission, will then result in random interference and a "smeared" look of the eye pattern. As the center of the eye pattern closes, it becomes more and

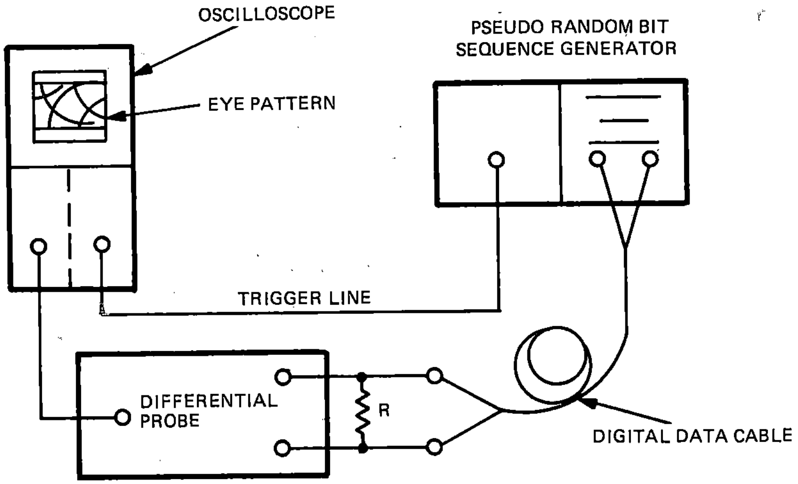

Figure 2.8 **"Eye" Pattern Measurement Setup**

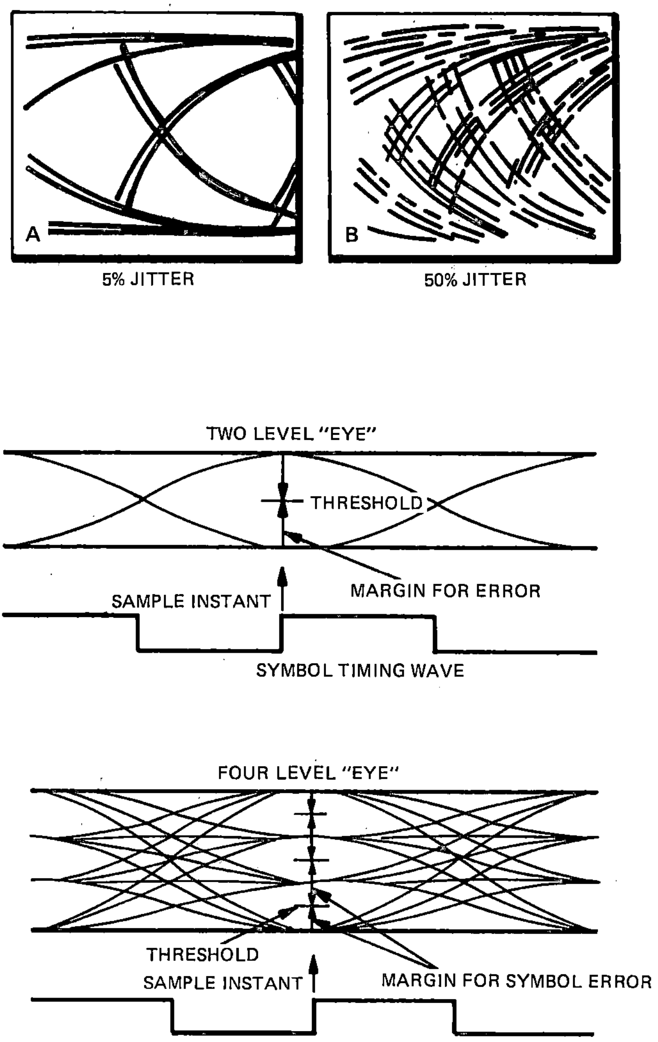

Figure 2.9 **Typical "Eye" Patterns with 5% and 50% Phase Jitter**

more difficult and costly for the receiving modem to distinguish between a binary "0" and a binary "1". When the eye closes completely, this distinction becomes impossible.

3. Transmission Bandwidth: Bits, Bytes, and Baud

MAXIMUM TRANSMISSION SPEED OF A VOICE-BAND CHANNEL

A voice-band channel on the switched Public Telephone Network in the United States has a bandwidth of approximately 3000 Hz; an overseas telephone channel has a bandwidth of approximately 2500 Hz. Typical measured characteristics of voice-band telephone channels were shown in Figures 2.6 and 2.7. In 1928, a Bell Laboratories mathematician, Harry Nyquist, derived a relation between channel bandwidth and the number of signal changes which a channel can transmit. His theorem states that the maximum number of possible signal changes in a channel of bandwidth B is $2 \times B$. In practical applications, it was found that the maximum number of possible signal changes is actually slightly less than B. Thus the application of the Nyquist theorem leads to an apparent limitation of the maximum transmission speed for a voice-band channel to less than its bandwidth, typically 2400 bps for a half-duplex and 1200 bps for a full-duplex circuit, with frequency separation of the opposite signal flows.

Fortunately, there is an easy way to get around the Nyquist limitation, namely by assigning more than 1 bit of information to each signal change. The old measure of telegraph transmission, a Baud, determines the rate of modulation, at which signals are being transmitted. If the signals are all the same, e.g., 5 V for a "1" and 0 V for a "0," then the modulation rate in Baud equals the bit per second transmission speed. The Bell 103A type modem, using frequency shift keying type of modulation (FSK), would be an example of such a system, since it is strictly a two-state modem. It is thus limited to the maximum theoretical transmission speed of 1200 bps in full-duplex operation. The telephone channel can therefore comfortably support the low 300-bps transmission speed of the 103A type modem.

A 1200-bps full-duplex modem such as the 212A assigns 2 bits (called a dibit) to each transmitted signal, thus effectively doubling the transmission speed. The full-duplex transmission speed of 1200 bps is equivalent to a modulation rate of only 600 Baud (1200 bps divided by 2 bits per signal element). Similarly, for higher speed modems, 4 bits can be assigned to each signal, doubling the transmission speed to 2400 bps, but still retaining the modulation rate of 600 Baud. Increasing the number of bits per signal element thus increases the effective transmission speed. It is somewhat similar to transmission of characters and words rather than bits when talking to another person. Saying the word "Hello" takes considerably less time than saying a long sequence of zeroes and ones corresponding to the binary representation of the same word. What then is the theoretical limit of transmission speed, the channel capacity, for a channel of bandwidth *W* in Hertz? It is clear that by increasing the number of bits per signal element one cannot increase the transmission speed indefinitely, because the detection process becomes more and more difficult as the redundancy of the transmitted signal decreases. The maximum attainable transmission speed was derived by another Bell Laboratories mathematician Claude Shannon, in 1949. Shannon's theorem relates the channel bandwidth, the signal-to-noise ratio of the transmission channel and the capacity of the transmission channel into the following equation:

$$C = W \times \log_2 (1 + S/N)$$

Where C = Maximum channel capacity in bps
Where W = Channel bandwidth in Hz
Where S = Signal power in Watt
Where N = Noise power in Watt over the whole bandwidth

This formula finds the maximum theoretically possible transmission speed for a given transmission facility without consideration for circuitry, method of modulation, error correction, or coding required to approach this limit. Figure 3.1 evaluates the above formula for a voice-band channel with a bandwidth of 3000 Hz. A typical dial-up voice connection in the United States will have a bandwidth of approximately 3000 Hz and a signal to noise ratio of 30 dB.

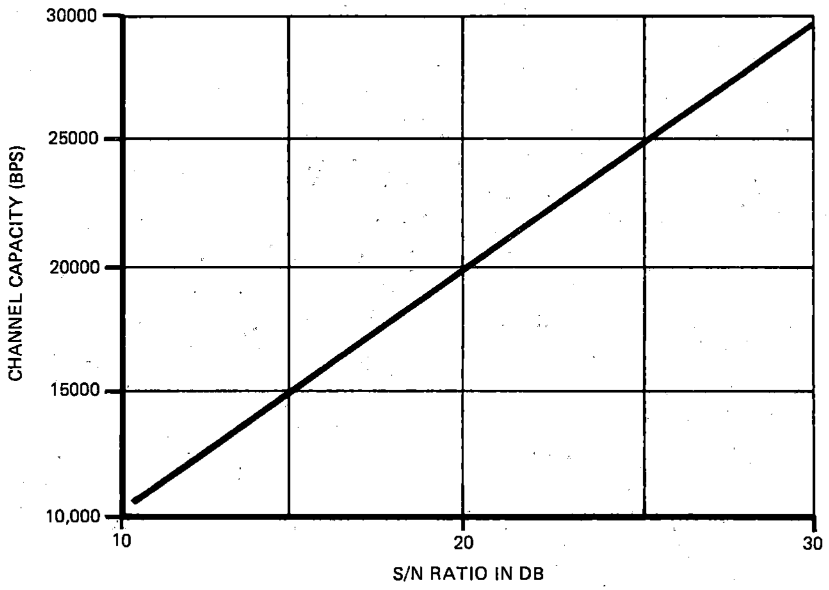

Figure 3.1 **Maximum Channel Capacity For an Ideal 3000 Hz Facility**

Looking up the S/N ratio of 30 dB yields a theoretical channel capacity of approximately 30,000 bps. The commercial modems used on dial-up lines now reach 19,200 bps in half-duplex mode; therefore, there is still a way to go to reach the theoretical limit of transmission speed.

As the theoretical transmission limit is being approached, the transmitting and detecting circuitry is becoming exceedingly complex and expensive. It is much more difficult to detect amplitude and phase relations between successive signal samples, as in the Quadrature Amplitude Modulation (QAM), than it is to simply distinguish between two frequencies, as in the FSK type modulation scheme. When transmission facilities with better signal-to-noise ratios are developed, based mainly on fiber optics transmission, then both the theoretical and the practical transmission speed limits will be pushed up even further.

RELATIONS BETWEEN VARIOUS MEASURES OF TRANSMISSION SPEED

Transmission speed of a modem is alternately given in bits per second (bps), characterrs per second (cps), words per minute (wpm) or in Baud. In this section I will show the relation between these four measures.

The basic transmission speed, or data signaling rate, of a modem is given in bits per second. It is typically 300, 1200, or 2400 bps. A modem rated at 1200 bps will transmit a maximum of 1200 binary digits of information, 0's and 1's, each second, or one pulse, or absence of it, every 0.833 ms. An effective data transmission rate of a synchronous modem will be close to this rate, the effective data transmission rate for an asynchronous modem will be about 30% less because of start, stop, and parity bits required for each character. If no binary data is arriving from the computer, then a synchronous modem sends a fixed sequence of bits, for example, 010101..., to synchronize the receiving modem. An asynchronous modem, on the other hand, will only transmit a continuous sequence of stop bits 111111... when it does not receive binary data from the computer.

The data fed into the modem consists typically of ASCII characters, translated into a sequence of 1's and 0's. At least 7 bits are required to transmit an ASCII character. Seven bits will produce 2^7 or 128 different combinations which covers the first half of the ASCII alphabet and includes upper- and lowercase letters, digits, and control codes. See also the ASCII Table in the Appendix. If graphic data is transmitted, then the eighth bit may also be required to send one of 2^8 or 256 different combinations. To transmit an ASCII character in synchronous mode thus requires 7—8 bits per character and an occasional frame synchronizing byte.

Asynchronous transmission requires in addition to the 7 or 8 data bits, a start bit to indicate the start of a character, 1 or 2 stop bits to indicate that the transmission of a character is completed, and 1 parity bit to check for errors in transmission. To transmit one character in asynchronous mode requires between 10 and 12 bits, including data, start, stop, and parity bits.

The ratio between bits per second and characters per second thus is approximately 10 to 1. To convert characters per second (cps) into words per minute (wpm), one has to multiply cps by 10, to account for the average word length of five characters followed by a space, and for the 60 seconds in each minute. A 1200-bps modem can thus send approximately 120 characters per second or 1200 words per minute.

The other measure of transmission speed is the modulation rate in "Baud," named after Emil Baudot, who invented in 1874 the first constant length teleprinter code. One Baud is equal to one code or signal element transmitted each second. If one code element represents 1 bit of information, like in the FSK 300 bps modem, then bps and Baud are the same. The Bell System 103A type modem using FSK modulation transmits at 300 bps and its modulation rate is 300 Baud. Higher speed modems, for example, the 1200 bps Bell System 212A and its equivalents, use the relative phase position of each transmitted signal, to represent *two* successive bits. The equivalent modulation rate in Baud is therefore one half of the transmission speed in bps, or 600 Baud. Similarly, a 2400-bps modem represents 4 successive information bits by each transmitted signal and thus also operates at 600 Baud. Modem literature and specifications frequently confuse the bps and Baud and erroneously use the same numbers for transmission speed and for the modulation rate in either units without consideration for the type of modulation.

To summarize: the prime measure of modem transmission speed is bits per second (bps) which is directly related to characters per second (cps) and to words per minute (wpm). The modulation rate in Baud is related to bps by a factor determined by the type of modulation. A 212A type modem transmits at 1200 bps, 120 cps, 1200 wpm, and 600 Baud. A 103A type modem transmits at 300 bps, 30 cps, 300 wpm, and 300 Baud.

4. Modulation Techniques

A digital signal transmitted over a voice-band telephone circuit contains significant energy components between DC and about three times the basic modulation rate. For a modulation rate of 600 Baud, the signal energy would thus span the frequency range between 0 and 1800 Hz. Most of the signal

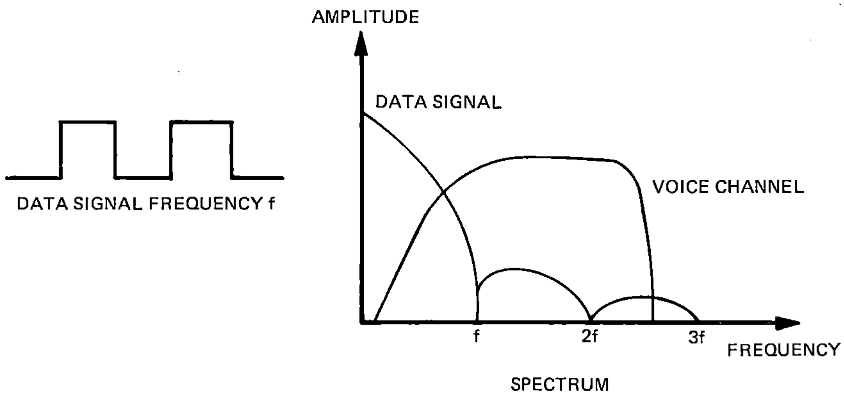

Figure 4.1 **Energy Spectrum of Data Signals vs. Channel Bandwidth**

energy would be concentrated at low frequencies below the modulation rate, or below 600 Hz. The analog telephone network, over which the digital signal is to be transmitted, unfortunately will not pass frequencies below 300 Hz and above 3200 Hz. The cutoff limits on circuits, which include underwater cable links are even more stringent. The energy distribution of a digital signal and the passband of the telephone network are superimposed in Figure 4.1. To "fit" the digital signal of 0 to 1800 Hz (at 1200 bps) into the 300—3200 Hz passband of the telephone network, the signal has to be modulated on carrier frequencies located in the flat portion of the passband of the transmission facility.

The instant value of a carrier frequency *Y* can be represented at any given time *t* by a sinusoid with three parameters, the maximum amplitude *A*, the frequency *F* and the phase *P*:

$$Y = A \times \mathrm{Sin}\ (2\pi F \times t + P)$$

Consequently, if the carrier wave is to carry digital information, all three parameters, the amplitude, frequency, and phase of the carrier wave, have to be separately or jointly modulated by the digital signals. The methods most frequently used in modem technology are frequency modulation, phase modulation, and a combined phase/amplitude modulation. An older method of modulation, the amplitude modulation, finds only limited use in modem technology. The type of modulation used by a particular modem depends on what specification or standard the modem adheres to; e.g., the Bell 103A, 212A, or 202 standards, the CCITT V.22 bis or other standard. In general, frequency modulation is used at transmission speeds of up to 300 bps, phase modulation at 1200 bps, and phase/amplitude modulation at higher transmission speeds. We will describe these methods of modulation in more detail; for complete descriptions of appropriate modulation schemes consult the CCITT V. series modem recommendations listed in the Bibliography.

AM MODULATION

The simplest method of modulation, namely, amplitude modulation (AM), finds only limited use for data transmission because of its susceptibility to noise and need for a wide frequency spectrum, twice the highest modulating frequency. The largest application of AM modulation is in carrier telephony, specifically the Frequency Division Multiplex (FDM) system, where one of the two sidebands generated during modulation process is suppressed in order to conserve the frequency spectrum. AM modulation is of course still widely used in the form of AM radio and television signals. The main advantage of AM modulation, which is the simplicity of the receiver demodulation circuit — a diode followed by a low pass filter — lost its importance with advances in electronics.

FREQUENCY MODULATION

This relatively simple modulation technique translates the digital 0's and 1's into preassigned discrete frequencies. The standard designation for this type of modulation is Frequency Shift Keying (FSK). Figure 4.2 shows a simulated oscilloscope picture of an FSK modulated signal. Frequency assignments used for the 300 bps Bell 103A FSK modem are shown in Table 4.1, while Figure 4.3 displays how these frequencies fit in the voice-band spectrum.

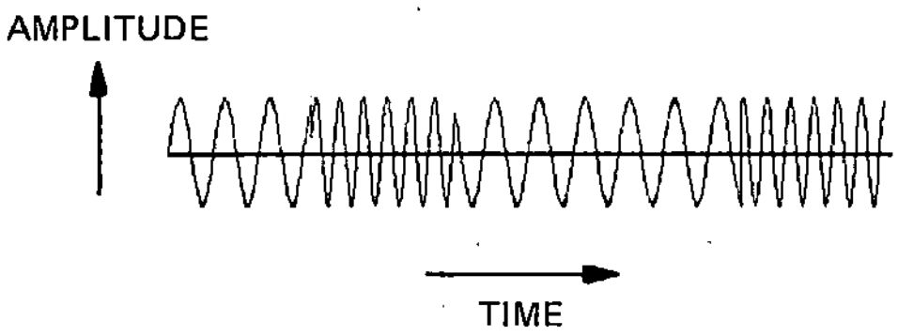

Figure 4.2 **Frequency Shift Keying (FSK) Modulated Signal**

Table 4.1 **Bell 103A Frequency Assignments**

Direction of transmission	Data signal	Frequency
Originating	Mark (1)	1270 Hz
Originating	Space (0)	1070 Hz
Answering	Mark (1)	2225 Hz
Answering	Space (0)	2025 Hz

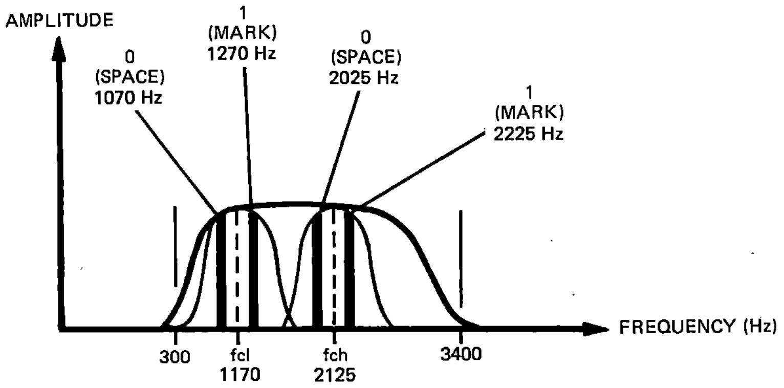

Figure 4.3 **Bell 103A Modem Frequency Assignments**

The circuitry required for FSK modulation and demodulation is relatively simple by today's standards, which makes this type of modem very inexpensive. The modulator requires only an electronic switch to select one of two frequencies for the originating or answering mode. The demodulator requires a phase locked loop or bandpass filters, followed by a detector, to determine which frequency is being received. No synchronization between the receiving and transmitting modem is required for proper demodulation. An example of implementation of a Bell 103A equivalent modem is shown in Figure 4.4. The design is based on a single chip modem made by the National Semiconductor Corporation.

CONSTELLATION DIAGRAMS

The next two modulation schemes, the differential phase modulation keying (DPSK) and the combined phase/amplitude modulation (QAM) can best be explained by means of the so-called constellation diagrams. A constellation diagram is a vector diagram, which shows the phase and amplitude relations associated with each combination of bits. The constellation diagram in Figure 4.5 for the Bell 212A modem shows phase assignments for each dibit combination. The frequency and relative phase assignments for 212A

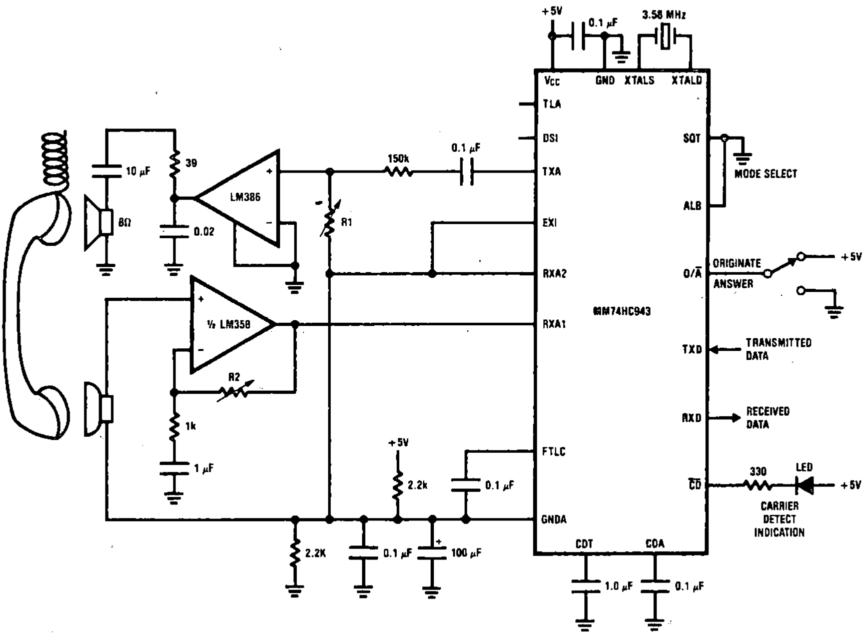

Figure 4.4 **Implementation of the Bell 103A Modem**

modems are shown in Table 4.2. Figure 4.6 displays how these frequencies fit into the voice-band spectrum.

Table 4.2 **Bell 212A Frequency and Phase Assignments**

Direction of Transmission	**Frequency (Hz)**
Originating Modem Send	1200
Originating Modem Receive	2400
Answering Modem Send	2400
Answering Modem Receive	1200

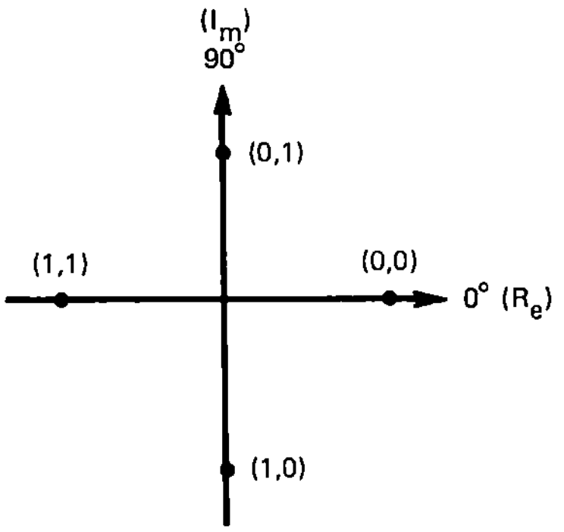

Figure 4.5 **Constellation Diagram for Bell 212A Modem**

Table 4.2 **(continued)**

Dibit	Phase Shift (degrees)
01	0
00	90
10	180
11	270

Another important interpretation of the constellation diagram is to consider two sinusoids, the second one shifted by 90 degrees from the first one. The maximum amplitude of the first sinusoid is the projection of the data point in the constellation diagram on the X axis; the maximum amplitude of the second sinusoid is the projection of the data point on the Y axis. The modulated signal is then the sum of the two sinusoids. This interpretation of the constellation diagram can be used to visualize the transmitted signal and also to design the modulating and the demodulating circuitry. The modulator sets the proper amplitude of the two sinusoids before combining them and sending the resulting waveshape over the transmission line. The demodulator shifts the received modulated sinewave by 90 degrees, and then recovers information from the shifted and the unshifted components of the received signal.

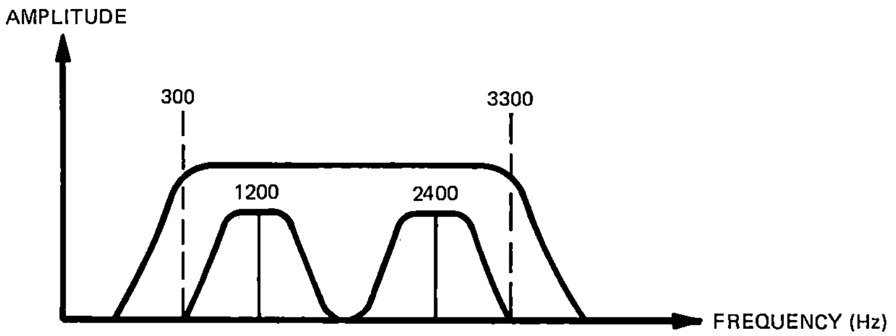

Figure 4.6 **Frequency Allocation for Bell 212A Modem**

DIFFERENTIAL PHASE MODULATION

The modulation technique commonly used for 1200-bps data transmission is a variation of the simple phase modulation, called Differential Phase Shift Keying (DPSK). The technique uses phase changes relative to the previously sent signal as indicators of the signal value. For example, in two consecutive sequences of data 00 and 11, the dibit "00" will give a phase change of 90 degrees, while the dibit "11" will change the current phase by 270 degrees. Relying on phase changes, rather than on the absolute phase value of the carrier frequencies, as would be the case in pure Phase Modulation (PM), to detect the transmitted signal obviates the need for keeping an absolute time standard at the transmitting and at the receiving terminals. Still, a synchronization procedure is required for all phase modulation techniques to assure that the initial conditions are correct and that the received signals are properly interpreted. The synchronization between the transmitting and the receiving terminal is performed by sending a fixed pattern of 1's and 0's which can be recognized by the receiving terminal during the handshake procedure at the beginning and at periodic intervals during the transmission of data.

An example of a simulated DPSK signal is shown in Figure 4.7. Notice that the maximum amplitude of the signal does not change with modulation.

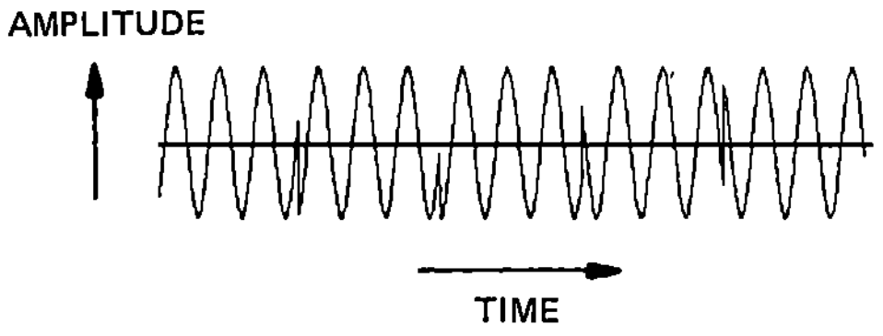

Figure 4.7 **Differential Phase Shift Keyed (DPSK) Signal**

The two methods to detect phase changes are the comparison and the coherent methods. In the comparison method, in which there is a circuit introducing delay equal to time between signal elements, two successive signal elements, one delayed and one not delayed, are compared. Comparison of two signals differing by a certain phase angle is usually accomplished by timing the zero crossings of the respective sinewaves. The coherent detection of phase modulated signals consists of comparing the received signal with an internal reference carrier being kept in phase lock with an internal clock. A decision is then made for each received signal about which phase position it represents, depending on its relation to the local clock. The local clock receives its synchronization from the received data during the handshake period, and continuously adjusts itself based on some error criteria.

COMBINED PHASE/AMPLITUDE MODULATION (QAM)

This technique, often referred to as the Quadrature Amplitude Modulation (QAM), is being used in many modem designs, at transmission speeds above 1200 bps, in particular at 2400 bps, 4800 bps, and 9600 bps. To be able to send data at these transmission speeds over the telephone network, several bits have to be combined in groups of 2, 4, or 8 bits, so that the modulation rate in Baud, equal to the transmission rate in bits, divided by the number of bits in each group, does not exceed 1200 for a full-duplex connection or 2400 for a half-duplex or for a simplex (one way) connection. Figure 4.8 shows constellation diagrams for various 2400 bps, 4800 bps, and 9600 bps standards. As the phase changes are relative, the same bit combinations appear in all four quadrants. For example, a 90 degree phase shift will move a phase vector from quadrant 1 to quadrant 2, from quadrant 2 to quadrant 3, etc. Figure 4.9 shows a modulated carrier wave according to the 2400 bps V.22 bis protocol. Notice changes in both amplitude and phase due to the QAM modulation. Demodulation of a QAM signal is a quite complex operation, consisting of detection of phase differences, followed by a decision about the value of the received amplitude. Only recent advances in Very Large Scale Integration have made a QAM modem economically feasible, in particular for personal computer modems.

TRELLIS MODULATION

Several manufacturers have recently introduced 9600-bps voice- band modems, which can operate on the two-wire switched Public Telephone Network circuits in full-duplex mode. These modems follow the CCITT V.32 protocol and employ the so-called "trellis" modulation. The trellis modulation provides a slightly better noise immunity than the 9600-bps CCITT V.29 protocol, which can be used only on private lines or in half-duplex mode on the Public Telephone Network. In the trellis modulation technique the data stream is grouped into 4 bits at a time and an additional fifth redundant bit is generated for error correction from each group of 4 bits.

The trellis constellation diagram in Figure 4.10 shows the phase and amplitude values for each combination of 5 bits in each group. The fifth bit is used for error detection and correction by the receiving modem. The receiving modem uses the Viturbi decoder, which performs the so-called "soft bit" detection. The more common "hard bit" detector decides after reception of each bit whether that bit represents a binary "0" or a binary "1." This decision depends on the amplitude of the received bit in the "eye" diagram as compared to a threshold value. After detection in the "hard bit" detector, the analog bit value, as it was received, is discarded. In a "soft bit" detector, as implemented in the Viturbi decoder, the analog value of the received bit is compared with other bits in a group and the actual decision whether a received bit was a "0" or a "1" is made only after a number of bits (up to 32) were received. The name "trellis" modulation comes from the picture of the decision tree used by the Viturbi decoder, which looks like a wooden trellis.

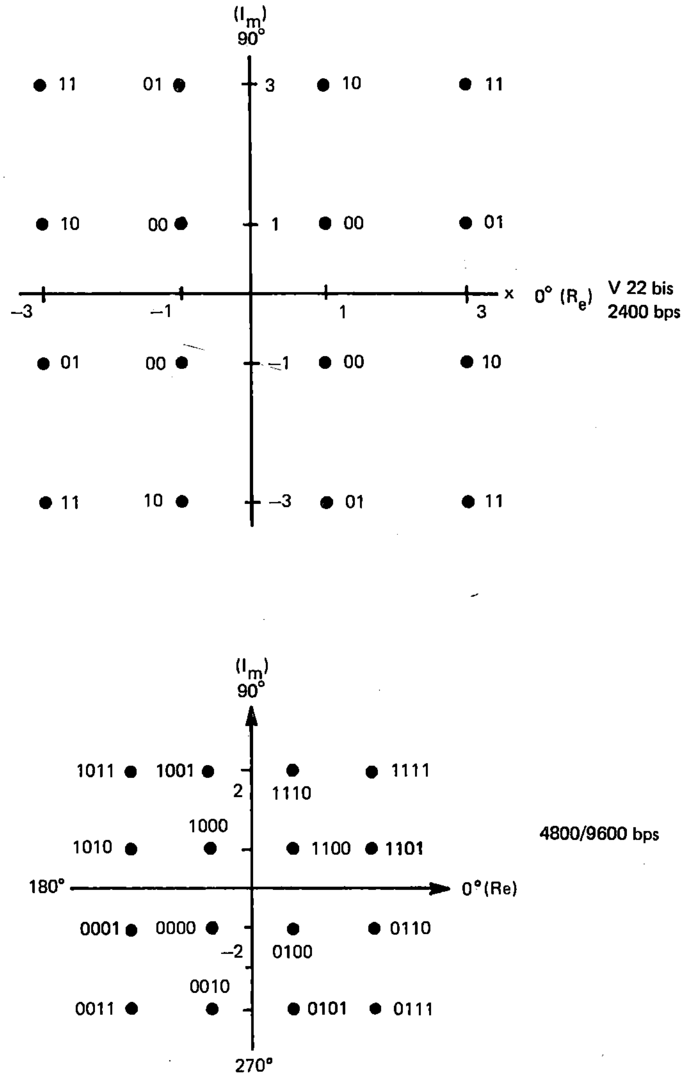

Figure 4.8 **Constellation Diagrams for 2400/4800/9600 bps Modems**

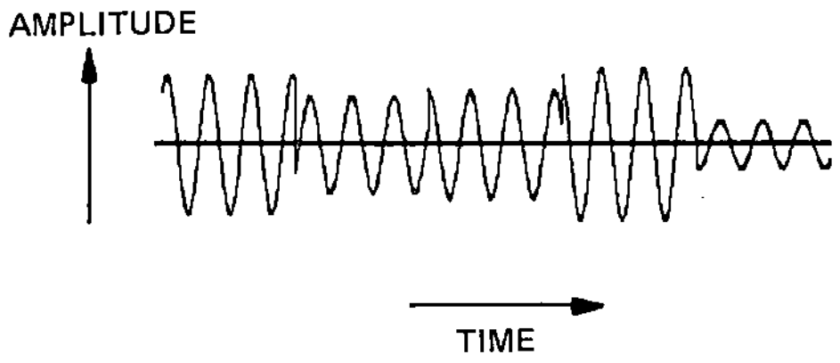

Figure 4.9 **Quadrature Amplitude Modulation (QAM) Signal**

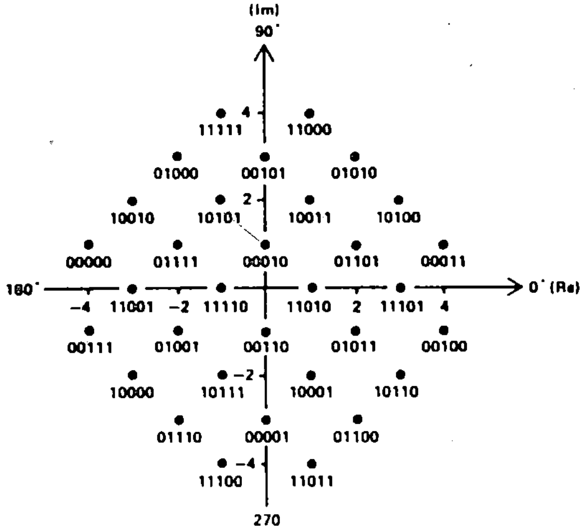

Figure 4.10 **Constellation Diagram for 9600 bps Trellis Coded Signal**

The actual decision tree is not described in the V.32 standard. The decision tree of various V.32 modems using trellis coding is proprietary and is independently arrived at by modem manufacturers. The trellis modulation scheme is also referred to as forward error correction and is supposed to provide 3—5 dB additional noise immunity. As the 9600 bps signal at 2400 Baud occupies the whole voice-band frequency spectrum, to achieve full-duplex operation over two-wire facilities, modem manufacturers employ various echo cancellation techniques.

MODULATION METHOD VERSUS SUSCEPTIBILITY TO IMPAIRMENTS

As the number of amplitude and phase levels increases with each successive, more complex modulation method, both the transmitting and the detecting circuitry become more complicated and costly. The simple FSK modulation requires only frequency discrimination; the DPSK modulation requires detection of successive relative phase positions; the QAM modulation requires detection of both phase and of amplitude changes, a formidable undertaking, in particular as the transmission seed increases in each successive modem generation. Finer distinctions between detected data signals in terms of phase and amplitude make it more difficult for the receiving modem to decide whether the signal is a "0" or a "1." As discussed previously the Shannon's theorem gives the upper bound of the transmission speed as function of the signal-to-noise ratio for a given transmission facility. This upper bound is being slowly approached with more and more complex modulation schemes.

Bit Error Rate

The Bit Error Rate (BER) of a specific modulation method easily can be computed as a function of the sugnal to noise ratio. Most BER formulas use the Gaussian error function or the complement error function as their arguments, because the thermal noise is assumed to have a Gaussian distribution of its energy as a function of time. The theoretical bit error rate, as a function of signal-to-noise ratio, for various modulation methods is given by the following formulas:

Several calculator and computer programs have been developed by this author and others to evaluate these and other BER formulas. They are listed in the Bibliography. Actual BERs measured on a 3002 unconditioned line are shown in Figure 4.11. The instrument setup used for this measurement is shown in Chapter 14, Figure 14.8. The actual BER is not only a function of the modulation technique and the type of telephone line used, but it will also be determined by the modem circuit design of a particular manufacturer. A modem manufactured by one company may have quite a different noise sensitivity from a modem manufactured by another company. It should be noted that the 300 bps FSK type modem is extremely impervious to noise showing a S/N ratio of only 8 dB required to achieve an error rate of 10^{-5}, or one error in 100,000 bits of data.

Formula 4.1 **Probability of Error Pe Versus S/N Ratio**

1. On-Off Keying (OOK), Coherent:

$$Pe = \frac{1}{2}\,\mathrm{Erfc}\left(\frac{1}{2}\sqrt{\frac{S}{N}}\right)$$

2. Frequency Shift Keying (FSK), Coherent
   Amplitude Shift Keying (ASK), Coherent
   Pulse Code Modulation (PCM), Unipolar

$$Pe = \frac{1}{2}\,\mathrm{Erfc}\sqrt{\frac{S}{2N}}$$

3. PCM, Polar
   Phase Shift Keying (PSK)

$$Pe = \frac{1}{2}\,\mathrm{Erfc}\sqrt{\frac{S}{N}}$$

4. FSK, Noncoherent

$$Pe = \frac{1}{2}\,e^{-\frac{S}{2N}}$$

5. Differential Phase Shift Keying (DPSK)

$$Pe = \frac{1}{2}\,e^{-\frac{S}{N}}$$

6. ASK, Noncoherent

$$Pe = \frac{1}{2}\,\mathrm{Erfc}\left(\frac{1}{2}\sqrt{\frac{S}{N}}\right)$$

The function Erfc (complementary error function) related to the Gaussian noise distribution is defined as follows:

$$\mathrm{Erf}\,(x) = \frac{2}{\sqrt{\pi}}\int_0^x e^{-t^2}\,dt \qquad \mathrm{Erfc}\,(x) = 1 - \mathrm{Erf}\,(x)$$

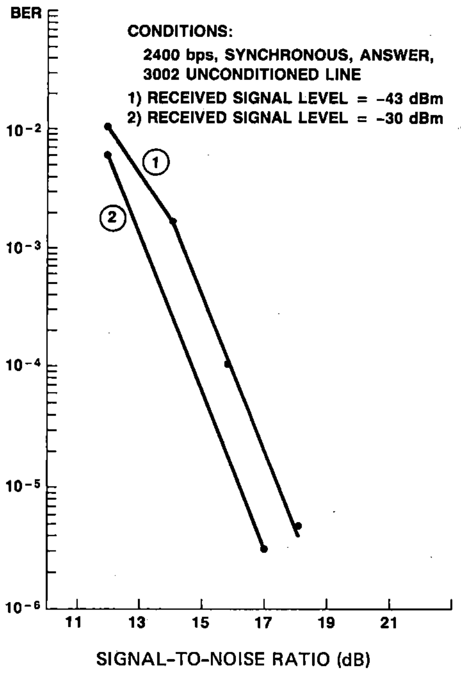

Figure 4.11 **Typical BER Curves for a 2400 bps Modem**

5. Asynchronous and Synchronous Transmission

There are two ways by which data can be exchanged between two or more computers equipped with modems, the asynchronous and the synchronous methods. Synchronization refers in this context to synchronization on characters, and not to synchronization of clocks required for proper demodulation of, for example, a DPSK signal. Each ASCII character, when expressed as a binary number, is composed of a sequence of seven or eight 0's and 1's. The receiving terminal therefore needs some indication to determine where bits belonging to one character end, and where the next character begins. In asynchronous operation, when no data is being sent, a steady stream of 1's (mark) is being transmitted. To alert the receiving terminal that a character is being sent, a start bit "0" (space) is transmitted, which is then followed by 7 or 8 data bits, a parity bit, used for error detection, and 1 or 2 stop bits "1" (mark). Figure 5.1 shows, as an example, the character "A" being transmitted. It starts with a start bit, followed by 7 bits "1000001" corresponding to A, followed in turn by a parity bit and, finally, by a stop bit. If the parity is odd, then the parity bit will be 1, if the total number of 1's in the previous 7 or 8 data bits is odd. It will be 0 otherwise. Similarly, if the parity is even, then the parity bit will be 1, if the total number of 1's in the previous 7 or 8 bits is even. It will be 0 otherwise. After the last bit associated with A is sent, either more 1's will follow or another start bit will precede the next packet of data bits associated with the next character.

Figure 5.2 shows the decision process at the receiving modem during

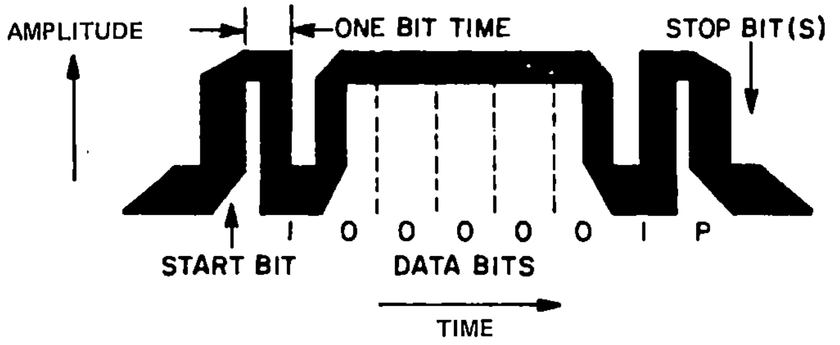

Figure 5.1 **Diagram of the Serial Transmission of the Letter "A"**

reception of individual bits comprising a character. As each character in asynchronous mode of operation is surrounded by start and stop bits, both the transmitting and the receiving modems are always synchronized by those bits on a character-by-character basis. No synchronization is required between characters. The asynchronous method is particularly suitable for manual exchange of data, where the two participants type at their respective terminals. The hardware implementation for the asynchronous mode of transmission is relatively simple, which is another reason for its popularity.

In the synchronous mode of operation no start or stop bits are transmitted, which can speed up the transmission by up to 30% (7—8 instead of 10—11 bits per character). The data is now sent in a steady stream. The local and remote modems synchronize themselves by means of special framing signals surrounding large blocks of data and by extracting timing information from data itself. In some commercial applications a clock signal is sent separately from the data on a special circuit. Figure 5.3 shows a block of data (TEXT) with synchronizing, error checking, and framing characters surrounding it.

Many medium- and high-speed modems (1200 bps and up), in particular those used in commercial environment, are equipped with the synchronous transmission option. Though integrated circuit manufacturers provide both asynchronous and synchronous options in most of their modem chip sets, the synchronous option is usually not implemented in lower priced modems, due

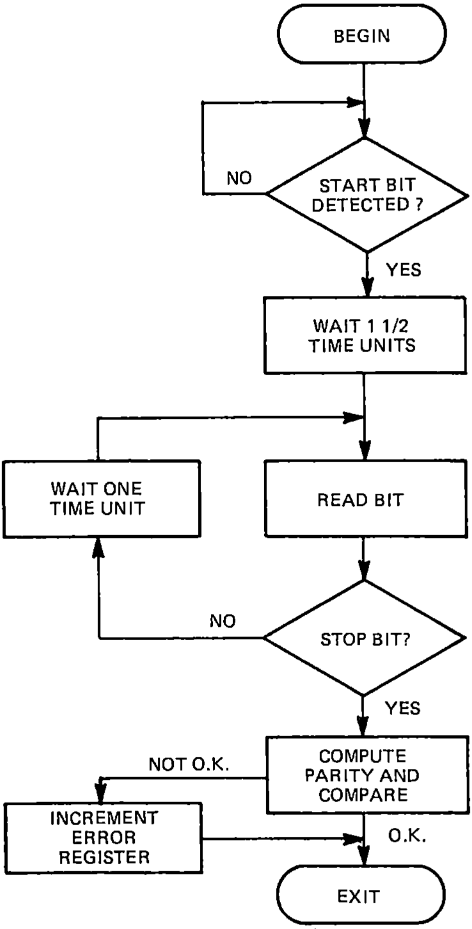

Figure 5.2 **Decision Tree for Detection of a Serially Transmitted Character**

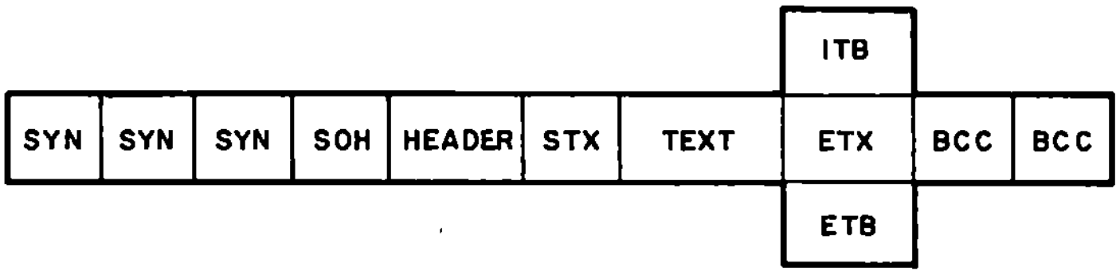

Figure 5.3 **Block of Synchronous Data With Synchronizing and Framing Bits**

to the limited public interest in that option. Only a few personal computing modems implement the synchronous option, e.g., Hayes SmartModem 2400 and the Ven-Tel 2400 Plus. In the commercial environment, synchronous modems are often used in polled and multipoint private networks. Synchronous operation permits higher transmission speed and sophisticated error recovery systems.

SYNCHRONOUS TRANSMISSION PROTOCOLS

As in other areas of data transmission, there is also a need here for common protocols, so that synchronous terminals can communicate with any other synchronous terminals and understand each others' signals. The number of framing characters and their composition is determined by the protocols used. The most commonly used synchronous transmission protocols are the Binary Synchronous Communication Protocol (BISYNC) and several High Level Data Link Protocols (HDLC). The BISYNC protocol developed by IBM in 1964 is a half-duplex character oriented procedure most often used on polled multipoint networks. The HDLC protocols are attempts to improve on BISYNC by providing full-duplex operation and being bit- rather than character-oriented. IBM's own Synchronous Data Link Control Protocol or

SDLC belongs in this category of protocols. The SDLC protocol developed in 1973 independently manages each link between terminals. SDLC can be used to control a link between a terminal and the concentrator or between the concentrator and the host computer.

The overall network control is performed by additional software in the concentrators and in the host computer. Other HDLC protocols were developed by the Digital Equipment Corporation and by other manufacturers. Another contender for a dominant synchronous protocol standard is the Hayes Synchronous Interface (HSI) protocol introduced by the Hayes Corporation. Hayes placed the protocol itself in the public domain. However, the company charges the developers a $100 license fee for use of drivers required by the protocol to interface with various Hayes compatible modems. The HSI protocol, unlike other HDLC protocols, is specifically designed to operate on personal computer modems. The HSI protocol should allow synchronous transmission at 2400 bps through a standard RS-232-C serial port. The HSI protocol will be part of the Hayes software and its Smartmodem 2400 series of modems. Should this protocol be accepted by major software vendors, then Hayes could become a dominant figure in the synchronous modem field, as it is currently in the asynchronous modem field.

Network protocols are a big subject in themselves and their detailed discussion is beyond the scope of this book. For further studies consult the Reference Section.

Following is a short summary of control characters and their ASCII equivalents in hexadecimal notation, where available, as they are used in Synchronous Transmission Protocols:

SYN	**16H**	Used to establish and maintain synchronization. Fills time in absence of data between 2 and 5 SYN characters required in each frame.
SOH	**01H**	Start of Header, user defined. Includes source/destination codes, parity, date. Terminated by STX.
STX	**02H**	Start of Text segment block. Text may be divided into several blocks.
ITB		Used to separate messages into multiple blocks. No reply required until ETB or ETX sent. Followed by BCC.
ETB	**17H**	End of Text Block for multiblock messages. Requires response from receiving station. Followed by BCC.
ETX	**03H**	End of Text, terminates a block of text. Requires reply. Followed by BCC.

BCC		Block Check Character used for error detection. Computed by Cyclic Redundancy Check from block data.
EOT	04H	End of Transmission, resets all stations on the line. Response to a poll if nothing is sent.
ACK	06H	Acknowledge, positive response, message received correctly.
NAK	15H	Negative response, message not received or incorrect. Determined by agreement of received data with BCC.
WACK		Waiting for acknowledgment.

HARDWARE CONSIDERATIONS

For proper operation in synchronous mode, both the receiving and the transmitting terminals have to use the same kind of data communications hardware and software. In addition, the serial interface on the computer and the serial cable should have pin 15 (Transmit Signal Element Timing), pin 17 (Receiver Signal Element Timing), and pin 24 (Transmit Signal Element Timing) all connected through and implemented. Both terminals also have to agree on proper timing option, namely, whether the modem provides its own clock, whether the clock will be generated by the computer, or whether the clock will be derived from the receiving modem in the so-called "slave" mode of operation. They also have to agree on the number of bits used for each character. These options are usually selected by switch or strap settings.

One of the problems inherent to synchronous transmission is that dialing and other modem commands, e.g., the AT commands, have to be sent from the computer to the modem in asynchronous mode. The communication between the computer and the modem is always asynchronous, even when the modem-to-modem transmission is synchronous. Therefore, one cannot use the escape code (+++) in synchronous mode to change from the on-line to off-line command mode, as would be the case in asynchronous operation.

The final option to be selected is the dialing mode. In dialing Mode 1, the call is placed in the standard asynchronous fashion. When the connection is established, the modem switches automatically to the synchronous mode. In dialing Mode 2, the modem automatically dials a stored number when the DTR lead is high. This number must be previously stored in the modem by means of asynchronous data transmission. In dialing Mode 3, the operator dials manually using a standard telephone set or dials a stored number using one of the modem panel buttons.

There are only three conditions under which the modem will change from the synchronous to the asynchronous operation, each of them terminating the previously established connection:

1. One can terminate a synchronous connection by pressing a front panel disconnect button normally provided on a modem.

2. When the computer drops the DTR line, the connection is terminated.

3. When the modem detects the loss of carrier, the connection will also be terminated.

Considering all the above options and settings, it is no wonder that the synchronous transmission is used mostly for specialized applications in commercial environment. However, if implemented, it can considerably speed up data transfer.

6. The Serial Interface

A computer needs a set of formalized procedures in both hardware and in software to be able to communicate with the outside world through a modem. The lower level of such procedures generally describes the hardware interfaces — plugs and jacks, electrical interfaces, voltage or current levels, timing interfaces, and signal interfaces, whether synchronous or asynchronous transmission should be used. Higher level procedures also provide rules for establishing a connection between the sender and the receiver by describing the handshake rules, granting the sender access to the physical channel, defining the message format and blocking rules, and providing message acknowledgment and recovery methods. A set of low level procedures is called an interface protocol. The most common interface protocol for communication between a computer and a modem is the serial interface. The word "serial" means that data is transmitted in sequence or serially, one bit after another, over a single wire with a ground return, or over a pair of wires balanced to ground. This differs from the parallel interface, commonly used to transfer data from a computer to a printer, where 8 bits are transmitted simultaneously over eight separate wires with ground returns.

The most common serial interface protocol is the RS-232-C standard, which is described below in detail. Because of the technical obsolescence of the RS-232-C standard, other standards have also been proposed. Still, because of the large installed base of equipment using the RS-232-C standard, these newer standards have not taken over the market. Quite to the contrary, except for some special applications, including the military, or high-speed data transmission, the RS-232-C still reigns supreme. A short review of other serial interface standards, besides the RS-232-C, is given later in this chapter.

RS-232-C SERIAL INTERFACE

The serial interface, as implemented in the RS-232-C standard, is the most common way of connecting a computer to a modem. The RS-232-C standard was developed by the Electronic Industries Association (EIA) in the stone age of computing in August, 1969. The full name of the standard is "Recommended Standard 232 Version C, Interface Between Data Terminal Equipment and Data Communications Equipment Using Serial Interface." The EIA standard describes functions of 25 leads connecting the Data Terminal Equipment (DTE), typically a terminal or a computer, to the Data Communications Equipment (DCE), typically a modem. The serial port on most computers and on most communications devices only uses between 9 and 11 leads out of the 25 leads shown in Figure 6.1. The 9 to 11 leads are sufficient for most control applications and are also sufficient for operating a modem.

Most modems, printers, controllers, and other devices in the data communications market follow selected subsets of the RS-232-C standard. There is also a European equivalent of the RS-232-C, namely, the CCITT recommendation (standard) V.24. The V.24 recommendation not only describes the electrical interface like the RS-232-C does, it also specifies many more than the 25 leads listed in the EIA standard.

Though many communications devices claim to adhere to the RS-232-C standard, they may still be incompatible with each other. The reason for incompatibility is that the RS-232-C standard, as written in the EIA specifications, covers only some aspects of the communication protocol. For example, though most RS-232-C devices use a 25-pin male or female D-shell connector, the connector is not mentioned in the EIA standard. The standard also does not say which connectors should have male and which ones should have female gender. This ambiguity alone spawned a whole family of gender changing cables and connectors. The RS-232-C standard assigns specific functions to 22 leads and lets the equipment manufacturers assign the remaining 3 leads. The pin assignments of the leads to the 25-pin D-shell connector, as used by most manufacturers complying with the RS-232-C standard designations, are shown in Figure 6.1. However, some companies, e.g., Apple in their Macintosh line of computers, and IBM in their AT computers, use 9-pin D-shell connectors (DB-9) with only a subset of the 25 leads of the RS-232-C standard. The IBM PCjr,

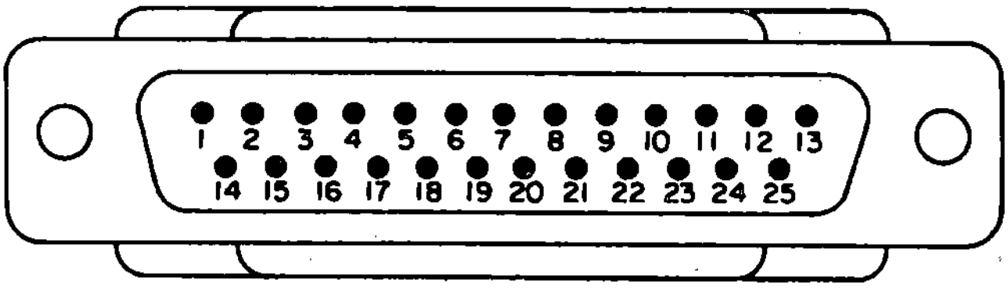

Abbrev.	Pin No.	Circuit	Description	Signal Type	Function	Direction To:
PG	1	AA	Protective Ground	Ground	Ground connected to the equipment frame or power cord ground.	
TD	2	BA	Transmitted Data	Data	Information sent from the local terminal.	DCE
RD	3	BB	Received Data	Data	Information received at the local terminal.	DTE
RTS	4	CA	Request to Send	Control	A control signal from the local terminal to determine if a transmission can be sent. This control is most useful for half duplex operation where data are transmitted in both directions, one at a time, over a single communication line. It is not necessary on full duplex (communication in both directions simultaneously) but is often implemented.	DCE
CTS	5	CB	Clear to Send	Control	A control signal to the local terminal which indicates that data transmission to the remote terminal may commence. This is in response to a Request-to-Send-command.	DTE
DSR	6	CC	Data Set Ready	Control	A handshake signal to the local terminal indicating that the data communication equipment is connected and ready to operate.	DTE
SG	7	AB	Signal Ground (Common Return)	Ground	The ground connection to which other RS-232 signals are referenced.	
RLSD	8	CF	Received Line Signal Detector	Control	Carrier Detect is a handshake to the local terminal indicating that an acceptable signal is being received on the communications line between DCEs.	DTE
	9	—		—	Reserved for data set testing.	DTE
	10	—		—	Reserved for data set testing.	DTE
	11	—	Unassigned*	—		
SRLSD	12	SCF	Secondary Received Line Signal Detector	Control	Auxiliary carrier detect used when signals on pins 14 and 16 are implemented.	DTE

*While unassigned in RS-232-C, some of these pins are used for specialized functions by the manufacturers of DTE and DCE equipment.

Figure 6.1 **RS-232-C Connector and Lead Description**

Abbrev.	Pin No.	Circuit	Description	Signal Type	Function	Direction To:
SCS	13	SCB	Secondary Clear to Send	Control	An auxiliary handshake used when signals on pins 14 and 16 are implemented.	DTE
STD	14	SBA	Secondary Transmitted Data	Data	An auxiliary channel by which low speed data or special control functions are sometimes transmitted.	DCE
TSET	15	DB	Transmission Signal Element Timing (DCE Source)	Timing	Used for synchronous transmission.	DTE
SRD	16	SBB	Secondary Received Data	Data	A low speed data or control function received from the remote DCE.	DTE
RSET	17	DD	Receiver Signal Element Timing (DCE Source)	Timing	Used for synchronous transmission.	DTE
	18	—	Unassigned*	—		
SRS	19	SCA	Secondary Request Send	Control	An auxiliary handshake used when signals on pins 14 and 16 are implemented.	DCE
DTR	20	CD	Data Terminal Ready	Control	A handshake from the terminal to prepare the DCE for communication.	DCE
SQD	21	CG	Signal Quality Detector	Control	Indicates to the local terminal that there is a low-grade signal on the communications line which could result in a high error rate. This signal is normally used on long distance telephone communications.	DTE
RI	22	CE	Ring Indicator	Control	A handshake sent to the local terminal indicating that a ringing signal is being received on the communication line. This signal would be used on an auto answer telephone communication system.	DTE
DSRS	23	CH/ CL	Data Signal Rate Selector (DTE/DCE Source)	Control	A handshake used on a telephone communication system to indicate and/or select one of two bit rates. This signal gives the user the option to operate with different speed communications equipment at the remote end.	DCE
TSET	24	DA	Transmit Signal Element Timing (DTE Source)	Timing	Used for synchronous transmission.	DCE
	25	—	Unassigned*	—		

*While unassigned in RS-232-C, some of these pins are used for specialized functions by the manufacturers of DTE and DCE equipment.

Figure 6.1 **(continued)**

even further out on a limb, uses a rectangular Berg connector as serial interface. Pin assignments used in the Macintosh serial interface are shown in Figure 6.2; those for the PCjr are shown in Figure 6.3.

By definition, a data communications device (a terminal or a modem) complies with a standard as long as it does not violate it. If one device adheres to one subset of the RS-232-C standard and another device adheres to a different

Pin Number	Macintosh Signal Name	RS-232 Signal Name
1	Chassis Ground	Chassis Ground (1)
2	Plus 5 Volts (+5)	
3	Signal Ground	Signal Ground (7)
4	Transmit Data + (TXD+)	
5	Transmit Data – (TXD–)	Transmitted Data (3)
6	Plus 12 Volts (+12)	Data Terminal Ready (20)
7	HSC Input	Data Carrier Detect (8)
8	Receive Data + (RXD+)	Chassis Ground (1)
9	Receive Data – (RXD–)	Receive Data (2)

Macintosh to Modem Connecting Cable

Macintosh Connector	Modem Connector (DCE)	Function
DB-9P	DB-25P	
(Pin Numbers)		
8	1	Chassis Ground
3	7	Signal Ground
5	3	Data Mac to Modem
7	8	Carrier Detect (HSC)
9	2	Data Modem to Mac
2	6	Data Set Ready
6	20	Data Terminal Ready

Figure 6.2 **Macintosh DB-9 Serial Interface Connector**

subset, then although both devices adhere to the RS-232-C standard, they may be incompatible with each other. To confuse things even further, the RS-232-C standard refers always to Data Terminal Equipment (DTE) and to Data Communications Equipment (DCE). This designation is fine, if one always attaches a terminal, DTE, to a modem, DCE. But how should one designate a terminal which has a printer attached to it and is connected directly to a computer? It may be considered a DTE or a DCE. Some printers are also configured as a DTE and some are configured as a DCE.

The RS-232-C standard does not cover the communication protocols, such

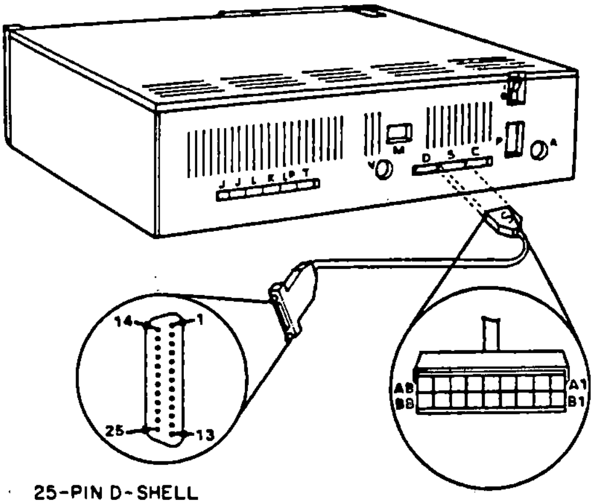

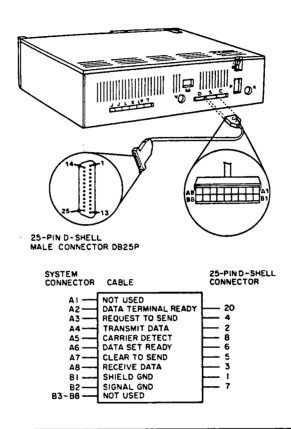

25-PIN D-SHELL
MALE CONNECTOR DB25P

SYSTEM CONNECTOR	CABLE	25-PIN D-SHELL CONNECTOR
A1	NOT USED	
A2	DATA TERMINAL READY	20
A3	REQUEST TO SEND	4
A4	TRANSMIT DATA	2
A5	CARRIER DETECT	8
A6	DATA SET READY	6
A7	CLEAR TO SEND	5
A8	RECEIVE DATA	3
B1	SHIELD GND	1
B2	SIGNAL GND	7
B3-B8	NOT USED	

Figure 6.3 **PCjr Serial Interface Connector**

as type of transmission (asynchronous or synchronous), or the number of bits per character. The features which the RS-232-C standard covers best are the electrical characteristics of the data signals. The received data signals, according to the RS-232-C standard, are interpreted as follows: –3 to –15 V is a "mark" — a binary "1"; +3 to +15 V is a "space" — a binary "0." Voltage levels between –3 and +3 V are not defined. Similarly, negative voltages on control leads indicate the OFF or LOW condition, positive voltages indicate the ON or HIGH condition. These relations are shown in Figure 6.4. In real-life use, what is referred to as the RS-232-C interface is a subset of the above

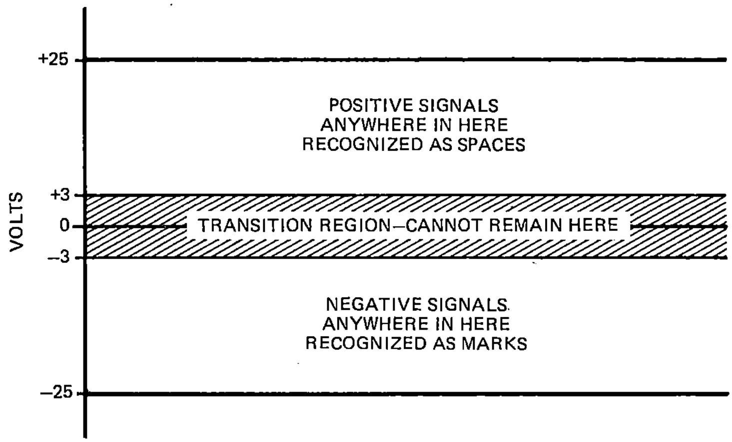

Figure 6.4 **RS-232-C Signal Levels**

electrical requirements combined with asynchronous serial transmission of data.

One important safety feature of the RS-232-C standard is that any lead can be connected to any other lead without causing damage to the equipment. Cross-connecting assorted leads may not help in establishing a data connection, but at least it will not "fry" anything. The "null" modem described later in this chapter, as well as various "cheater" cords like those described in Chapter 7, all rely on this "nondamage" feature of the RS-232-C standard.

At a recent computer convention I heard about a computer salesman telling a customer how easy it is to interconnect various devices, as long as they follow the well-established RS-232-C standard. The customer then asked whether he needed a 25-pin male or a 9-pin female cable, and whether the data leads should be reversed or straight. The salesman's answer was that the store carries every "standard" cable and if they do not have one, they will make it.

After reading all this, one may probably wonder how two RS-232-C devices ever communicate with each other. Well, sometimes they do, and sometimes one has to put some extra effort to achieve successful exchange of information.

Before explaining how to connect a modem to a computer through the serial port I will show how to transfer data between two computers without a modem, or to be precise, by means of a "null" modem.

COMPUTER-TO-COMPUTER COMMUNICATION VIA "NULL" MODEM

Use of the serial port allows one to send files directly from one computer to another. If the two computers are located near each other, one only needs a connecting cable and a so-called "null" modem to do it. For example I have used a null modem to transfer text, data, and program files between the AT&T PC6300, the IBM PC, the TRS-80 Model I, and the TANDY Model 100. This technique is particularly useful if the disk formats of the two computers are not compatible. For example, one computer may use 5.25-in. and the other 3.5-in. disks, and one may have a need to transfer data or program files between them.

The reason why a null modem is frequently necessary is that most computers are configured as DTEwith data being transmitted on pin 2 and data being received on pin 3, rather than as a DCE, where data is transmitted on pin 3 and received on pin 2. The "null" modem cable is required to make one of the computers appear to the other computer as a terminal (DTE). If one connects for example, two IBM PCs, one will need either two modems back to back, or as a simpler solution, one will need a short piece of cable which interchanges the Receive Data and the Transmit Data signals on pins 2 and 3, as

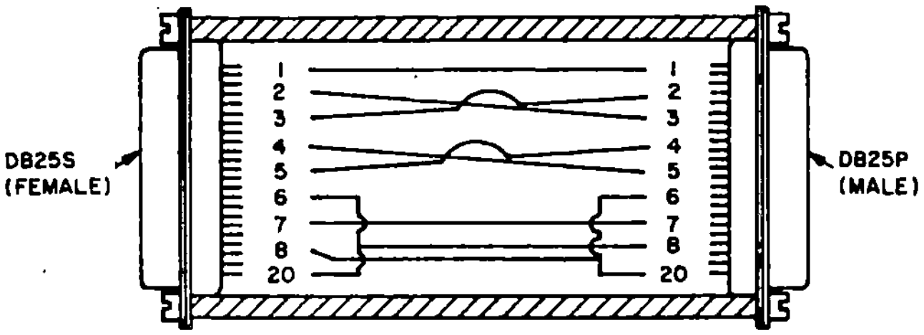

Figure 6.5 **Diagram of a "Null" Modem**

well as all the appropriate control signals. The control signals indicate if the transmitting terminal is ready to send and if the receiving terminal is ready to receive data. Such a cable, which is electrically equivalent to two modems connected back to back, is called a null modem.

The physical implementation of a null modem may be in a cable or in a large plug with DB-25 connectors at both ends. Figure 6.5 shows a typical implementation of a null modem. Notice in particular the crossed leads #2 and

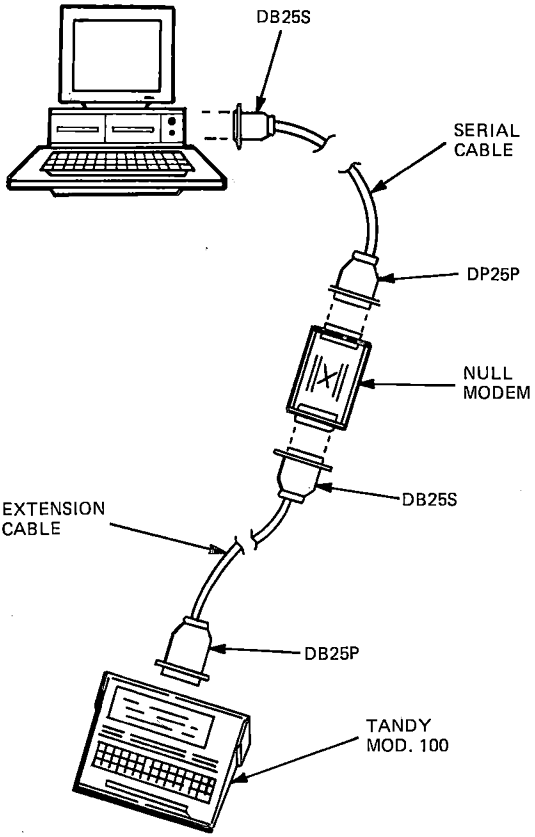

Figure 6.6 **Hook-Up of an IBM-PC and Tandy 100 Via a "Null" Modem**

#3. If the null modem cable is not available, one can easily put one together following that figure. The RS-232-C 25-pin male and female D-shell connectors can be easily found in most electronic and computer supply stores. When buying a null modem, or when building one from individual components, one should check for gold-plated pins on all connectors. Gold makes the best electrical corrosion-proof contacts. Figure 6.6 shows connections required to transfer files between an IBM PC and TANDY Model 100 by means of a null modem. The same Figure 6.6 would apply to most other computers equipped with a serial interface. After making the proper connections you may now send a letter or a BASIC program listing from the IBM PC to the TANDY Model 100. Just remember to first save the BASIC program to be transmitted as an ASCII file with the

```
SAVE "filename",A
```

command, because the simple file transfer programs work only with standard ASCII characters. The simple communications programs get confused by special characters present in non-ASCII files (e.g., tokenized BASIC files) and interpret them as control characters, carriage returns, form feeds, disconnects, etc.

To initiate the file transfer one should first redirect the IBM PC printer output to the serial port by entering the following commands while in DOS:

```
MODE COM1:600,n,7,1,p
MODE LPT1:=COM1
```

The display should then look as follows:

```
A>MODE COM1:600,n,7,1,p
Resident portion of MODE loaded
COM1: 600,n,7,1,p
A>MODE LPT1:=COM1
Resident portion of MODE loaded
LPT1: redirected to COM1:
A>
```

The first command sets the transmission parameters for the serial port "COM1" to 600 bps, no parity, 7 data bits, 1 stop bit, and "p" to continuously check for time-out errors. The second command redirects the printer (LPT1) to the serial communication port. Change COM1 to COM2 in both commands if you have a printer, an internal modem, or some other device installed in the system unit of your PC as COM1. The internal modem is then referred to as COM1 and the serial port is then referred to as COM2. Based on experience, I find the above MODE statements foolproof. In particular, 600 bps seems to be the fastest common denominator for reliable transmission between various computers, serial printers, operating systems, and communications programs.

When transmitting to the TANDY Model 100, call its resident terminal program TELCOM/TERM and set its serial parameters (bit rate, parity, start and stop bits) to the same values as for the IBM PC. Now load into the PC's memory the program which you want to transmit to the other computer, and then type LLIST. The program listing, instead of going to the printer, will now go via the serial interface to the TANDY Model 100. The program can then be saved on the Model 100, and if the two BASIC dialects are compatible, it can also be executed. Similarly, a file of text can be transmitted from the IBM PC using the TYPE command from DOS. If you are transmitting to a computer other than the TANDY Model 100, then the only difference would be, that you would have to load an appropriate terminal communications program into the target computer before starting transmission, unless it has a resident terminal program already builtin as in the TANDY Model 100.

Terminal programs, which translate a string of characters, including special characters, into a series of ASCII codes, have been developed for nearly every computer and are either in the public domain or can be purchased at a reasonable cost. Chapter 9, Communications Software, describes such programs in more detail. These programs initialize the integrated circuit doing the parallel-to-serial data translation in the computer or on the internal modem card, the so-called UART (Universal Asynchronous Receiver and Transmitter), by supplying it with the bit rate, parity information, and other parameters. The terminal programs also load the files, which are to be transmitted (not necessarily in ASCII format) from disk into memory and vice versa, provide feedback, echo to the transmitting terminal, and take care of other nitty-gritty details.

CONNECTING A SERIAL PORT TO A MODEM

If the transmitting and the receiving computer are separated by a substantial distance, then instead of the simple connection using a null modem, as

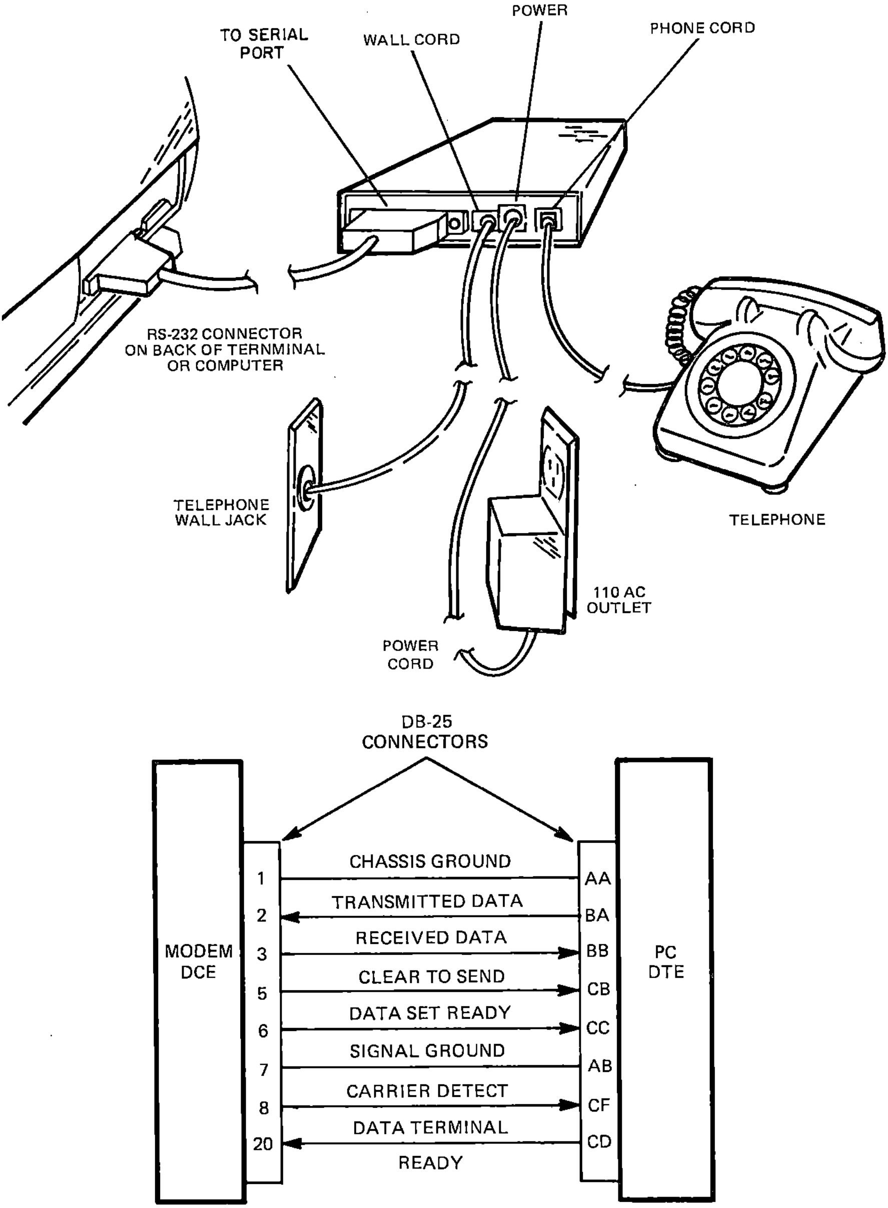

Figure 6.7 **Hook-Up of a PC to an External Modem and to a Telephone Outlet**

described in the previous paragraph, a data path including a modem and a telephone connection has to be established. The basic connections and typical pin assignments between an external modem, the computer's serial port, the phone, and the phone outlet are shown in Figure 6.7.

Certain pins like pin 15 (TC), pin 17 (RC), pin 12 (SCD), and pin 18 (SRS) may not be implemented in the computer or in the modem. The same considerations as those described in the previous paragraph about choosing COM1 or COM2 will still apply. In general, the DB-25 jack on the computer will be male and the one on the modem will be female. The start-up handshake sequence between the serial port and the modem is shown in Table 6.1.

Table 6.1 **Start-Up Sequence (Control Signals)**

RS-232-C Signal	**Description**
DTR	Normally high when DTE is ON
DSR	Normally high when DCE is ON
RTS	Goes high to request service
CTS	Goes high after typically 100 ms delay, connection is now established (dialing)
CD	Goes high to indicate received carrier
TD	Starts sending from DTE to DCE
RD	Starts receiving from DCE to DTE

To start the handshake sequence, the computer sets the DTR lead to ON. The modem responds by setting the DSR lead ON. Next, the computer signals that it is ready to send data by setting the RTS lead ON. The modem responds, after a specified delay time, that it is ready to accept data by setting the CTS lead ON. The final step before transmission of data is confirmation by the local computer that the carrier was received from the remote modem by setting the CD lead ON. The data exchange then proceeds on the lead TD and on the lead RD.

NON RS-232-C SERIAL INTERFACES

The RS-232-C developed in 1969 has severe limitations in terms of maximum transmission speed of 19200 bps and maximum distance between DTE and DCE of only 50 ft. Therefore, a number of other standards have been

Table 6.2 Non-RS-232-C Serial Standard Pin Assignments

RS232C/CCITT V.24	CCITT V.35	RS449	
25 Pin	34 Pin	37 Pin	9 Pin
1—Protective Ground	A—Protective Ground	1—Shield 37—Send Common	1—Shield 9—Send Common
2—Transmitted Data	P—Transmit Data (A) S—Transmit Data (B)	4—Send Data (A) 22—Send Data (B)	
3—Received Data	R—Received Data (A) T—Received Data (B)	6—Received Data (A) 24—Received Data (B)	
4—Request to Send	C—Request to Send	7—Request to Send (A) 25—Request to Send (B)	
5—Clear to Send	D—Clear to Send	9—Clear to Send (A) 27—Clear to Send (B)	
6—Data Set Ready	E—Data Set Ready	11—Data Mode (A) 29—Data Mode (B)	
7—Signal Ground	B—Signal Ground	19—Signal Ground	5—Signal Ground (C)
8—Carrier Detect	F—Receive Line Signal Detect	13—Receiver Ready (A) 31—Receiver Ready (B)	
9—Reserved for Testing	m—Reserved for DSU Testing		
		20—Receive Common	6—Receive Common
10—Reserved for Testing		10—Local Loop (A) 14—Remote Loop (A)	
11—Unassigned		3—SPARE 21—SPARE	
12—Sec. Carrier Detect		32—Select Standby	2—Sec. Receiver Ready
13—Sec. Clear to Send			8—Sec. Clear to Send
14—Sec. Transmitted Data			3—Sec. Send Data
15—Transmit Clock (DCE Source)	Y—TX Signal Element Timing o—TX Signal Element Timing	5—Send Timing (A) DCE Source 23—Send Timing (B) DCE Source	
16—Sec. Received Data			4—Sec. Received Data
17—Receive Clock	V—RX Signal Element X—RX Signal Element	8—Receive Timing (A) 26—Receive Timing (B)	
18—Unassigned		18—Test Mode (A) 28—Term in Service (A) 34—New Signal	
19—Sec. Request to Send			7—Sec. Request to Send
20—Data Terminal Ready		12—Terminal Ready (A) 30—Terminal Ready (B)	
21—Signal Quality Detector		33—Signal Quality (A)	
22—Ring Indicator		15—Incoming Call (A)	
23—Data Signal Rate Selector		2—Signaling Rate Indicator (A)	
		16—Signaling Rate Selector (A)	
24—Transmit Clock (DTE Source)		17—Terminal Timing (A) 35—Terminal Timing (B)	
25—Busy		36—Stand by Indicator	

developed since 1969 to enable operation at higher transmission speeds and at longer distances.

Some of these newer interface standards were developed by the same EIA committee as the RS-232-C and start with letters RS, some were developed by the European standard body CCITT and start with the letter V, and some were developed by the U.S. military and start with the letters MIL-STD. The standards are frequently as confusing as the RS-232-C standard, occasionally leaving out the hardware specifications.

Table 6.2 lists pin assignments of the most common non-RS-232-C serial interface standards in current use, RS-449 and CCITT V.35, and compares them with the RS-232-C standard.

The most important of these standards, the RS-449, defines only the mechanical interface, the 37-pin and the 9-pin connectors. It defines 10 new leads beyond those already specified by the RS-232-C standard, and it uses two additional electrical standards, the RS-422 and the RS-423. It is interoperable with RS-232-C and is equivalent to MIL-188-114. The big disadvantage of the RS-449 standard is the need for two connectors and the associated heavy cables.

The RS-422 standard provides signals which are balanced to ground. Both data and control signals require a pair of wires for each signal. The standard can operate at transmission speeds of up to 100 kbps at distances of 1 km and at 10 Mbps at distances of up to 10 m. The inherent advantage of a balanced circuit is that it is less affected by ambient electrical noise. The RS-422 generator has two outputs, which connect to two transmission lines. The receiver responds to the voltage difference between these two lines, rather than to voltage difference between a line and ground, as in the unbalanced RS-232-C interface. When the transmission lines are subject to electrical noise, the noise affects both lines to about the same degree, so that the difference, as measured by the receiver, is less noticeable. The RS-422 installations frequently use inexpensive twisted-pair telephone cable, which is mentioned in the appendix to the RS-422 standard.

The RS-423 standard provides signals which are unbalanced to ground, similar to RS-232-C. Because of this limitation the interface can only operate at up to 3 kbps at distances of 1 km and at 300 kbps at 10 m.

The V.35 interface based on the CCITT recommendations is popular with high-speed modems and multiplexers. It is specified as interface for various high-speed digital services. The data and control lines are balanced to ground using multipair twisted cable. The V.35 interface uses a rectangular connector, as shown is Table 6.4.

INTERFACE CONVERTERS

When two pieces of data communications equipment use different and incompatible interfaces, it may be possible to find an interface converter. The following is a list of interface converters listed by a modem and interface manufacturer, the Black Box Corporation of Pittsburgh.

RS-232-C to RS-422 Converter
RS-232-C to V.35 Converter
RS-422 to V.35 Converter
RS-232-C to MIL-188 Converter
RS-232-C to Current Loop Converter
RS-232-C to RS-449 Converter
RS-232-C to Burroughs TDI Converter

Each of the above converters consists of a small box with jacks to accommodate the two incompatible interfaces. For example, the first converter interconnects the electrically balanced RS-422 with the unbalanced RS-232-C equipment. All supported leads are converted to their electrical equivalents. Both DCE and DTE equipment is supported and the interface conversion occurs in both directions of transmission. Mechanical connection is to a 25-pin connector on the RS-232-C side and to a 37-pin and a 9-pin connector on the RS-422 side. Both synchronous and asynchronous operation is supported.

Nearly every interface comes with its own set of connectors. Some interfaces, for example, the RS-232-C, even come with a variey of different plugs and jacks, though the DB-25 connectors are most prevalent. Table 6.3 compares specifications of various serial interfaces, while Table 6.4 shows connector types associated with serial and other interfaces.

Table 6.3 **Serial Interface Specifications**

	RS-232-C	**RS-422-A**	**RS-423-A**	**RS-485**	**RS-449**
Recommended Maximum Distance (feet)	50	4000	4000	---	200
Maximum Signaling Rate (bits/sec)	20k	10M	100k	10M	20k/2M
Generator Levels (V)					
Open Circuit	<25	≤6	≤6	<6	RS-422 /423
On, Space, 0	+5 to +15	+2 to +6	+3.6 to +6	+1.5 to +5	
Off, Mark, 1	–5 to –15	–2 to –6	–3.6 to –6	–1.5 to –5	
Maximum Receiver Levels (V)	±3 to ±25	±12	±12	–7 to +12	RS-422 /423
Balanced/ Unbalanced	U	B	U	B	U / B
Connector	25-pin D	---	---	---	37- and 9-pin D

Table 6.4 **Interface Connections**

INTERFACE	CONN. TYPE	NO. OF PINS	APPLICATION
	DB 25	25	RS-232
	DB37	37	RS-449
	DB50	50	DataProducts, Datapoint, UNIVAC, & others
	DB15	15	DSU, CSU, TI, NCR POS, & others
	DB9	9	449 Secondary, ATARI, DAA, & others
	V.35	34	V.35
	M/50	48	Data Products, UNIVAC, DEC, & others
	Champ	36	Centronics, Champ, Printronics, Epson & others
	IEE-488	24	IEEE-488
	MATE-N-LOK	8	Current Loop
	RJ-11	4	Telephone
	RJ-45	8	Telephone

RS-232 Interface

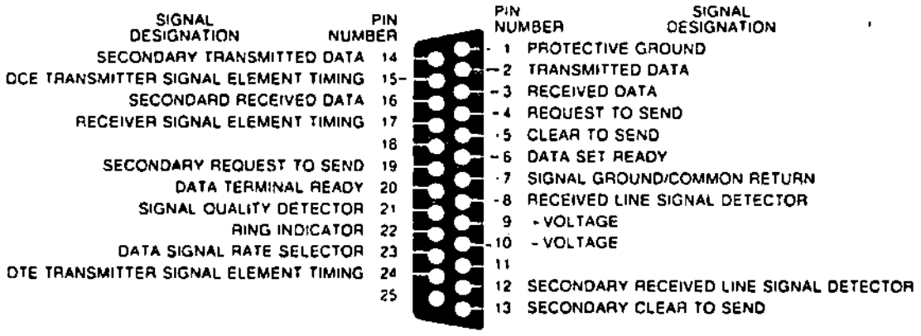

RS-449 Interface

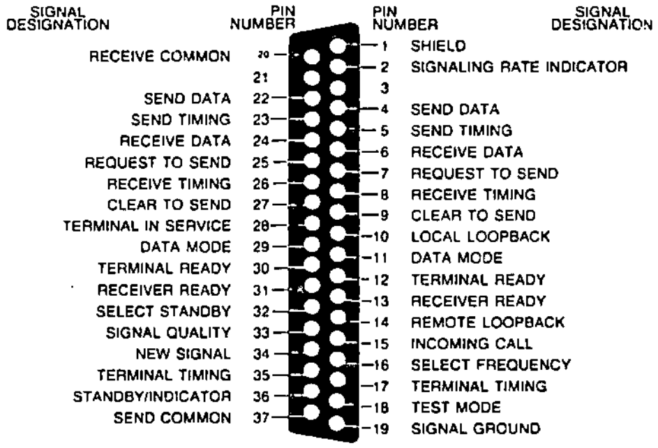

Table 6.4 **(continued)**

Centronics Interface

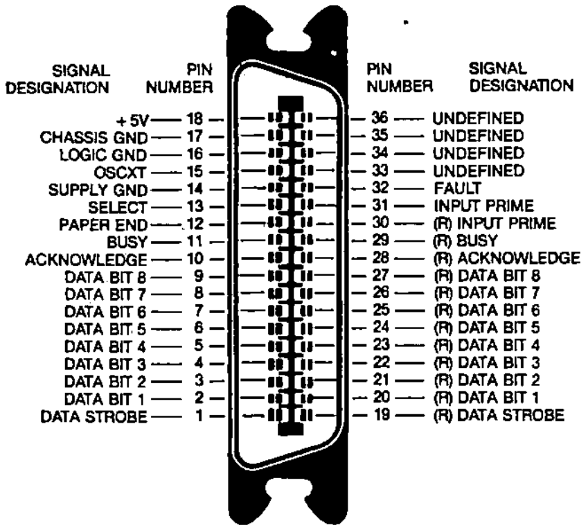

(R) INDICATES SIGNAL GROUND RETURN

V.35 Interface

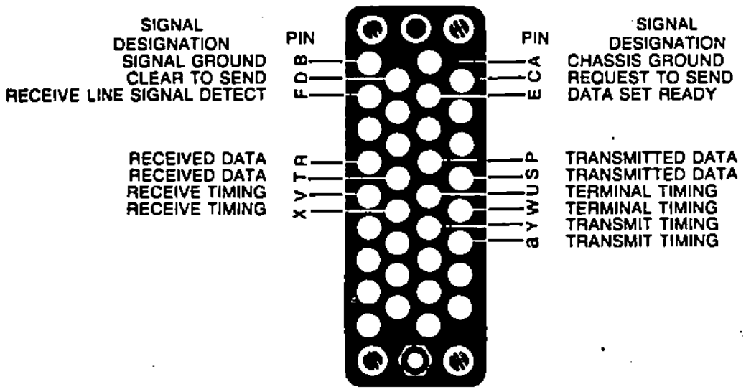

Part Two
Modems for the Personal Computer User

Owners of personal computers are the principal users and purchasers of modems. The explosive growth of personal computers, and of modems associated with them, is due to low prices, high quality, and adherence to common standards by most manufacturers. This makes for easy exchange of data between modems attached to different computers.

In Chapter 7, the reader will find a description of features and options available to the personal modem user, and advice about their relative importance. In Chapter 8, there is a description of a set of features, commonly referred to as the Hayes standard, to which most personal modems adhere, and of various extensions to this standard. In Chapter 9 comes the communications software and the error detecting and correcting protocols. In the final Chapter 10 of Part 2, there is a discussion of a set of Large Scale Integration chips, which comprise the "guts" of a 300/1200/2400 bps modem.

7. Modems for Personal Computers

In many low- and medium-speed applications, at transmission rates of 2400 bps or less, the personal computer and the personal modem associated with it provide a convenient and economical way to exchange digital information. The terms ''personal'' computer and ''personal'' computer modem apply only in part to the private ''home'' market. Though large, the home market is overshadowed by business applications of the personal computer with its evergrowing capabilities. In terms of sheer numbers, the personal computer market is the principal user of modems. The reason for the popularity of modems, particularly in the United States, is the nearly complete lack of restrictions for connecting modems to the Public Telephone Network, availability of high quality communications software, standardization and low cost of personal computer modems. Thanks to standardization of hardware and software, users can exchange data with each other, even if their modems and computers come from different manufacturers or use different operating systems. All that is required is that data communications parameters such as bit rate, number of data and stop bits and parity are the same at both ends of a data connection.

Personal modem sales are of the order of 2 million modems per year, with the Hayes Corporation still holding a predominant but declining share of the market. In 1986, Hayes had between 40% and 50% of the personal modem market. This is a substantial decline from the 68% market share which, according to Future Computing Inc., Hayes held in 1984. An ever growing share of the personal modem market is currently taken by other U.S. manufacturers like Ven-tel, Rixon, Novation, US Robotics, UDS and by various Far East imports.

Thanks to ingenuity of designers, competition, and availability of inexpensive modem chip sets, many modem features which were previously found only in the commercial market are now available at low prices in the personal modem market. For example, only a few years ago I tried to establish from my home phone a data connection to a main-frame computer. Unfortunately the main-frame access required a certain touch-tone code, while my home phone used a rotary dial and the acoustically-coupled modem was not equipped with an automatic touch-tone dialer. Finally, using some ingenuity the problem was solved by recording the touch-tone signals from another phone with a tape recorder and then playing the tape back to the main-frame computer after the connection was established using the rotary dial. The one serious problem left was that the connection established with so much effort would break down when anybody would make a loud noise in the house. The sound would be picked up by the acoustic modem coupler, the only type of personal modem used only a few years ago, and would ruin the connection.

Today the same connection can be established in a few seconds by means of an auto-dialing direct-connect modem. The data communications software resident in my home computer now uses a script file, which sends the proper codes and passwords upon receiving a prompt from the main-frame computer.

MODEM STANDARDS FOR PERSONAL COMPUTERS

Modems currently used with personal computers follow one of three standards, which have evolved over the last several years:

a. 300 bps, asynchronous, based on the Bell 103A protocol

b. 1200/300 bps, asynchronous, based on the Bell 212A protocol

c. 2400/1200/300 bps, asynchronous, based on the CCITT V.22 bis protocol

The higher speed modems (b) and (c) are downward compatible, i.e., the 2400-bps modem can operate at 300 or 1200 bps; the 1200 bps modem can also operate at 300 bps. In general, the calling modem will recognize the maximum transmission speed of the called modem during the handshake sequence. If this speed is lower than the maximum speed of the calling modem, then the calling modem will automatically adjust its transmission speed to that of the called modem. The so-called "intelligent" operation, which includes auto-dialing and compatibility with the Hayes AT command set, is a standard feature of some 300-bps and of most 1200- and 2400-bps personal computer modems. All personal computer modems can communicate over the switched telephone network in full-duplex mode. With the continuing price erosion in the personal computer field, the 300-bps modem is now becoming nearly obsolete as 1200-bps modems can be purchased for under $200 and 2400-bps modems for under $300. Currently, the 1200-bps modem has approximately 50% of the personal modem market. It is slowly being replaced by the 2400-bps modems. The 2400-bps modem, based on the CCITT V.22 bis recommendation, is the preferred choice for new modem applications.

A recent study conducted by PC Magazine compared the minimum signal-to-noise ratios of transmission lines required for error-free communication between modems from various manufacturers at different transmission speeds. The interesting conclusion was that although 2400-bps operation over switched telephone network was frequently found unreliable, the same 2400-bps modems worked much better at 1200-bps than the 1200-bps only modems. The main cause of good performance of 2400-bps modems at 1200-bps is use of adaptive equalizers and of more precise filters, without which acceptable performance at 2400-bps would not be possible. Good performance at 300-bps and at 1200-bps would be thus another reason to purchase a 2400-bps modem, even if it is only being used in the 1200-bps mode.

BUILT-IN AND EXTERNAL MODEMS

A personal computer modem can be purchased as either an internal built-in card or as an external unit, which is then connected to the computer with a serial cable. We will discuss later the advantages and disadvantages of each configuration. Figures 7.1 and 7.2 show pictures of the two modem implementations.

Some of the modem components will be found in both built-in and external units; others are specific to either one or the other configuration. The most important components of both a built-in and an external modem are the signal processing integrated circuits, either a specialized modem chip set, or a general purpose microprocessor with a program stored on a Read Only Memory (ROM) chip. An internal modem will have, in addition, a Universal Asynchronous Receiver and Transmitter (UART) circuit, which translates the parallel signals coming from the computer bus (1 byte, equal to 8 bits, at a

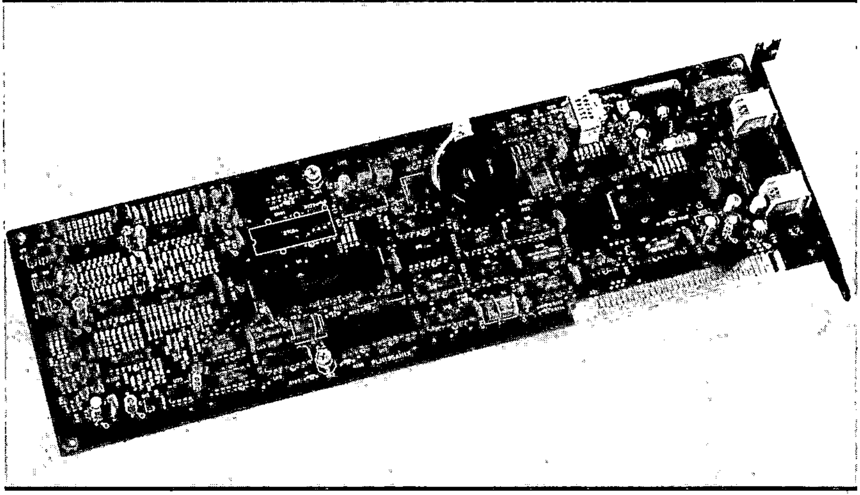

Figure 7.1 **Picture of an Internal Modem**

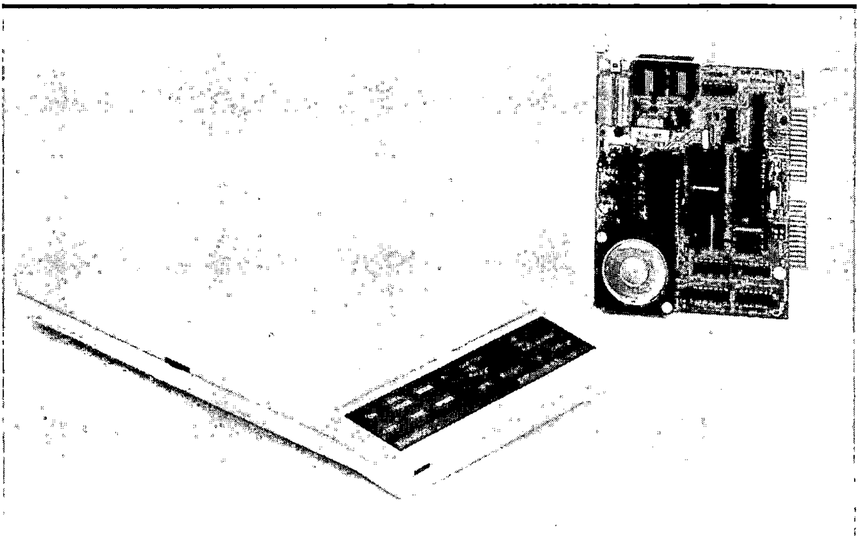

Figure 7.2 **Picture of an External Modem**

time), to serial signals (1 bit at a time). The serial signals are then sent to, or are received from, the remote terminal.

Both an internal or external modem should also have a speaker with a volume control to monitor the ring, busy, and dial tone signals on the telephone line. On the outside, an internal or an external modem will have one or two RJ11C telephone jacks. All external modems and some internal ones will also have a DB-25 jack for the RS-232-C interface. Many modems will also have Read/Write Memory (RAM) chips to store the configuration values entered by the user. One will also find on a modem a set of jumpers or DIP switches for setting various parameters. These parameters will be discussed later in this chapter. An essential part of each modem is the Direct Access Arrangement (DAA) circuit, which isolates the modem and the computer from all "bad" influences of the telephone line and vice versa. The telephone company and the FCC insist on the DAA circuit to protect other telephone users from defective modems, which could interfere with the Public Telephone Network. Block diagrams of the two modem configurations showing the individual components are shown in Figures 7.3 and 7.4.

A built-in modem and an equivalent external modem should not differ in

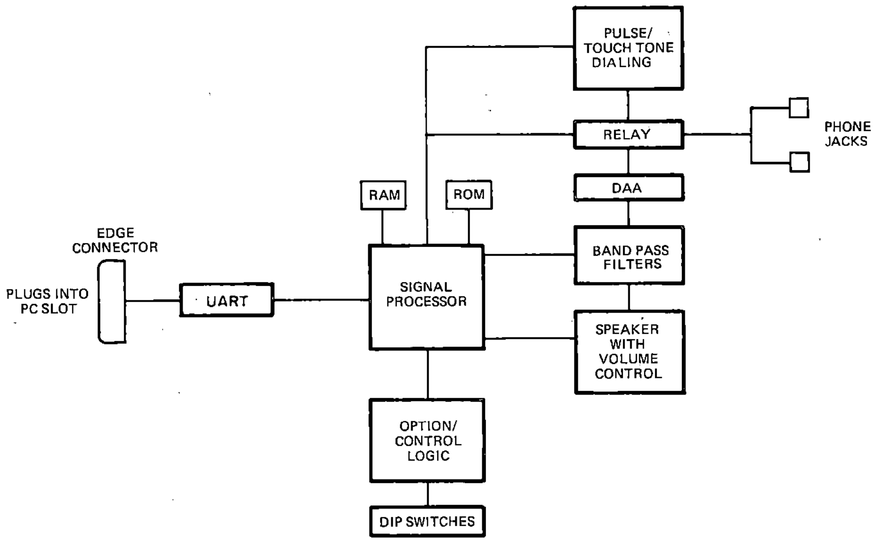

Figure 7.3 **Block Diagram of an Internal Modem**

terms of transmission quality; still, each is built differently and each has its advantages and disadvantages. Choosing the proper type may be very important.

The differences in modem hardware should be transparent to the user. The difference, as mentioned before, consists mainly of the internal modem being equipped with a UART circuit, which translates between the parallel data on the computer bus and the serial data stream being sent to the remote modem. To compensate for the cost of the UART, the internal modem does not require an external power supply, as it derives its power directly from the computer bus. Savings on the power transformer, which would be required in an external power supply, on enclosure, and on indicator lights make the internal modem less expensive by about 20% than an equivalent external modem.

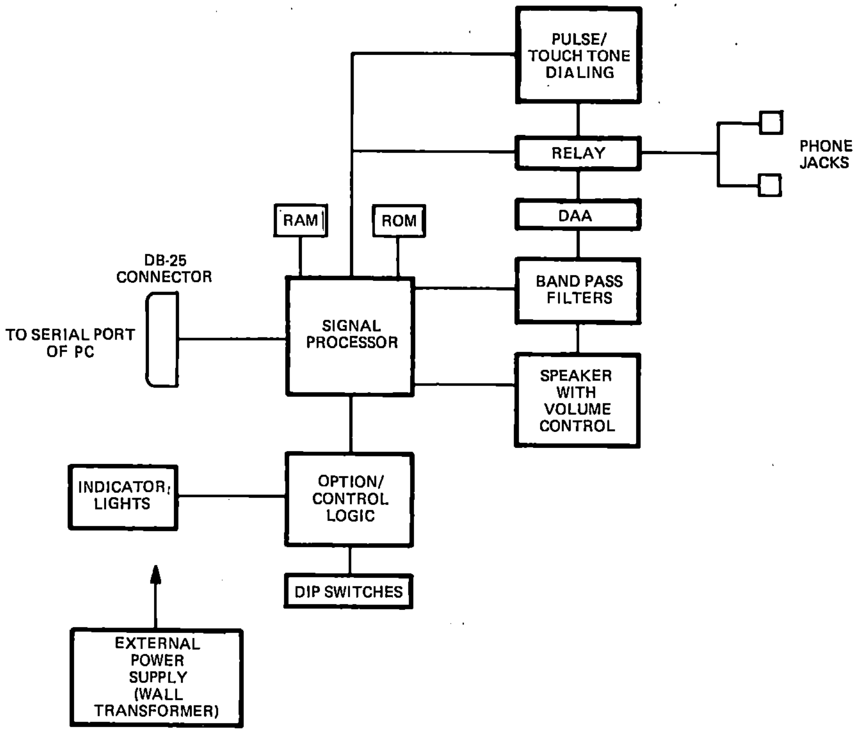

Figure 7.4 **Block Diagram of an External Modem**

The advantage of power being derived from the computer bus results not only in saving on the power transformer, but also in lack of an external cable leading to the wall-mounted power transformer. Still, some external modems operate on portable batteries to avoid the clutter of a power cable. A possible disadvantage of the internal modem is additional load on the computer power supply, which may not be adequate to support it.

While an internal modem provides its own serial RS-232-C port, an external modem uses a serial port built into the computer. It may be a separate card, as on the IBM-PC/XT series, or it may come "free" on the computer mother board, as on the ATT PC6300. On most computers a serial port is a separate option, a circuit card which plugs in the computer bus. The DB-25 jack with 25 pins, or the DB-9 jack with 9 pins, protrudes in back or on the side of the computer. The serial cable completes the connection between this jack and the external modem.

The internal modem does not need a separate serial port, since all serial port hardware is already included on the modem plug-in card, which mounts in the computer cage. Its only external connections are two RJ11C jacks, one for the cable connecting to the telephone outlet and the other for the cable connecting to the telephone set. Again, this arrangement results in reducing the clutter on the computer desk by doing away with the thick serial cable required for the external modem.

One other point to consider when deciding between an internal and an external modem is the fact that an internal modem occupies a card slot in the computer chassis, which may be required for other cards performing important functions not necessarily related to data communication, e.g., additional memory or graphics cards. The advantages of the external modem are its indicator lights, which may pinpoint a problem in a data connection, and its portability allowing it to be attached to any computer with a serial interface, e.g., an IBM-PC, a Commodore C64, an Apple IIc, or even an early vintage TRS-80 Model I or III. However, although an external modem plugs into the normally available serial port and does not require any additional hardware, if the available serial port is already occupied by another device, e.g., a printer, a plotter, or a "mouse," then an additional RS-232-C serial card will have to be purchased and installed in the computer.

The final point to consider is that, if the two standard serial ports COM1 and COM2 are already used, then an internal modem can often be assigned to COM3 or COM4, which are supported by MS-DOS but cannot be accessed by an external modem.

Figure 6.7 showed a typical connection between the computer, an external modem, the telephone outlet, and the telephone set. Figure 7.5 shows a similar connection for an internal modem. Unless the computer is used only to access bulletin boards, computerized information services, and other fully automated services not requiring human assistance, it is a desirable feature for a modem to be equipped with two, rather than with one, RJ11C jacks to plug in a telephone set. This way, one can easily go back and forth between data and

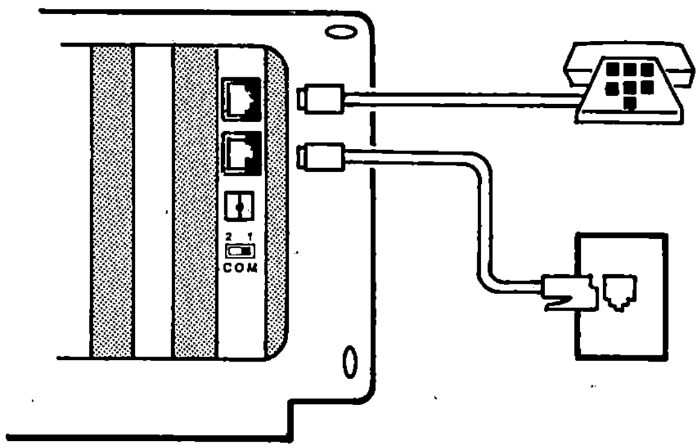

Figure 7.5 **Internal Modem Connections With Two Telephone Plugs**

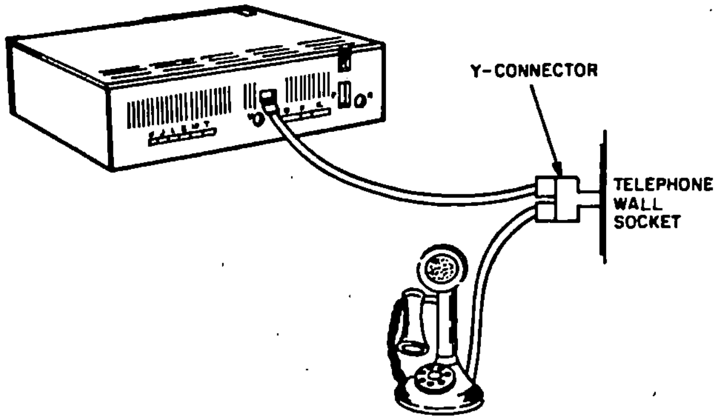

Figure 7.6 **Modem Connections With One Telephone Plug and a "Y" Connector**

voice communication. Lack of a second jack may require a Y-connector to plug in a telephone set as shown in Figure 7.6.

INITIAL SETTINGS

Both the internal and external modems require a few one-time hardware or software settings, to make the modem compatible with the computer and the communications software. Depending on the modem manufacturer and the specific model, these settings are done with software commands stored in nonvolatile memory, with pluggable jumpers, with DIP switches, or with any combination of hardware and software. In some modems, a jumper or DIP switch setting becomes the default setting, which can still be changed with a software command. The settings control important modem parameters described in the following paragraphs. An improper setting will make exchange of data with another computer impossible.

The first and the most important setting is the selection of the serial port. Computer architecture provides for a number of serial ports, not all of which are normally implemented. These ports are designated COM1, COM2, etc. An IBM-PC and its compatibles are limited in general by hardware considerations to two serial ports COM1 and COM2, although the operating system recognizes two additional ports. An external modem should be assigned to one of these two ports and should not interfere with other devices assigned to the same port as the modem. Otherwise it cannot operate properly. If, for example, the printer is assigned to COM1, then the modem should be assigned to COM2. In a built-in (card) modem this assignment is made with jumpers or switches. In an external modem it is done by plugging the cable from the modem into the DB-25 jack assigned to the proper serial port on the computer. Some internal modems give the option of using serial ports COM3 and COM4. If the communications software recognizes these ports, then a modem can operate, e.g., as COM3, while a printer operates with COM1 and a "mouse" with COM2.

Other software, jumper, and switch settings on the modem card or on the external modem determine how the modem will react to certain RS-232-C interface signals. These settings are particularly important for auto dialing and to some extent depend on the communications software. Frequently, the default settings, the way the modem leaves the factory, have to be changed to operate with specific sofware packages. The default settings will vary between modems from different manufacturers and even between different models from the same manufacturer. Table 7.1 shows a list of selectable switch settings found in a personal computer modem (Avantek 1200). It shows the default settings and also the settings required to operate with the popular Crosstalk XVI communications software.

Table 7.1 **Modem DIP Switch Settings**

Function switch up	Switch down	Default	Xtalk XVI
Sense DTR signal	DTR forced ON	Down	Up
Messages in words	In numbers	Up	Up
Messages not displayed	Displayed	Down	Down
Local Echo Enabled	Disabled	Up	Up
Auto Answer Enabled	Disabled	Down	Down
Sense CD signal	CD forced ON	Down	Up
Sense CTS signal	CTS forced ON	Down	Down
Does not recognize the AT command set	Will recognize	Down	Down

As can be seen from the table, if the DTR and CD switches are left in the default position, then Xtalk XVI will not operate properly.

Another setting which should be made on both internal and on external modems is the volume control adjustment of the internal speaker. The speaker is bridged on the telephone line and "plays" the call progress tones, like dialing, busy, ring, and answer. Listening to the call progress tones gives the first indication if the connection is being properly established. Once the connection is established, the communications software turns the speaker off since it is no longer necessary. A proper setting of the volume control is required to avoid loud annoying beeps coming from the modem while listening to the call progress tones over the ambient noise and the whirring of the computer fan.

MODEM INCOMPATIBILITIES

Considering the large number of different types of modems and of personal computers on the market, it may occasionally happen that no combination of jumper and DIP switch settings will result in satisfactory modem operation. In such cases, where everything else fails, a ''cheater'' cable may be the only solution. A cheater cable straps internally certain serial interface leads and forces them to be HIGH (OFF) or LOW (ON) to satisfy the handshake protocols. Fortunately, the RS-232-C standard allows one to connect any interface lead to any other interface lead without causing permanent damage. Of course, an incorrect strap, though not resulting in subsequent damage, will not set up a data connection. For example, in a handshake sequence, the DTE side of the circuit, the Personal Computer, expects the Carrier Detect (CD) lead to be HIGH when it sets the Request To Send (RTS) lead HIGH. The cheater cord then simply straps the RTS and CD leads on the PC side and thus forces the CD lead to HIGH.

Figure 7.7 shows a cheater cable which does away with the whole handshake protocol between the computer and the modem. The only leads carried between the modem and computer are the TD, RD, and the signal ground. The danger of this arrangement is that transmission will continue, even if the respective terminals are for some reason not ready to accept data. In such cases the transmitted data may simply get lost. However, even use of the cheater

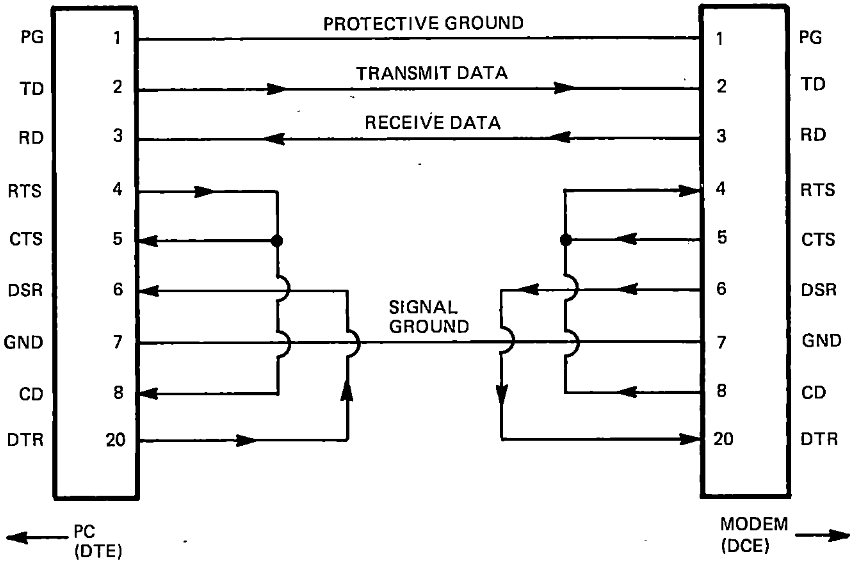

Figure 7.7 **Example of a "Cheater" Cable**

cable still allows for certain error correcting block protocols to operate properly. Such protocols do not have to rely on the condition of the RTS and CTS leads for retransmission of blocks of data, but may instead use control characters exchanged between the two terminals to control data flow. Such data flow protocols are referred to as XON//XOFF protocols. The XON character is ASCII 17 (DC1/Ctrl-Q) and the XOFF character is ASCII 19 (DC3/Ctrl-S).

OPTIONAL MODEM FEATURES

Like a typical American automobile with hundreds of expensive options, the personal computer modem comes with dozens of optional features, each touted by the respective manufacturer as the most important feature of the decade. The features differentiate basically similar models, following the same basic standards listed in the beginning of this chapter. Some of these features are of real importance, some are more like tail fins. Of course, what one person finds to be of limited value can be very important for another's special application. If one modem user makes a lot of calls to different data services, then auto-dialing is very important. If a person makes one call per day, then even manual dialing would be acceptable. Studying the list of available features and comparing them with actual needs should help in making correct buying decisions. Some of these options are fairly standard today, and if a modem from an XYZ manufacturer does not feature them, then the modem is probably obsolete, or the manufacturer is unaware of the current market needs.

Many modem features are discussed in detail throughout this book; what follows is a summary of major modem features offered by various manufacturers for the personal modem market and their evaluation by this author. To help in making a quantitative comparison between similar units I assigned a value of between 1 and 10 to each feature. Values 1 to 3 are of limited importance, 4 to 6 are nice to have, and as far as 7 to 10 are concerned — you do not want to be without them! In your specific circumstances, these subjective numbers may have to be changed.

Auto Dial with Rotary and Touch-Tone Option

This is the most important option and it should be included in any modern modem. A preferable hardware implementation is an electromagnetic relay, rather than a semiconductor switch. A relay, though slightly more expensive, will provide a complete isolation between the telephone line and the computer, when modem is not in use. Inadequate isolation may interfere with the phone conversations even when the modem is not being used. Value = 9.

Full-Duplex Operation

This is a standard feature of all personal computer modems and is part of the appropriate standards. It is always included. Value = 10.

Direct Connect Capability

This is an option which depends on the specific use of the modem. If it is being used "on the go," then an acoustic modem is preferable. This would apply to reporters and writers who have to file their daily "copy" from hotel rooms and phone booths. However, for a stationary operation, a direct connect modem should always be used to lower interference from ambient noise sources. For stationary operation, value = 10; for portable operation, value = almost 0.

Hayes Compatibility

Importance of the compatibility with the Hayes AT command set depends on the availability of data communications software. As most of the software is based on the Hayes commands, even if you are now using data communications software written by the XYZ Corporation based on an obscure command set, and are satisfied with it, you may still want to change in the future to different software with new features. Unless you use a modem with a standard set of commands, the chance of finding appropriate software in the future is rather remote. Value = 10.

Automatic Answer Capability

This, and the next two features, Originate/Answer capability and the Automatic Speed Select, are of importance if you exchange data with other people and do not limit yourself to bulletin boards, information services, etc. The feature is somewhat similar to an automatic answering machine. When you are not home, your friends can still call you and leave "digital" messages. Value = 6.

Originate/Answer Mode Capability

Somewhat similar to the previous feature. All bulletin boards and information services operate in the Answer mode, with the subscribers modem in the Originate mode. However, if you try to communicate with another modem and both modems can only operate in the Originate mode, than a connection cannot be established. Value = 6.

Automatic Speed Select

If another modem calls your modem, your modem will set itself to the proper transmission speed. This feature is of importance only if you operate with many callers using different transmission speeds. Value = 5.

Call Progress Tone Recognition

This feature will recognize Dial and Busy tones. With proper software it is possible to avoid "blind" dialing and to get easier access to busy bulletin boards by repeated automatic redialing. Value = 6.

Front Panel Indicators

This feature is only available on external modems. However, if you have an external modem, with its associated jungle of cables, this feature should be implemented. An external modem should have at least 5—6 indicator lights. Functions of these indicator lights are described in detail in Chapter 14. For external modems only. Value = 8.

Number of RJ11C Telephone Jacks

Both an internal and an external modem should have two female telephone jacks, or one jack and one telephone cable terminated with a male telephone plug. One of these jacks or cables connects to a telephone line, the other to a telephone set. Modems equipped with a single jack and no cable should be avoided, since connecting a telephone set via a Y-type connector then becomes a major inconvenience. For double jacks, or for one built-in jack and one cable with a jack. Value = 9.

COM1, COM2, COM3, and COM4 Capability

This feature applies only to internal modems. Access to COM3 and COM4 serial ports gives an added flexibility, if several devices are already assigned to ports COM1 and COM2. In any case a modem should have at least the option of COM1/COM2 selection. For COM1 only, value = 0; for COM1/2, value = 6; for COM1/2/3/4, value = 8.

Testing Capabilities

Many modem modems allow for several types of diagnostic tests, described in detail in Chapter 14. In case of poor transmission, it is a nice feature to have. Value = 6.

Clock/Calendar

Some modems provide their own time and date information for time "stamping" of received and of transmitted files. This is a duplication of functions found in the great majority of personal computers. Only if your computer has no permanent clock function, value = 6; otherwise, value = 0.

Storage of Telephone Numbers

This feature, though highly touted in many advertisements, is of very limited importance, except for security modems. In general, communications software takes care of storing a directory of numbers, which can then be dialed by the modem. If this feature is provided, make sure that there is a battery backup, and that it is supported by communications software. Value = 3.

Demon Dialer

This feature related to the storage of telephone numbers will repeatedly call one or more numbers stored in modem's memory. The modem will detect the busy signal and keep dialing, alternating between two or more telephone numbers, if so instructed. This feature can usually be duplicated by communications software. Value = 5.

Data Buffer

Some modems will store the incoming data in a large buffer, typically 64 or 128 kbytes, which corresponds to between 25 and 50 typewritten pages. Although this function is normally performed by communications software, it may be advantageous to have the modem save data automatically as a back-up. In some modems the buffer can also be used as the printer buffer for off-line printing. Value = 6.

Data/Voice Capability

This feature is of importance when the computer is used as a memory dialer for making regular telephone calls. It can also be used in conjunction with the previously mentioned Demon Dialer feature. Occasionally this feature can avoid embarrassment when a data call is made by mistake to a wrong number and a person answers. Value = 6.

Touch-tone Decoder

Some modems have the ability to decode the incoming touch-tone signals. This feature, if recognized by the software, allows one to add security features to the modem by excluding callers not sending a specific number code with their touch-tone phone. Value = 5.

Ability to Operate with 80286-based and Other High-Speed Computers

Computers equipped with the 80286 or 80386 processor operate at higher clock speeds than the 8088 or 8086 type machines. Before purchasing a modem for this type of computer it should be ascertained that the modem can operate in that environment. For high-speed machines only. Value = 10.

Size of the Modem Card (Internal Only)

Older versions of built-in modems come on a full-size card; newer versions, using more LSI circuits, usually fit on a half-size card. As there is only a limited number of full-size slots inside a PC, and the slots are frequently already occupied by other cards, a smaller modem card is definitely preferable. For a half-size card. Value = 5.

Small Size of an External Modem

Migent Corporation introduced recently the Pocket Modem, a truly miniature Bell 212A compatible external modem, which fits into a shirt pocket. This was followed by Touchbase Systems Inc. bringing to market a similar product named WorldPort 1200. The value of miniaturization in an external modem is, however, questionable. Value = 1.

Error Correction

Some modems include built-in proprietary error detecting and correcting protocols. In general, the called modem should be of the same type as the calling modem. The error correcting modems are used only for specialized applications, generally on point-to-point and multiple point private networks. Value depending on specific application.

Speaker with Volume Control

A speaker with volume control should be included in each modem to be able to listen to call progress tones. If an incorrect number was dialed and a person answers, one would like to be aware of it. Value = 10.

Ease of Setting of Internal Switches

Switches should be easily accessible, without having to disassemble the complete modem. Software switches, which are "remembered" by the modem, using low power CMOS memory are preferable to DIP switches, which in turn are preferable to pluggable jumpers. On the bottom of my list are soldered jumpers. Assigned values are as follows: software switches, value = 10; easily accessible DIP switches, value = 9; hard to access DIP switches, value = 6; pluggable jumpers, value = 5; soldered jumpers, value = 0.

FCC Approval

Each modem used in the US should be approved by the FCC. Lack of such approval will prevent you from legally connecting the modem to the telephone network and may also result in fines, confiscation of equipment, and in embarrassment. Value = 10.

INFORMATION SERVICES

Proliferation of personal computer modems led to development of commercial and user supported nonprofit services such as private and commercial bulletin boards, banking and information services. Availability of such services then convinced more people to buy modems and attach them to their computers. Some of these services appeal to specific professions, for example, the LEXUS service for the legal profession. There is even a service, which computes telephone rates for a given time of day, originating location and terminating location.

The power and need for such services is clear from the following example. While writing this book, I needed a reference relating to the CCITT modem standards. It was 10 P.M., but the library service was still on the air. I called the appropriate number and saw on my computer display a list of relevant titles with a short summary of each book. In about 5 minutes I was able to select the appropriate book and had it delivered to my desk the next morning.

Inn Western Europe, information services are provided, or at least are regulated, by the national PTT administrations, as extension of the regular telephone service. In the United States they are operated by a few large commercial enterprises such as CompuServe, The Source, Dialog, Byte Magazine (BIX), General Electric (Genie), and by hundreds of nonprofit organizations such as computer clubs or even private individuals. In addition to information service providers, there are a number of packet switching networks, the largest of which is TYMENET, which allow one to avoid toll charges by dialing a local telephone number and getting a direct connection to the supplier of information.

One of the reasons for proliferation of private bulletin boards is that the complete cost of setting up such a board can be less than $3000, including all hardware and software. Commercial services give access to large data bases, e.g., the legal profession can find every judgment and proceeding connected with asbestos litigation, or a medical doctor can find references to articles in professional journals describing a rare disease. Large bulletin boards also have specialized user's groups, which are frequently referred to as conferences. There may be groups interested in amateur radio, stamp collecting, or the Commodore-64 computer. All these services can be easily accessed from a personal computer equipped with a modem. The access charges vary from being free to about $300 per hour for commercial services. The most expensive are legal search services.

A more detailed discussion of information services, and examples of calls to such services, are shown in Chapter 9, which deals with the communications software.

FCC AND TELEPHONE COMPANY REQUIREMENTS

Each personal modem offered for sale in the United States for use on the switched Public Telephone Network, and not on private or leased lines, should be type tested and should carry an FCC registration number, according to Part 68 of the FCC Rules and Regulations. The ringer equivalence number, indicating line loading requirements in terms of a standard telephone set, should also be provided with each modem. The modem user is required to register the modem with the local telephone company, before connecting it to the telephone network, by giving the telephone company the FCC registration number, the modem model number, its manufacturer, and the modem ring equivalence number. One of the reasons for this last requirement is that if too many phones, modems, and other devices are hooked up to the same telephone line, then the current reaching the ringer in a telephone set will not be sufficient to ring the bell and calls will remain unanswered. Currently, there are no charges associated with the modem registration. This may change, however, and telephone companies may impose a fee for modem users in the future.

Direct connection to the telephone lines may only be made through standard plugs like the RJ11C. No direct modem connections are allowed through party or coin-phone lines. A connection between the computer and an external modem should be made with a shielded cable. Since each modem is type approved by the FCC, the user is not allowed to make any modifications or to perform unauthorized repairs. If the modem malfunctions and interferes with telephone communication, then the telephone company may notify the user and ask him or her to disconnect it. If the defective modem is still attached to the telephone network, then the telephone company may temporarily disconnect telephone service. In case of an unlikely dispute with the local telephone company, there are formalized appeal procedures to the Federal Communications Commission and to the state regulatory bodies.

8. Hayes Modem Standards

Hayes Corporation, the pioneer and long time leader in development of dial-up modems for personal computers, established a set of modem programming commands and hardware implementations which became a de facto standard for the personal computer industry. The commands are frequently referred to as AT commands because of the uppercase "AT" prefix usually required. The AT prefix instructs the modem to start paying attention to whatever follows, and to interpret the character string following AT as an internal modem command, rather than as data to be transmitted to the remote modem. A Hayes or a Hayes compatible modem will, depending on the specific command given to it, dial a remote computer using pulse or touch-tone, set data transmission parameters such as number of data bits, parity, number of stop bits, and transmission speed, and then, after establishing connection, will start transmission of data. The AT commands, besides dialing, also control speaker operation, initiate various diagnostic procedures, and read or write to various modem registers controlling the modem status.

In addition to standardization of the AT commands, various internal modem registers, the so-called S-Registers, originally introduced by Hayes and described later in this chapter, also became a de facto standard and are common throughout the industry. For example, the S0 register stores a number which is equal to the number of rings before the modem answers in the self-answer mode. Sending the command ATS0=3 will make the modem wait for three rings before answering a call. The advantage to modem manufacturers in using the same commands and registers as Hayes is that the majority of communications software will then work on their modems.

Many modem manufacturers developed extensions to the Hayes command set. For example Avantek 1200B modem features a "help" file with menus which appear on the terminal screen when the "AT?" command is sent to the modem. Manufacturers who provide some unique features in their modems, e.g., the error detection and correction in the MNP modems have extensions to the AT set to call those features. Similarly, most 2400 bps modems based on the CCITT V.24 bis protocol, provide assorted self-testing features. These tests are activated by an additional set of "AT&T" commands described in more details in Chapter 14. Other manufacturers, like IBM, tried to completely bypass the Hayes command set by developing their own commands and appropriate data communications software to use those commands. These efforts have been largely abandoned, as the majority of users decided to stay with the Hayes "standard."

AT COMMAND STRUCTURE

The AT prefix is required for all commands, except for the "A/" command. In most modems the characters "AT" have to be in uppercase; the remainder of the command also has to be in uppercase on some modems, or it can be in either upper- or lowercase on other modems. One or more commands can follow the AT prefix with optional intervening blanks. A command consists of a letter identifying it, e.g., "H" for the command designating the on-hook/off-hook condition, followed by an optional parameter value. If the parameter value is not given, e.g., ATH, then the parameter value is assumed to be equal to 0. Thus the ATH command is equivalent to ATH0 (hang-up and disconnect). Several commands can be linked together into a character string, generally not exceeding 40 characters, and limited by the RAM memory in the modem. Each command string has to be terminated by a carriage return. The backspace key can be used to edit a command before the carriage return is pressed. The important AT commands shared by most modems are listed in alphabetical order in Table 8.1.

Table 8.1 **Principal AT Commands**

A/ — Repeat last command. A/ is the only command which is not preceded by AT or followed by a carriage return. Each AT command is loaded into a buffer before it is being executed. It remains in this buffer until the next command is loaded. When the modem encounters the A/ command it pulls the contents of that buffer and executes it.

A — Put the modem in Answer mode. When this command is executed the modem will go immediately into the answermode regardless of the condition of the register S0, which when set to 0 would normally prevent the modem from answering a call.

D — Dial, puts the modem in originate mode, ready to dial a number. If followed by T it uses tone dialing, if followed by P, pulse dialing. An example of this command would be ATDT 1-(213)-555-1212. A comma "," instructs the modem to wait a specified number of seconds for a second dial tone. The wait time is determined by the status of the register S8. A semicolon at the end of the dialing sequence puts the modem in off-line mode after dialing. Off-line and other operating modes are discussed later in this chapter. Notice that dashes and parentheses are ignored when they are a part of the dialed number. A call from a PBX, where 9 has to be dialed first, followed by a 6 second wait, with pulse dialing could be done with ATDP 9,,,1-(213)-555-1212. Notice that the command set gives no capability to wait for a second dial tone after dialing 9. The wait time is fixed by the three commas to 6 seconds. If "R" is the last character in the dialing string, e.g., ATDT555-1212R, then the call will be dialed in the Answer mode, rather than in the Originate mode. The difference between the Answer and Originate mode is the choice of carrier frequencies. On a connection, one modem always has to be in the Originate mode and the other modem in the Answer mode. Normally the calling modem is in the Originate mode. This feature is required, when placing a call to an Originate only modem.

E — Echo ON/OFF, echoes characters to the local terminal. The setting of this parameter depends on the setting of the called modem. Normally on a full- or half-duplex connection the called modem will echo each character to the calling modem. However, if the screen is blank while you are typing, this parameter has to be turned ON by typing ATE1.

H — On-hook/Off-hook command. Sending ATH or ATH0 command to the modem will cause the modem to terminate the telephone connection (go on-hook). If all the normal log off procedures for your bulletin board do not work, this is the command of last resort. A simple way to test this command is to type ATH1. This is the same as lifting the phone receiver and the dial tone should be heard through the modem speaker.

I — Indicate product or version code of the modem. Typing ATI should return the modem designation.

M — The M command controls the modem built-in speaker used for listening to call progress tones (dial tone, ring, busy, etc.) In the default setting (M1) the speaker is turned on until the carrier is received from the remote modem, then it is turned off. ATM2 will leave the speaker turned on for the entire connection. ATM0 will leave it off during the entire call including the dialing period.

R — Reverse originate and receive frequencies to let the modem dial an Originate only modem. This command modifier was discussed under dialing commands.

O — Switch the modem to on-line mode after executing commands in the on-line command mode. This command is not followed by a parameter value, e.g., the only correct use is ATO and not, for example, ATO1.

Sr= y — Set the r register to value y (decimal). For example, sending ATS8=5 to the modem would make each comma in the dialing sequence correspond to 5 seconds instead of the default value of 2 seconds.

Sr? — Display status of the r register. If after sending the command ATS8=5 the command ATS8? is executed, the modem will return "005" to the terminal.

&Tx — Perform one of the diagnostic tests described in Chapter 14, where x is the test number. These commands will vary greatly from modem to modem with the more expensive modems providing a larger selection of tests.

Z — Restore all default settings. This command, similar to the O command, has no parameter values. ATZ is the only acceptable form of it. The Z command can be used like the H command to disconnect the modem.

The difference is that the Z command will reinitialize all registers based on the various switch settings.

After executing a command the modem will send back to the monitor the result code. Depending on jumper or switch settings the code can be either numeric, e.g. "1" or it can be a word, e.g., "CONNECT". Table 8.2 lists the result codes, their numerical equivalents and their meaning:

Table 8. 2 **AT Result Codes**

Code	Equivalent	Explanation
0	OK	Command was executed without an error
1	CONNECT	The carrier was detected, the handshake sequence was successfully completed, and the modem is ready to communicate.
2	RING	There is an incoming call. Unless the modem is set to answer mode, the call will go to the telephone set.
3	NO CARRIER	Either the modem timed out after dialing or the carrier was lost during a call.
4	ERROR	The command just sent to the modem contains an error. This could be a syntax or typing error or the command exceeds 40 characters, the size of the buffer.
5	CONNECT	This code means that a connection with a 1200-bps modem was successfully established.
6	BUSY	Busy signal was detected at the far end modem.
7	ABORT	Dialing or handshake was interrupted due to user's interaction.
8	DISCONNECT	For some reason the connection has been lost.

The AT commands can be sent to the modem through the data communications software, when the modem is in the local or in the on-line command mode. For a quick test, the AT commands can also be sent directly from DOS level bypassing any data communications software. An example is a short DOS file called MYPHONE.BAT shown below. Such a file could easily be written by means of any text editor, e.g., EDLIN, Sidekick in Note Pad mode, Wordstar, or Wordperfect in nondocument mode, etc.

```
REM MYPHONE.BAT dials via modem connected to COM1 port
MODE COM1:120
ECHO ATZ COM1
ECHO ATDT555-1212 COM1:
PAUSE
ECHO ATH COM1:
```

Typing MYPHONE at the DOS level will dial the number 555-1212, display a DOS message "press any key..." and put the relay in the modem in the off-hook position. Pressing any key will send the ATH message to the modem which will disconnect the phone and put the modem relay in the on-hookposition.

The modem can also be accessed directly via computer internal ports. These ports can be addressed with assembly programming or with certain commands in higher level languages. For example, the BASIC function INP(123) will return the status of port #123. The statement OUT 123,222 will send the decimal byte value of 222 to the port #123. The port addresses assigned to a built-in modem or to a serial port connected to a modem vary from computer to computer and can usually be found in the technical manual. For example, the IBM-PC assigns port addresses 3F8-3FF (hex) to COM1 serial port, while the IBM-PCjr assigns ports 2F8-2FF. Setting of parameters and serial communication could be performed by reading and writing to these ports. Control of the modem via these ports requires considerable programming experience and is not recommended to a novice.

S-REGISTERS

Modems are frequently described as "smart" or "dumb." The smartness of the modem is associated with dialing features and its capability to respond to the software commands. All smart features set by the data communications software, as a sequence of the AT commands described above, are stored in a series of internal modem stack registers, referred to as S-registers. These registers are in addition to any internal RAM modem memory, which may be required for storing passwords and acceptable telephone numbers in security modems or buffering data in some error correcting and other specialized modems.

The number of S-registers varies from modem to modem. For example, the Hayes Smartmodem 2400 uses registers S0 through S27, while Kyocera KM1200S modem uses registers S0 through S15. The 8-bit registers S0 through S12 store one number each, usually between 0 and 255. This number refers to a specific function, e.g., number of rings. Registers S13 through S15 assign a different function to each of the 8 bits. Thus one of these higher registers can store up to 8 different function values each numbered 0 or 1. A function could be 0 to indicate half-duplex and 1 to indicate full-duplex operation. Modem manufacturers in general agree more or less on function and setting assignments of the 16 registers S0 through S15, which are used by most software data communications packages. The higher numbered registers vary in function assignments from modem to modem. For detailed assignments of these registers, consult the user's manual which comes with each modem.

Table 8.3 shows the register assignments and describes the function of the 16 registers S0 through S15, which can be found on the majority of smart modems. Each register can be read with the ATSr? command and most of them can be changed or written to with the ATSr=y command, where r is the register number and y is the new assigned value.

Table 8.3 **Assignments of S-Registers S0 through S15**

Register	Default	Range	Description
S0	1	0–255	Sets the number of rings before the modem answers. If S0 = 0 the modem will not answer automatically. The AA indicator on the front panel will normally light up to show that the modem has been configured to the AUto Answer mode. On some modems, e.g., the Hayes Smartmodem 1200, the register also stores a number related to the quality of the telephone line. Changing the local command line and typing ATS1? will then return a number between 0 and 50. Any number below 40 indicates a poor telephone connection.
S10	0	0–255	Ring counter which is implemented during a call.
S2	43	0–255	Sets the ASCII value for the escape code. ASCII of 43 equals "+." If the register is set

			to a value larger than 127, then the escape sequence will be disabled.
S3	13	0—127	ASCII value used for the carriage return code. The character serves as the command terminator. If the communications equipment is nonstandard, then a value different from 13 may have to be assigned.
S4	10	0—127	ASCII value for the line-feed code. The line-feed character is generated by the modem after result codes are returned to the terminal.
S5	8	0—32,127	ASCIII value for the backspace code. It should not be set to a printable ASCII character (33-126) or to a value larger than 127, otherwise the modem will not recognize it.
S6	2	2—255	Dial tone wait time in seconds, time between off-hook condition and start of dialing. Used in the "blind" dialing mode.
S7	30	1—30	Wait time in seconds before the end of dialing and carrier detection. If carrier is not detected, modem will disconnect.
S8	2	0—255	Pause time in seconds represented by the comma in the dialing sequence, e.g., ATDT9,5551212. The pause is generally used when dialing through a PBX or when using an alternate long distance service.
S9	155	—	Time in ms between carrier recognition and its acknowledgment. The default value cannot be changed in most modems.
S10	3	1—255	Time in ms between carrier loss and disconnect. If set to 255 the modem will not disconnect due to carrier loss. The delay permits the carrier to disappear due to transmission fading or other reason without disconnecting. On a noisy line the default value should be increased from the current value.
S11	70	50—255	Controls the speed of the tone dialer (interval in ms between tones). The default is 7.1

			digits per second (tone of 70 ms + 70 ms interval between tones). Not used in some modems.
S12	50	20—255	Guard time before and after escape sequence (+++) required by the modem to recognize it. Increment is 20 ms, the default is 1 sec (50 × 20 ms). Care should be taken in choosing guard times shorter than transmission of a character. The time between the escape characters must be less than the guard time or the escape sequence will not be recognized by the modem.

Registers S13 through S15 assign specific functions to each bit. Table 8.4 shows bit assignments of these three registers.

Table 8.4 **Bit Assignments for S-Registers S13 to S15**

Register	Bit	Description
S13	0	Undefined
	1	0 - Basic result codes are selected 1 - Extended result codes are selected
	2	0 - Parity disabled 1 - Parity enabled
	3	0 - Odd parity 1 - Even parity
	4	0 - 7 data bits 1 - 8 data bits
	5	Undefined
	6	Undefined
	7	0 - 8th data bit set to space (if bit 4 = 1) 1 - 8th data bit set to mark (if bit 4 = 1)
S14	0	0 - Auto answer disabled (S0 = 0) 1 - Auto answer enabled (S0 0)

	1	0 - Local echo disabled 1 - Local echo enabled
	2	0 - Result codes enabled 1 - Result codes disabled
	3	0 - Reslt codes sent as digits 1 - Result codes sent as words
	4	Undefined
	5	0 - Tone dial 1 - Pulse dial
	6, 7	00 - Speaker disabled 01 - Speaker enabled until carrier detected 10 - Speaker always on
S15	0, 1	01 - 110 bps 10 - 300 bps 11 - 1200 bps
	2	0 - Answer mode 1 - Originate mode
	3	0 - Half-duplex 1 - Full-duplex
	4, 5	Same as bits 0 and 1
	6	0 - Local carrier off 1 - Local carrier on
	7	Undefined

MODES OF OPERATION

To establish a data connection, a computer with an attached modem using the Hayes command set has to first initiate the call. Unless otherwise agreed upon, that modem will remain for the duration of the call in the Originating mode while the remote modem will remain in the Answer mode. The two transmission modes are physically different as they use different assigned carrier frequencies. The modem initiating the call does not, however, have to operate in the Originating mode, though some modems can operate in only one mode. If calling a modem which can only operate in Originating mode, the call initiating modem must be able to operate in the Answer mode. The selection of the transmission mode is accomplished either manually by setting an appropriate switch or jumper or by the communications software. For example, the command ATDTxxx-xxxx, where xxx-xxxx is the called number, will dial the computer and put the calling modem in the originating mode. However, using the ATDTxxx-xxxx\R command will dial the number and put the call initiating modem in the Answer mode.

To better grasp the interaction between the modem, the data communications software, and the computer, one should understand the four operational modes of the modem and their transitions. The four modes are:

1. Local Command Mode

In this mode the modem is disconnected from the telephone line. It will accept dialing instructions and settings of data communications parameters, such as bit rate, parity, etc. When typing on the terminal, one communicates with the internal modem registers. This mode is changed to the handshake mode after a call has been dialed.

2. Handshake Mode

This mode is under the modem control. It consists of a check that the carrier was received from the remote modem. Once the connection is established, the originating modem may send a training sequence to adjust the remote adaptive equalizer. There is also a check for compatibility of the two modems. For example, if the called modem is set to 1200 bps and the calling modem is set to 2400 bps, the calling modem may fall back to 1200 bps. If handshake is successfully concluded, then the modem will shift to the On-line mode; otherwise a message "NO CARRIER" will be echoed to the terminal and the modem will go on-hook and revert to Local Command mode.

3. On-line Mode

This is the data transfer mode. All characters typed on the local terminal are sent to the remote terminal and vice versa. To get out of the On-line mode in

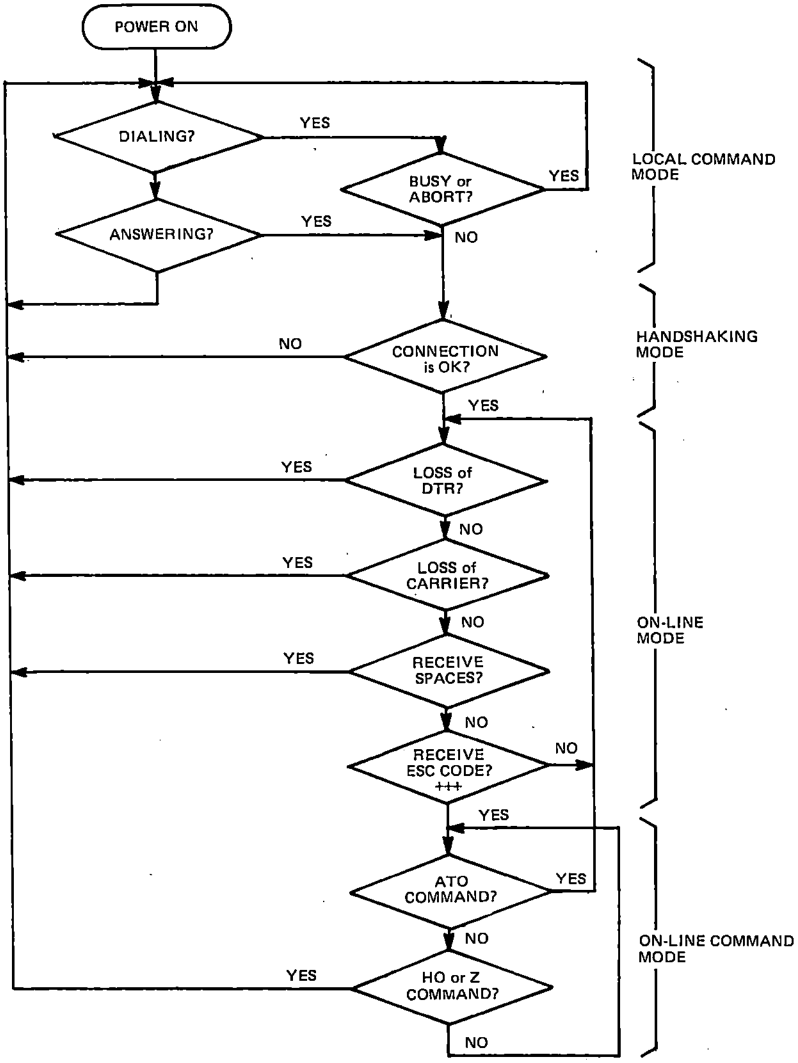

Figure 8.1 **Operating Mode Transitions**

order to communicate with the modem directly one has to send an escape sequence (by default "+++") with a 1 second "guard" pause before and after the sequence. Upon receiving the escape sequence, the modem will change into the On-line Command mode while still keeping the connection to the remote modem open. Loss of carrier will change the operating mode from the On-line to the Local Command mode.

4. On-line Command Mode (also referred to as Off-line Mode)

In this mode the connection remains open in the background (data can be sent or received), while one can send commands to the modem to perform some system operation. For example, one could open or close a memory buffer for received data, enable local echo, read the DOS directory, or terminate the call.

Figure 8.1 shows transitions between the four operating modes in terms of the internal modem commands. A software data communications package also gives the capability of shifting back and forth between various operating methods. For example, Xtalk XVI will switch from the On-line mode to the On-line Command mode when the Escape key is pressed. Similarly, hitting the Return key returns the modem to the On-line mode. To enter the Local Command mode from the On-line mode one has to type GO LOCAL, or one can type BYE to disconnect a call in progress.

WEAKNESSES OF THE CURRENT STANDARD AND POSSIBLE IMPROVEMENTS

The current Hayes AT standard has many weak points, which are fortunately being addressed in new modem designs, including modems designed by Hayes. The main limitation of the basic Hayes standard is that the modem dials without regard to the call progress tones. There is no command in the AT set to wait for the dial tone. For example, if due to traffic congestion there is a long delay in obtaining the dial tone, the modem will dial anyway and no connection will ever be established. Also, a Hayes compatible modem will not automatically hang up or take some other action after encountering a Busy signal. It will just time out after a predetermined time, since the carrier tone has not been received. A minor annoyance of the standard is that all commands have to be in uppercase. Another weak point of the Hayes standard is the lack of a HELP command. The assumption here is that the communications software will take care of the user's needs.

Newer modems, e.g., Hayes Smartmodem 2400, recognize call progress tones and can be programmed to wait for the dial tone or redial immediately upon encountering a Busy signal. Other modems, e.g., the inexpensive Avantek 1200HC, display two different Help files. The command AT? returns to the terminal a list of all operating and dialing commands and a list of operating options. A list of testing commands can be obtained by typing AT?T. The status of all S-registers can be displayed by typing AT?S. Similarly, the settings of all option switches and factory settings can be obtained by typing AT?C.

A technically minded user can benefit from these new commands by writing specialized script files applicable to his or her specific modem. However, unless the new modem features are somehow standardized between various manufacturers, there will not be enough incentive for software writers to produce good data communications software packages taking advantage of these features.

Concerning the hardware aspects of modems it would be nice to have some kind of standardization of configuration switches and indicator lights on external modems. Currently, different manufacturers provide different configuration switches and indicator lights and even call the same functions by different names. In fact, considering the lack of standardization of many modem features and the dismal style and contents of most instruction manuals, it is astounding that the majority of modem purchasers succeed in making them work.

9. Communications Software

The average computer user does not care about Hayes AT command set, the internal modem registers, or the details of the file transfer protocols. All he or she wants to do is to enter the phone number of the remote computer, request some information, or give the name of the file to be sent and let the computer do the rest. Alternately, the computer user may want to download some files from the remote computer, order a book from the library, send a memo to a coworker, or transfer $500 from checking to money market account. The function of the communications software is to perform all these functions unobtrusively and efficiently.

There are three ways in which communications software can be obtained: public domain (free) software, shareware, and commercial software. The public domain software costs nothing, but it is not supported by its author or authors after it has been released. The public domain software comes with some documentation, most often on disk, which may or may not apply to the specific computer/modem configuration of the user. It can be obtained from various computer clubs, downloaded from bulletin boards, or it even comes prepackaged with many modems. The next category of communications software, the shareware, can be obtained from the same sources as the public domain software, but it comes with a plea from the author to make a contribution, usually in the range of $25 to $75. Though shareware programs come with some form of documentation on disk, the author usually promises to provide the user with complete documentation after receiving the contribution. Public domain and shareware programs will satisfy many users, but they seldom provide features and support required by the business community. The commercial communications software typically costs between $100 and $400, which may be high for a hobbyist, but is of little importance in business applications. For that price the commercial software provides a wide range of options and user support with frequent program updates, which follow new developments in modem hardware.

BASIC SOFTWARE FEATURES

The first and basic function of the communications software is to make the general purpose computer behave at least like a computer terminal, frequently referred to as the "dumb" terminal or the "glass" teletypewriter. It means that if the user types "Hello," the word "Hello" should appear on the remote terminal. When somebody at the remote terminal types "I got your message," the same words should appear on the local terminal. If more than one line of text is being sent, then the previous line of text should scroll on the terminal to make a place for the next line. These are the absolute minimum requirements expected from communications software. In fact this type of basic software is usually supplied free with any modem.

As the next step, the communications software should allow one to transfer files between the local and remote computers. Of course, one should also be able to save the transmitted files on disk and/or print them locally. The communications software should also take care of all dialing chores, retrieve the phone number from a file, set up proper transmission parameters associated with the call, such as transmission speed, number of data and stop bits, parity, etc. and it should then dial the call. The data communications software should then keep track of the call progress tones indicating Busy, or No Answer, and should redial at prescribed intervals if no connection was established.

As soon as the carrier signal is received from the remote modem, the communications software should switch the local modem from the local command mode to the on-line mode and then start transfer of data. Other important parameters which should be set by the communications software are local echo, remote echo (also referred to as feedback), and the proper carriage return and line feed combination. The local echo makes every character transmitted from the local terminal appear on the screen of the local terminal; feedback sends each character received from the remote terminal back to the remote terminal to appear on the display. At least one of these options has to be active; otherwise one does not see what one sends to the remote terminal. If both local and remote echo are active at the same time, then each character will appear twice on the screen. Instead of "Hello" one would read "HHeellllloo."

TERMINAL EMULATION

Next come more esoteric but important features expected from modern communications software. For example, one should be able to emulate various popular terminals in addition to the "glass" teletypewriter. The important terminals, which the data communications software should be able to emulate, are the DEC VT100 series, Lear Siegler's ADM-3 series, Tele Video 912 series, and the IBM 3101 series. Of course, not all features of a specific terminal can be emulated, for example, the large size character option on the VT100 which is embedded in the terminal hardware.

The computer keyboard in the emulation mode should have certain keys reassigned as special keys present in the emulated terminals. Even more importantly, the computer in its emulation mode should duplicate certain "smart" features of the emulated terminals. The main difference between a dumb terminal and an smart terminal obtained through emulation is that a dumb terminal will let the user type at the keyboard and read from the screen moving the cursor only left and right on a single line, while a smart terminal allows the cursor to move up and down on the screen and perform on-screen editing. In the emulation mode the terminal will also respond to special codes specified for a particular terminal which may clear the screen, move the cursor, or define function keys. A smart terminal has the ability to make input forms on the screen with highlighted field for entering of data, underline, display reverse video fields, or make a field blink.

MENU-DRIVEN VERSUS COMMAND-DRIVEN PROGRAMS

The user "friendliness" in a communications program can assume various forms. The program designer has to weigh the simplicity of user interface versus program flexibility and consider the type of user community. In a commercial program the designer also wants to maximize the number of potential users, who range from neophytes to sophisticated users.

The easiest way to interact with the user is by presenting a few simple choices or an introductory menu on the screen. As the number of choices displayed on the screen is limited to between 15 and 20, the program can display additional menus after the initial selection. A menu-driven program assumes only a minimal knowledge on the part of the user, as choices are always displayed on the screen, but it has its limitations. A large number of choices leads to hierarchical menus which may make a menu-driven program very cumbersome.

An example of a simple menu-driven program is PFS:ACCESS. The opening menu displays a list of information services such as The Source, Dow Jones, CompuServ. All transmission parameters for these services are stored in program memory; the user just has to provide the access telephone number. Then the program displays a menu of modem choices such as Hayes Smartmodem 1200, IBM PCjr built-in modem, etc. After the choice is made, the program will automatically dial the selected service and then will establish a data connection giving the proper user name, password, etc.

An alternate method of user interface is a command-driven program, which is frequently combined with a menu-driven program. In a command-driven program the user, instead of choosing from a limited number of options displayed on the screen in a menu, issues short commands from a separate dictionary. The dictionary of any size can be a written document or an on-line

```
          Opening Screen of the Crosstalk XVI Program

                [-----   CROSSTALK - XVI Status Screen  -----]      Off line

 NAme   Template                                   LOaded    C:STD.XTK
 NUmber                                            CApture   Off

[-------- Communications parameters --------]   [------ Filter settings ------]
 SPeed 1200   PArity Even   DUplex  Full         DEbug     Off   LFauto   On
 DAta  7      STop   1      EMulate None         TAbex     Off   BLankex  Off
 POrt  2                    MOde    Call         INfilter  On    OUtfiltr On

[------------- Key settings ---------------]    [---- SEnd control settings --]
 ATten  Esc                 COmmand ETX (^C)     CWait     None
 SWitch Home                BReak   End          LWait     None

[-------------------------- Available command files ------------------------]

 1) ANSWER        2) BIX          3) DEC          4) FACIT        5) GEORGE
 6) HO            7) MOD100       8) NCSA         9) NEWUSER     10) PC-BLUE
11) SETUP        12) STD         13) YELLOW

Enter for file to use ( 1 - 13 ): _
```

Figure 9.1 **Crosstalk XVI Opening Menu**

help file. The user gains considerable flexibility at the expense of having to remember the various commands. The popular CrossTalk XVI program combines the two approaches by responding to a large dictionary of user commands and by displaying the most important ones in a menu on the screen. The opening screen of Xtalk XVI is shown in Figure 9.1. The beauty of a command-driven program is that it allows one to combine commands in a so-called script file, which can then be easily recalled and executed. The basic commands to be found in a communications software package and their use in command and script files wil be described in the next paragraphs.

BASIC COMMUNICATIONS PACKAGE COMMANDS

Again using as an example the Xtalk XVI program, I will list the principal commands available to the user in alphabetical order. There are a total of over 60 commands in a recent release of the program, not including commands associated with script files. This compares with about 25 commands in an older communications program ST80III used on an 8-bit computers. Looking at the partial list of Xtalk XVI commands in Figure 9.1 should give an idea of what can be expected from a modern communications program. You will also notice that none of the commands exercise nonstandard modem functions such as testing or nonblind dialing. Other communications packages will have a set of similar commands, although their names will most probably differ.

ACCEPT — Depending on the options, limits the calling modem to only reading, appending, or creating new files.

BLANKEX — The command, when called, will convert a blank line in a record being transmitted into a single space, thus saving transmission time.

BYE — Disconnects modem from the line, does not return to DOS.

CAPTURE — Opens and closes memory buffer to store the contents of the communication session.

CDIR — Changes the current directory in DOS.

CWAIT — Requests the program to wait between characters for a time specified by the option value when transmitting to another modem. This command may be necessary because certain computer systems cannot accept characters at full transmission speed.

DATA — Sets the number of data bits in a character. Typical choices are 7 or 8.

DEBUG — Depending on the value of this option, incoming control characters can be displayed on the screen in ASCII, Hex, or as, e.g., ^C.
DIR — Displays DOS directory.
DO — Starts executing a script file.
DPREFIX — Used to set the dialing prefix, for example, "ATDT" will dial the number using touch-tone frequencies.
DRIVE — Shows the amount of memory available on each drive in the system; also used to change the current drive.
DSUFFIX — Used to set the dialing suffix, typically a carriage return.
DUPLEX — Switches from half-duplex to full-duplex.
EMULATE — Selects the terminal to be emulated depending on the value of the option.
ERASE — Erases the contents of the memory buffer.
FKEYS — Sets and displays assignments of the function keys.
GO - Starts dialing.
HELP — Displays a short explanation of various commands.
LFAUTO — Inserts a line feed after each carriage return.
LIST — Displays settings of all parameters currently set by the communications program.
LOAD — Loads a command file associated with a specific bulletin board, information service, etc.
LWAIT — Puts a delay between lines when transmitting text files.
MODE — Gives choice of Call or Answer mode, where the modem waits for an incoming call.
NAME — Name associated with the number called for easy identification, e.g., "Yellow Pages Bulletin Board."
NUMBER — Phone number of the called modem.
PARITY — Sets the parity bit, e.g., "None," "Even," or "Odd."
PORT — Selects the communication port, COM1 or COM2.
PRINTER — Turns the printer on and off to print what appears on the screen.
QUIT — Ends the communication session and returns to DOS.
RQUEST — Requests file transfer from the remote modem.
RXMODEM — Tells the modem to expect a file transfer using the XMODEM protocol.
SPEED — Sets the transmission speed.
STOP — Sets the number of stop bits.
TYPE — Displays on the screen contents of any DOS file.

UCONLY — Converts from lower- to uppercase, if the terminal is not equipped for lowercase.

WRITE — Saves the contents of the memory buffer filled during transmission to a DOS file.

XXMODEM — Sends a file using the XMODEM protocol. Other commands transfer files using the proprietary Xtalk XVI protocol.

Command and Script Files

All but the simplest data communications programs will also support so-called command and script files. The user can store in these files settings of data communications parameters and responses to the handshake session with the remote information service. The command file is executed before a connection with a remote computer is established. It can be considered a static file. The dynamic script file executes in response to queries from the remote computer after the connection is established. A command file contains all parameters required to establish a data connection, such as the telephone number, number of data and stop bits, parity information, full or half-duplex setting. The script file contains the user's name and password for the particular service and standard responses to various questions asked by the information service. A script file is written in a special language, called a script language, which varies from one data communications program to another. Such script programs contains many conditional statements, to instruct the terminal to give certain answers, e.g., the password, after a specific interrogation. The data is saved for each service and is then recalled as needed. At the push of a function key the program will then dial the remote computer and, when the connection is established, will supply the user's identification or name and the password and will start an application session. Thus the primary user familiar with the data communications software does not even have to remember individual requirements of a specific connection, as they are all already stored in a file. A casual user does not need to have any familiarity with the data communications parameters and has only to know which function button to press on the keyboard to start a data connection.

Using as an example the Xtalk XVI data communications program we will look at a typical command and a script file. The program recognizes the files by their name and extensions. For example, the command file associated with the SOURCE information service would be called SOURCE.XTK and the corresponding script file would be called SOURCE.XTS. Command and script files for major services are supplied with most data communications programs.

A few generic command and script files are also supplied which can then be modified by the user.

The following are typical command and script files for Xtalk XVI; the lines with semicolons are comments.

Command file SAMPLE.XTK

```
NAME            MY SERVICE
NUMBER          1-212-555-1212
; List of transmission parameters
DATA            7
SPEED           1200
STOP            1
PARITY          NONE
PORT            COM1:
LFEED           ON
; Do not save initially to any file
; CAPTURE command saves all input/output to a file
CAPTURE OFF
PRINTER OFF
MODE            CALL
DUPLEX          FULL
; Set dialing prefix to ATDT (tone dialing)
DPREFIX ATDT
; Additional commands (function key assignments, etc.)
.
.
; Dial and repeat every 45 seconds if necessary, then wait
; 30 seconds for connection
GO R45/30
```

Script file SAMPLE.XTS

```
; Wait for 2 seconds after establishing connection
WAIT DELAY 20
```

```
; Wait for user prompt "user name:"
WAIT CHAR ":"
; Reply with system number ("|" stands for carriage return)
REPLY XYZ123|
; Wait for login prompt "login "
WAIT CHAR ""
; Reply with login and password
REPLY ID12345|
; Wait for prompt "" and request mail
WAIT CHAR ""
REPLY MAIL READ|
; Additional statements can be added to the script file or the connection
; can continue in manual mode.
```

A SESSION WITH A COMMERCIAL BULLETIN BOARD

I will describe how a connection is established with a popular bulletin board called BIX, short for Byte Information Exchange, a commercial venture of BYTE magazine. BIX can be accessed from any telephone in the United States via a packet switching network. A packet switching network, which in this case is operated by a company called TYMNET, provides local telephone access points throughout the United States. The local telephone numbers of TYMNET can be dialed by subscribers to BIX and many other services without incurring toll charges. As far as the user is concerned the TYMNET network is transparent. Transfer of data between the local terminal and the destination, the BIX computer in New Hampshire, is nearly instantaneous.

After having the modem dial the local TYMNET access point and getting a return carrier signal, a string of random characters appears on the screen. Pressing the letter "a" produces a "please login:" prompt. When TYMNET receives "a" it can determine the transmission parameters of the caller, in particular the transmission rate (300, 1200, or 2400 bps) and it can adjust its own parameters accordingly. At the "login:" prompt I typed "BIX," which then connected me to the BIX computer. A BIX logo then appeared on the screen, followed by the next prompt "Name:" requesting the assigned user code required for identification and billing purposes. The next prompt was "password:" to which I replied by giving my password. The password is assigned to the user when the account is established, and can be changed by the user at will anytime thereafter. If the "Name" and the "password" are recognized, then a message appears indicating if any "mail" is saved for the user. The mail can be read, answered, saved, or discarded. The user then has a choice of joining any of over 100 special interest groups or "conferences." Though most conferences cover computer related subjects, there is something for nearly everyone. Also a number of software and hardware companies "chair" a conference and answer questions from users of a particular product. Here is a sampling of selected conferences available on the BIX service:

4th.gen.langs	The 4th generation languages conference
a.t.and.t	The AT&T computers conference
ada	The Ada language conference
ai.theory	The conference on artificial intelligence theory
algorithms	Using algorithms to solve problems
apple	The Apple II family conference
ask.bix	Questions and answers about microcomputing
assembler	The assembly language conference
ataricorp	Atari's customer-support conference
aviation	Plane talk about computers in general aviation
basic	The BASIC language conference
bbs	Dial-up bulletin board systems: what's hot, what's not
byte.reviews	Hardware and software reviews
byte.uk	News from the United Kingdom
c.language	The C programming language conference
cats	Cats and computers
chess	A conference about the game of chess
cobol	The COBOL language conference
consultants	On the art and business of being a consultant
current.events	Discussing the news of the day
desktop.pub	Using micros for publishing
engineering	The conference on engineering programs
expert.sys	The conference on expert systems
food	Good eats
forth	The Forth programming language conference
games	The games program conference
grafic.disp	The conference on graphics displays
ham.radio	Computing, digital electronics, and amateur radio
handicapped	Computing and the handicapped

ibm.ps	IBM's new line of computers, the Personal Systems
idea.process	Beyond word processors and spreadsheets
lans	The conference on local-area networks (LANs)
lattice	The Lattice Inc. conference
law	Computers and the law
learn	A tutorial on using BIX
listings	Programs from BYTE and from the public domain.
logitech	The Logitech conference
macintosh	The Macintosh family conference
medicine	Computers in the medical and health services fields
microbytes.hw	New hardware products
microbytes.sw	New software products
music	Computers and music
newslet.excng	A conference for editors of club newsletters
packet.nets	The conference on packet switching networks
pascal	The Pascal language conference
postscript	The Postscript conference
sf	For science fiction and fantasy fans
soviets	Soviet computing, society, and foreign policy
space	Space exploration and development
tax.talk	Questions, answers, debates about the new tax laws
telecomm.tech	New telecommunications technology
television	The technology and uses of TV
unclassifieds	Buy, sell, and swap on BIX
writers	For writers, published or yet to be published

After joining a conference by typing, e.g., "JOIN CATS" at the ":" prompt, one gets a list of subtopics in that conference. Choosing a subtopic, e.g., "summary," gives one line summaries of recent messages. The next step is then to read and/or answer the messages. For example, the CATS conference included exciting messages referring to whether cats are color-blind, how to introduce new cats to established cats, and whether sawdust should be used as cat litter. The consensus of opinion was against it, because sawdust tracks all over the house.

Joining the law conference led to a lively discussion of recent litigation by Lotus Corporation concerning use of certain words like "Manuscript" as part of "Lotus Manuscript," against Pergamon Journals which has a product called "Manuscript Manager." There were also letters referring to the latest Supreme Court decisions and to the "crisis" in the liability insurance.

Anytime during a session with a bulletin board one can go back to the local command mode (Esc in Xtalk XVI) and start or stop the printer, save the contents of the screen to memory or to a disk file, or check contents of some other data file. One can also download programs from the bulletin board files by using any of the file transfer protocols, as described in the following paragraphs, e.g., Kermit or XModem, or one can upload one's own cherished programs for use by others.

After satisfying yourself with the contents of various conferences you quit by typing "q" at the prompt followed by "bye". The BIX service then returns you to TYMENET, which comes back with the "please login:" prompt. At this time you can simply break the connection by switching the modem to the local command mode and by typing BYE or QUIT.

TYMENET charges a flat rate of between $2 and $4 per hour of connect time independent of where the subscriber is located. On top of the TYMENET connection charges, BIX charges for their services at the rate of between $8 and $12 per hour, depending on the time of the day.

ELECTRONIC MAIL

A specialized form of a commercial bulletin board is the electronic mail, frequently referred to as E-Mail. The primary purpose of E-Mail is to transfer messages between individuals and organizations, each having an assigned electronic "mailbox" in the central computer's memory. An additional feature of E-Mail, not found on regular bulletin boards, is that for a small fee the message can be sent to the destination by regular first class mail or by express overnight delivery. The electronic message is then received at one of the E-Mail offices near the message destination, is printed on a high-speed printer, and is then brought to the nearest post office for final delivery. An additional feature of E-Mail is that the same message can be sent to a list of destinations, rather than to a single address.

E-Mail competes with such long established services as TWX and TELEX. The main difference is that TWX and TELEX use dedicated customer facilities and work more like a telephone. A data call from subscriber A to subscriber B is set up and electronic mail sent by subscriber A is printed on subscriber's B teletypewriter or printer attached to a dedicated computer. An acknowledging message is then sent to A confirming that his or her message was received. With E-Mail the message from subscriber A goes to the central computer from which it will hopefully be retrieved by subscriber B. The question arises, how can I send something to B and be sure that the message was received? Also, how often should I check my mailbox to make sure that I did not miss some important message? The final point to consider when deciding on a service is that TWX and TELEX are used mostly by business people, not by computer programmers, so ease of operating the system is of utmost importance. Even the "simple" menus of communications programs discussed earlier may sound arcane to an average business person. Questions like what is a stop bit, or what kind of parity do I need, were stopping many business people from using E-Mail until convenient software came along. This specialized software performs a limited number of functions, is less general than a typical communications software package, but is very easy to use. It does not require command or script files, since its functions are predetermined.

Software associated with E-Mail is very specialized and works best with a specific service. An example of such software is Lotus Express developed by the Lotus Corporation. The software package is specifically designed for the E-Mail service provided by the MCI Corporation. MCI Mail service can be reached through many MCI access telephone numbers in the United States or

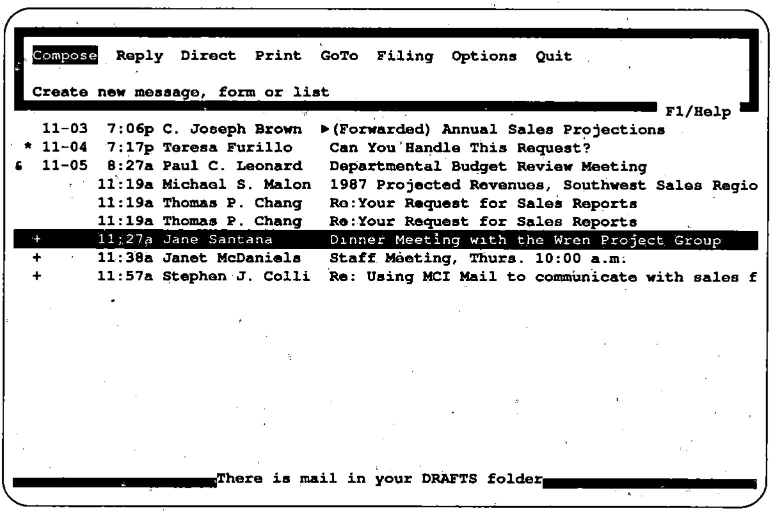

Figure 9.2 **Lotus Express Incoming Mail Summary**

```
Lotus Express  1.00 Reader                                12-15-86   8:52a
Folder: DRAFTS  (New draft)
                                                                 F1/Help
Via: 1
To: Mr. Andrew G. Gartner
 Company: International Systems, Inc.
 Line1: 325 West 57th St.
 Line2: Suite 3705
 City: New York
 State: NY
 Code: 10013
 Country:
   ■ Receipt  4Hour  Onite Charge:
 Options: 4hour,charge:newaccts█

                   There is mail in your DRAFTS folder
```

Figure 9.3 **Lotus Express Postal Address Form**

```
Lotus Express  1.00 Reader                                11-06-86   5:34p
Folder: DRAFTS  [3 of 3]
                                                                 F1/Help
Subject: XYZ Corp. Telephone Order Form

---------------------XYZ Corporation Order Form-----------------------------

Date order taken (MM-DD-YY) [         ]
Order taken by [                          ]
Invoice number [              ]

Customer Name      [                          ]
Street Address [                              ]  Apt. Number [     ]
       City        [                 ]  State [  ]  Zip [          ]
       Credit card [                 ]  V, M, or AE [ ]
       Expiration date (MM-DD-YY) [         ]

Product number [               ]        Quantity [   ]
Unit price     [               ]        Price [           ]
Delivery       [               ]        Tax   [           ]

Total due:     [               ]
                   There is mail in your DRAFTS folder
```

Figure 9.4 **Lotus Express Order Form**

through a packet switching network, such as TYMNET, described earlier. The Lotus Express program will make the access to the MCI Mail automatic by working in background, as soon as the computer is turned on, and at specific intervals calling the MCI or TYMNET and checking if any mail was added to the subscriber's mailbox. If any new mail was added, then the program running in the foreground mode, e.g., Wordstar or Lotus, will be temporarily interrupted to announce arrival of new mail. Similarly, any files or contents of the screen can be automatically sent via the MCI Mail to any other subscriber to the service. Incoming and outgoing messages can be assigned to individual "folders" and each folder can be opened, closed, or cleaned up. Thus the user can organize the incoming and outgoing mail into function related compartments.

All the information pertinent to calling MCI and identifying the caller is done during the Lotus Express installation procedure. The information, which has to be supplied during installation is the assigned MCI Mail User Name, password, and the local telephone access number. The program will also ask for the local time zone for time "stamping" of delivered messages and for the communication port (COM1 or COM2) assigned to the modem. Figures 9.2, 9.3, and 9.4 are displays produced by Lotus Express to show the user various aspects of the incoming and outgoing E-Mail messages. The program provides literally dozens of displays, to guide the user in sending, receiving, and cataloging messages.

ERROR CHECKING

Data communications software will call certain error checking protocols for file transfer. Every telephone connection will experience occasional bursts of noise which may result in a data error. If one transfers a long file of plain ASCII text an occasional error may not be important, but in a transfer of a binary file a single error will make the whole file useless. The most popular error checking protocols are Kermit, XModem, X.PC, and MNP. The protocols break the transmission in blocks and check parity and the Cyclical Redundancy Code (CRC) in each block. The difference between the simple parity check, sometimes referred to as Longitudinal Redundancy Check (LRC), and the more advanced CRC is that the parity check derives only a single bit (0 or 1) from each byte, in a CRC check all bits in a block of typically 128 bytes are examined and a "checksum" value of 2-byte length, the

Data Block

$$\frac{1101101011100011 \ldots \text{etc.}}{\text{CRC Constant}} = \text{some quotient} + \text{some remainder}$$

16 bits

Quotient is discarded
Remainder = 16 bits or 2 BCC characters

CRC 16=$2^{16} + 2^{15} + 2^{2}\ 2^{0}$ CRC CCITT=$2^{16} + 2^{12} + 2^{5} + 2^{0}$

Figure 9.5 **Cyclical Redundancy Check (CRC) Algorithm**

so-called Block Check Characters (BCC), is derived and transmitted following each block of data.

The detailed algorithm for the U.S. (CRC 16) and the European (CRC CCITT) implementation of the CRC check is shown in Figure 9.5. The CRC check is much more sensitive to errors than a simple parity check, as two errors in a single byte will make a parity check appear correct, but will be detected by the CRC check. If an error is detected by the parity or the CRC check within a block, then the whole block is retransmitted. Some protocols adjust the block size to the frequency of errors. On a noisy line with frequent errors the blocks are small. If the transmission is fairly error-free, then the block size will be larger. As each block adds some overhead for acknowledgment, the transmission on a "quiet" line will be faster with a protocol using variable block sizes. Following is a short description of the popular public domain XMODEM, the interesting proprietary MNP protocol, and a few less popular file transfer protocols.

XMODEM Protocol

This protocol was originally developed in 1979 by Ward Christensen and although it lacks certain modem features like variable block length, it is still very popular for personal computer data exchange. Several versions of the protocol exist, e.g., the XMODEM/CRC version, which instead of the simple 1-byte parity check (98% effective) uses the modern CRC error check (99.99% effective).

Once the protocol is initiated, the receiving modem starts sending a NAK signal (Not Acknowledged - ASCII 21) every 10 seconds. When the transmitting modem detects the signal it starts sending the file to be transmitted in blocks of 128 bytes. At the beginning of each block is the SOH (Start of Header - ASCII 01), followed by the ASCII character representing the block number, followed by ASCII character representing the one's complement of the block number. This is followed by 128 data bytes and a "checksum" byte derived from the data.

The receiving modem checks that the block started with SOH and that the block number and the "checksum" number are correct. If it finds that all three are okay, then it sends ACK (Acknowledged - ASCII 06) and the transmission continues. If one of the three numbers is incorrect, then a NAK is returned, which results in retransmission of the whole block of 128 bytes. At the end of the file the transmitting modem sends an EOT (End of Transmission - ASCII 04); the receiving modem acknowledges with ACK and the transmission is finished.

X.PC Protocol

This public domain protocol is one of the major contenders to become an accepted standard. It is supported by TYMENET and a number of users' groups. It is based on the ISO X.25 network level protocol used for packet switching of data.

The protocol provides the following features:

Multiplexing — The ability to support multiple data streams

Flow control — The ability to control, for each data stream, the flow of data between transmitting and receiving DTEs and DCEs

Error control — The ability to detect errors at the packet layer and to correct errors indicated by the link layer

Reset and restart — The ability to reinitialize the communication paths at the packet layer if serious errors occur.

Microcom Network Protocol (MNP)

The Microcom Corporation developed a series of hardware and software error correction schemes which are known by the collective name of MNP protocols. There are six levels of MNP protocols with each higher level more elaborate then the lower one. The first three levels are in the public domain and are based on CRC checks and block retransmission. The three higher proprietary levels of the MNP protocols levels 4, 5, and 6 are much more interesting. They feature a combination of software and hardware embedded in special modems. There are two aspects to this approach: error detection and correction, and improvement in data transmission efficiency by data compression. Using specialized modems gives the manufacture the advantage of being able to implement nonstandard and possibly better technologies; the disadvantage to the user is that modems at both ends of a communication link have to come from the same manufacturer. To be able to exercise special features of these modems may also require changes to the standard data communications software.

The proprietary MNP modems improve the data throughput by data compression. Data compression consists of buffering and analyzing the data and then, depending on frequency of appearance of various ASCII characters, coding each character into 4 to 12 bits. For example, the most common letter of the English alphabet "e" would be coded in 4 bits while the uncommon "X" would be coded in 12 bits. The assignments are dynamic and may change during a call. To further maximize the data throughput the block length of data is assigned dynamically and varies with the quality of the transmission facility. A quiet line would have long blocks, a noisy line would have short blocks. The special modems operate in synchronous mode by stripping start and stop bits. The combined MNP techniques in a level 6 protocol modem allow, according to Microcom, for effective transmission rates of up to 19200 bps on a switched telephone connection.

YMODEM/CRC Protocol

This protocol uses 1024 bytes per block versus 128 bytes in the XMODEM to reduce overhead. If more than 5 errors are encountered, the protocol reduces the block size to 128.

Kermit Protocol

This very popular public domain protocol is supported by Columbia University. The following description is derived from the official Kermit documentation, which can be obtained from many public bulletin boards. The protocol is intended for use in an environment where there may be a diverse mixture of computers — micros, personal computers, workstations, laboratory computers, and time-sharing systems from a variety of manufacturers. All these systems need the ability to communicate in ASCII over ordinary serial telecommunication lines.

Kermit was originally designed at Columbia University to meet the need for file transfer between DECSYSTEM-20 and IBM 370-series mainframes and various microcomputers. It turned out that the diverse characteristics of these three kinds of systems resulted in a design that was general enough to fit almost any system.

The Kermit protocol is specifically designed for character oriented transmission. The protocol is carried out by Kermit programs on each end of the serial connection sending "packets" back and forth; the sender sends file names, file contents, and control information; the receiver acknowledges (positively or negatively) each packet.

The packets have a layered design, more or less in keeping with the ISO philosophy, with the outermost fields used by the data link layer to verify data integrity; the next fields used by the session layer to verify continuity; and the data itself present at the application level.

Connections between systems are established by the user. In a typical case, the user runs Kermit on a microcomputer, enters terminal emulation, connects to a remote host computer (perhaps by dialing up), logs in, runs Kermit on the remote host, and then issues commands so that Kermit can start a file transfer from the remote computer, "escapes" back to the micro, and issues commands to the local Kermit to start its side of the file transfer. Files may be transferred singly or in groups.

Basic Kermit provides only for file transfer of ASCII files, although the protocol attempts to allow for other types of sequential files. Alternate microcomputer implementations of Kermit are expected to provide terminal emulation, to facilitate the initial connection.

Current implementations simplify the "user interface" somewhat by allowing the Kermit on the remote host to run as a "server," which can transfer files in either direction upon command from the local user.

DATA COMPRESSION

Data compression is used by many specialized modems and protocols including the previously mentioned MNP. Frequently the variable length Huffman code instead of the fixed length ASCII code is used to represent individual characters. This approach is similar to the Morse code, which assigns a single bit "." to the most common letter in the English alphabet "e." Frequently occurring words, such as "the," "and," "yours," "invoice," or numerical digits can also be compressed by "smart" algorithms, which analyze the data before transmitting it. Typical gains obtained through data compression are 30—50% in the throughput transmission. Even larger gains can be obtained when transmitting graphic image files, which contain much redundancy.

A user can also take advantage of data compression without any special modems or protocols by using popular archiving programs, some of them being in public domain. The only requirement is that both the sender and receiver use the same version of the archiving program. Before transmission the file is "squeezed" by means of the archiving program; it is then transmitted and "unsqeezed" at destination.

EFFECTIVE SPEED OF FILE TRANSFER

A direct file transmission without an error detection protocol occurs at the full modem transmission speed. As explained earlier, a 1200-bps modem will send approximately 120 characters per second. However, once an error controlling protocol is in effect, things slow down considerably. A minimum loss in speed due to error detection and correction is approximately 50% but it can get considerably worse. A recent study by the Software Digest Ratings Newsletter showed the ratio of effective transmission speeds between the fastest and the slowest communications software package to be 3 to 1. This information can usually not be found in the software specifications and can only be determined by an actual test consisting of sending a file of several pages over a telephone line to a computer equipped with a similar modem and software. Such a test may also show one software package to be better on a high-quality line since it uses large blocks of data, and another package to be better on a poor, noisy connection since it uses short blocks. The best overall transmission speed should be obtained from a communications protocol and software using variable block sizes.

10. Modem on a Chip

Until now, we have treated the modem as a separate subsystem, a black box located between the computer/terminal and the telephone line or some other transmission facility. In this chapter we will look in more detail at the individual circuits inside the black box.

The current trend in miniaturization by means of Very Large Scale Integration (VLSI) led to development of single and multiple chip sets of integrated circuits, which perform most of the modem functions. Adding a few discrete components results then in an inexpensive single board modem. Modems based on VLSI circuits are not only smaller and less expensive than earlier modems using discrete components, but they perform more functions and provide better transmission performance. This is due to implementation on VLSI chips of complex circuits, like adaptive equalizers, which were omitted in earlier modem designs. Because of high initial costs, modem chip sets have only been developed for the most popular modem types, namely, those based on 300-bps, 1200-bps, 2400-bps, and facsimile protocols. There are several single chip implementations of 300-bps and 1200-bps modems from various manufacturers. The current price/performance ratio still favors, however, multiple chip sets for 2400-bps modeems. A possible one-chip implementation of 2400-bps modems using hybrid technology is not yet price-effective.

There are three basic approaches to design of modem chips. The easiest and fastest approach is to translate the earlier analog designs from discrete components into integrated components by means of analog ICs, such as operational amplifiers and comparators, and retaining analog filters for frequency discrimination. The disadvantage of this approach is that all problems inherent in analog design, such as sample variations, are retained. The second, more difficult approach is to use digital signal processing with a general purpose microprocessor and with programs stored in ROM. The third and the initially most costly approach is to design a specialized digital chip set from scratch and to provide it with all appropriate functions. The last two approaches are similar in nature, but by designing a specialized digital chip set, one can obtain and optimize certain features in firmware, which would be difficult to implement at a sufficiently high speed using a general purpose microprocessor.

The question arises of how the basically analog signals transmitted over telephone lines or other analog facilities can be handled by digital modem circuits. What the modem designers do is to provide both analog-to-digital (A/D) and digital-to-analog (D/A) converters as interfaces between the digital chips and the analog world. Many analog functions such as frequency filtering and modulation can be performed more easily with full repeatability in the digital time domain. Multiplication of transfer functions in frequency domain, which is equivalent to filtering or modulation, becomes convolution in time domain, a special multiplication of digital signal representation. Similarly, sampling an analog signal at the sampling rate of $2 \times F$ per second is equivalent to passing the same signal through a low pass filter with cut-off frequency of F Hz.

We will look here specifically at the R2424DS, a three-chip implementation of a 2400/1200/300 bps modem from a major modem chip manufacturer, the Rockwell International Corporation. This particular three-chip set is a good example of current trends in VLSI based modem technology. Many modem manufacturers use the R2424DS set as their building blocks; other modem manufacturers use similar designs. The chip set is a mixture of digital and analog design with functions apportioned to the digital and analog sections. The set supports the following protocols, which are user selectable by applying ground or a positive voltage to specific pins of the modem chip set:

Bell 103A	0—300 bps Asynchronous
Bell 212A	1200 bps Synchronous
Bell 212A	1200 bps Asynchronous
CCITT V.22A	1200 bps Synchronous
CCITT V.22B	1200 bps Asynchronous
CCITT V.22A	600 bps Synchronous
CCITT V.22B	600 bps Asynchronous
CCITT V.22 bis	1200 bps Synchronous
CCITT V.22 bis	1200 bps Asynchronous
CCITT V.22 bis	2400 bps Synchronous

CCITT V.22 bis 2400 bps Asynchronous

Other basic characteristics of the R2424DS chip set are as follows:

2-wire full-duplex operation
Adaptive and fixed compromise equalization
Auto/manual answer mode
Auto/manual dial mode
Tone or pulse dialing
Call progress tone detector
Multiple test modes
Variable character length in asynchronous mode 8—11 bits
Interface — RS-232-C functional, TTL electrical
Supply voltages: +5 V, +12 V, –12 V
Power consumption –3 W

Functional Description

The Rockwell R2424DS set of three VLSI chips partitions the modem functions into two sections, the Digital Signal Processor and the Integrated Analog Device. The high-speed Signal Processor requires two chips; the low-speed Integrated Analog Device is located on one chip.

Signal Processor

The Signal Processor is a two-chip specialized 16-bit microprocessor designed for intensive numeric high-speed applications, like those required by A/D and D/A conversion, adaptive equalization, scrambling, and data conversion. One of the two chips is the Sample Rate Device, which performs tasks at the rate at which a data signal is sampled. The other chip is the Baud Rate Device, which performs tasks associated with groups of bits contained in each transmitted or received signal element. The assorted modem characteristics, like those associated with a 1200-bps 212A type modem, or with a 2400-bps V.22 bis type modem, are stored in the internal 1024 × 16-bit Read Only Memory (ROM), the specific modem configuration, selected by the

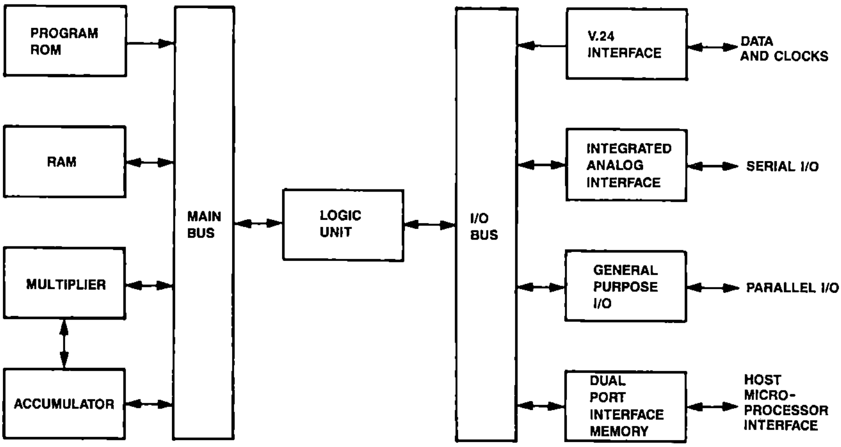

Figure 10.1 **Basic Building Blocks of the Signal Processor (RS2424DS)**

user, is stored in the internal 256 × 16 bit Random Access Memory (RAM). The signal processor uses 16-bit words and a 32-bit accumulator to perform internal computations. The Signal Processor is implemented in *N*-type Metal Oxide Semiconductor (NMOS) technology particularly suited for high-speed digital applications. Basic building blocks of the signal processor chip are shown in Figure 10.1.

Integrated Analog Device

The third chip of the R2424DS set performs a multitude of miscellaneous functions normally associated with discrete analog circuits. In discrete designs such circuitry would occupy up to 80% of the board size; therefore use of an integrated circuit contributes much to the potential modem miniaturization. The chip uses switched capacitor technology which allows the substitution of small integrated circuit capacitors for resistors, thus saving much of the silicon area on the chip. The principle of switched capacitor

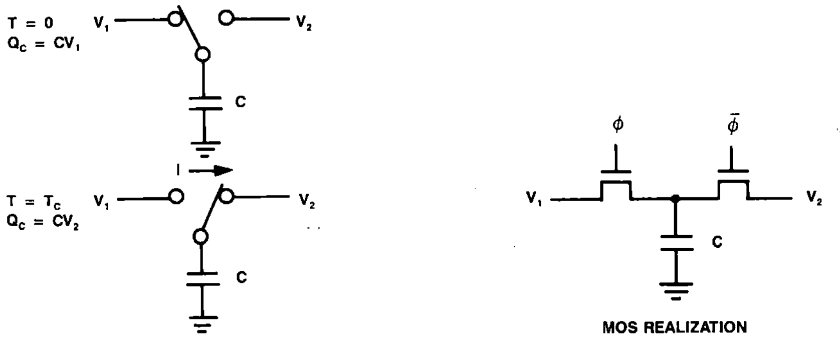

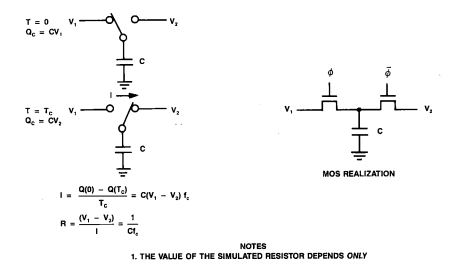

$$I = \frac{Q(0) - Q(T_C)}{T_C} = C(V_1 - V_2)\,f_c$$

$$R = \frac{(V_1 - V_2)}{I} = \frac{1}{Cf_c}$$

NOTES
1. THE VALUE OF THE SIMULATED RESISTOR DEPENDS *ONLY* ON THE CAPACITANCE AND THE SWITCHING FREQUENCY.
2. RC PRODUCTS ARE DETERMINED BY CAPACITANCE RATIOS AND SWITCHING FREQUENCY.

Figure 10.2 **Switched Capacitor Design**

design is shown in Figure 10.2. The technique allows the implementation of large capacitor and resistor values on an integrated circuit chip. The integrated analog device chip performs many functions related to interfacing the modem to the transmission facility and the serial interface in the computer. Interface to the telephone line includes the Data Access Arrangement (DAA) circuitry required by the FCC to protect the telephone network. Figure 10.3 shows the assorted functions located on the analog device chip. The chip is implemented in Complementary Metal Oxide Semiconductor (CMOS) technology, which is best suited for analog designs

INDIVIDUAL MODEM BUILDING BLOCKS

Depending on the configuration selected by the user, the modem can assume different "personalities." Figures 10.4 and 10.5 show in more detail block

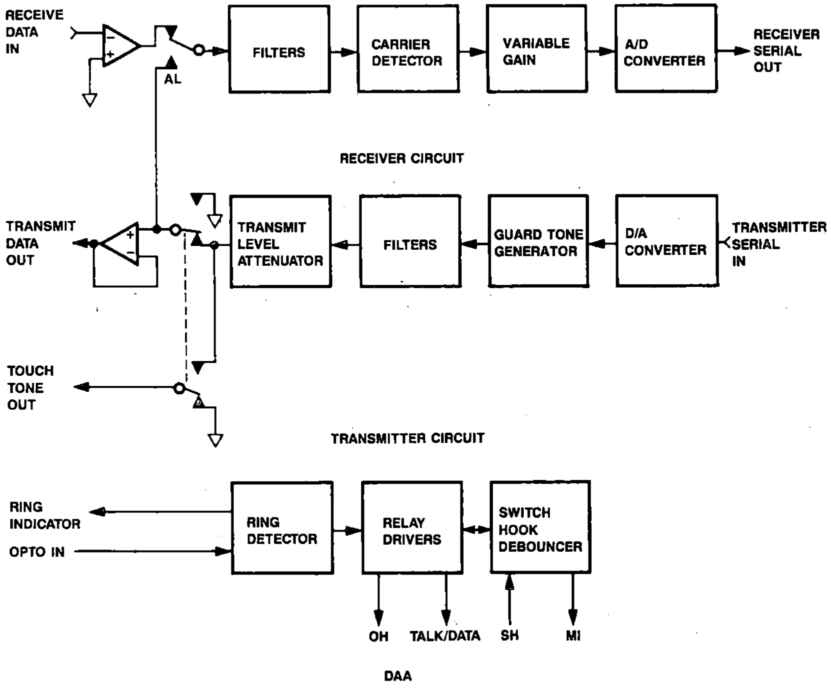

Figure 10.3 **Basic Building Block of the Analog Chip (RS2424DS)**

diagrams of the transmitting and of the receiving section of a modem configured for asynchronous operation at either 1200 bps or at 2400 bps. Next we will describe in more detail the major blocks shown in these two figures.

Data Input Control

This circuit controls the data flow from the computer via the RTS and DTR serial interface leads. In the test mode, the internal test generator would feed a test pattern at this point without regard to the status of the RTS and DTR leads.

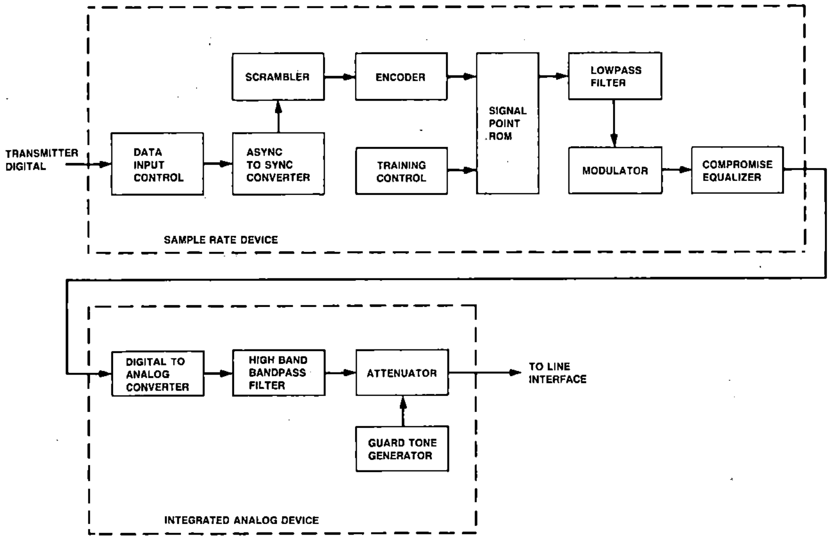

Figure 10.4 **Transmitting Modem 1200/2400 bps, Asynchronous**

Asynchronous to Synchronous Converter

The converter is required only in the asynchronous operating mode. When the modem is in synchronous operation this circuit is bypassed. The function of the circuit is to fit the gaps in asynchronous data flow so that the remaining circuits can operate under clock control, as if the data would be flowing continuously.

Scrambler

The purpose of this circuit is to assure a semi-randomness of the data stream, even if the data consists of a long string of 1's and 0's. The receiving terminal is namely dependent on the semi-randomness of received data to extract from it the timing information. The scrambling algorithm is part of a

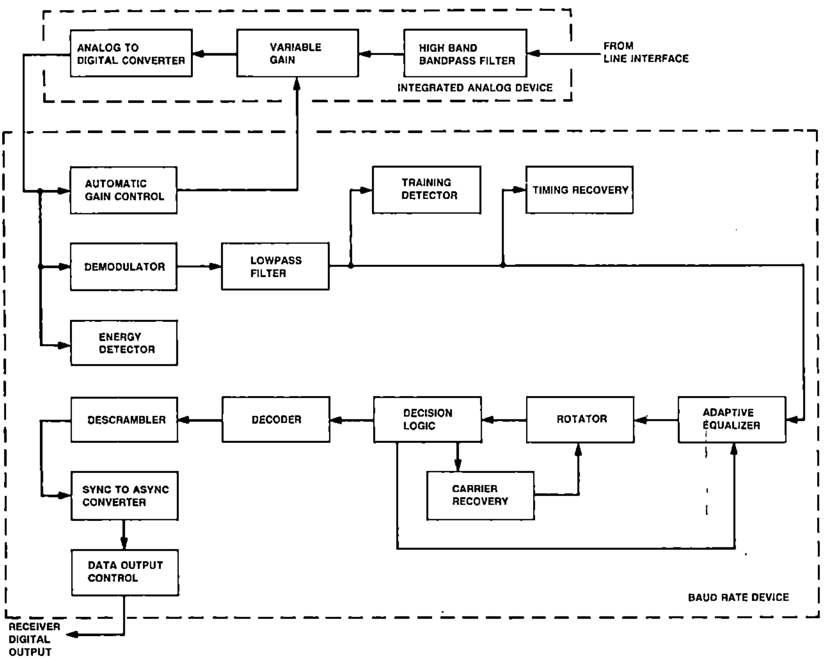

Figure 10.5 **Receiving Modem 1200/2400 bps, Asynchronous**

specific CCITT or Bell protocol and has to be the same for the receiver and for the transmitter. The scrambler has nothing to do with data security as the algorithms are public, are a part of the appropriate protocols, and are the same for a specific modem type. The scrambling algorithm, the scrambling and the descrambling circuits for the Bell 212 and V.22 bis protocols are shown in Figure 10.6. The square boxes are shift registers, each introducing a 1-bit delay. By inspection, or by writing a short BASIC program, one can see that a string of 1's will be translated into a pseudorandom sequence, but a string of 0's will remain a string of 0's after passing through the scrambler. The solution is to add a "kick" circuit which throws in a "1" after a sequence of 0's of predetermined length. The scrambler circuit is not used in 300 bps operation, since the FSK modulation does not require timing recovery from the data stream.

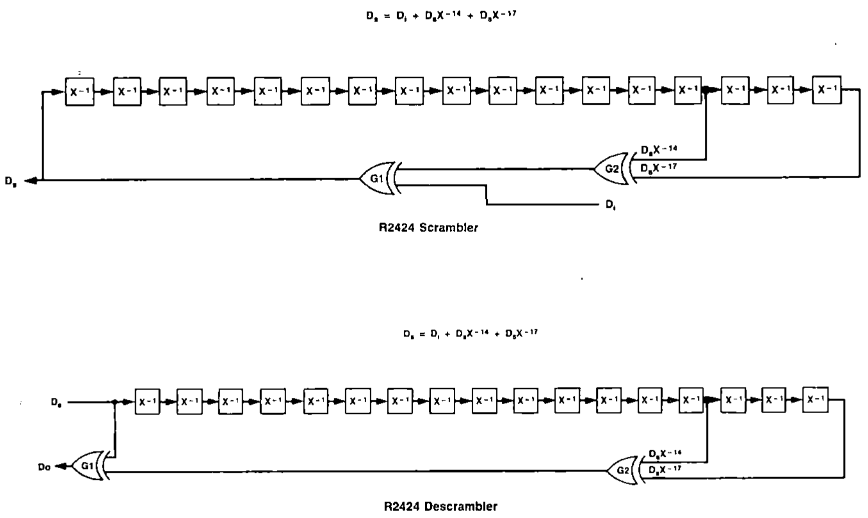

Figure 10.6 **Scrambling and Descrambling Algorithm and Circuit**

Encoder and Signal Point ROM

The encoder arranges successive data bits in groups of 2 (dibits) or groups of 4 (quadbits) depending on the transmission speed. Then, depending on the value of each dibit or quadbit, the signal ROM assigns the appropriate amplitude and phase values to each signal. As discussed in Chapter 4, the assigned amplitude/phase values are based on constellation diagrams associated with the appropriate protocol.

Modulator and Low Pass Filter

The modulation rules depend on the protocol chosen. The Bell 103 type protocol uses FSK modulation with two frequencies for the originating modem and two frequencies for the answering modem. The 212A protocols use DPSK modulation with carrier frequencies at 1200 Hz and 2400 Hz, while the V.22 protocols use the combined phase/amplitude QAM modulation with the same carrier frequencies as 212A. Encoding of 1, 2, or 4 bits per signaling sample is also made according to the appropriate protocol. Figure 10.7 shows the complex DPSK and QAM modulator. The corresponding demodulator in the receiving modem is the mirror image of the modulator. Both the modulation and the demodulation are performed in the time domain on digital samples of the data signal.

The signal sampling rate required for time domain filtering is 7200 samples per second, which is equivalent to a low-pass filter with 3600 Hz cut-off frequency. The sampling process generates repeated spectra around harmonics of that frequency. To avoid "ringing," caused by these harmonics, which could result in intersymbol interference, the data has then to be filtered by an analog low pass filter. A so-called raised cosine filter, with the shape similar to the shape of the cosine is chosen as the optimum filter. Since the signal consists of phase shifted x and y components there are actually two filters provided to shape each component.

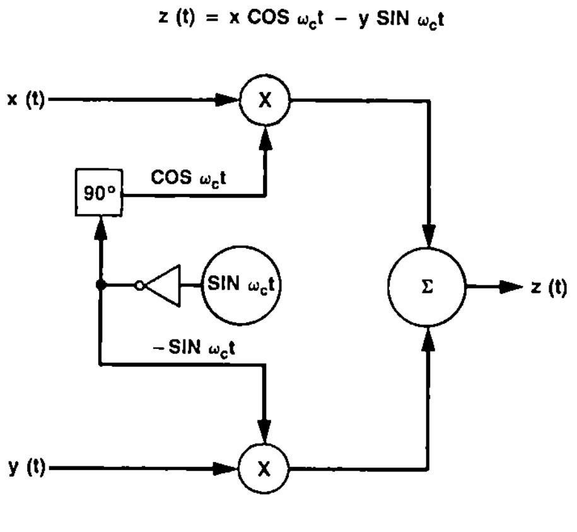

Figure 10.7 **DPSK/QAM Modulator**

D/A Converter, Band Pass Filter, and Interface

The digital modulated signal is first filtered by convoluting its digital values with the appropriate functions corresponding to a bandpass filter. The signal is then transformed by the D/A converter into an analog signal, which after band limiting, so that it does not interfere with signals modulated on adjacent carrier frequencies, is sent over the telephone line to the remote modem.

Compromise Equalizer

The compromise equalizer predistorts the signal to be sent over the telephone line or some other transmission facility, with a mirror image of the expected attenuation and delay line distortion. The fixed-form equalizer compensates for the average and not for the actual distortion of the transmission facility, since it cannot be known in advance.

Adaptive Equalizer

Most of the building blocks in the receiving modem are equivalent to similar blocks in the transmitting modem. A unique building block found only in the receiving modem is the adaptive equalizer.

At the receiving modem based on the R2424DS chip set, the actual remaining transmission channel distortion, transmission facility distortion less the predistortion of the compromise equalizer in the transmitting modem, is compensated by means of an adaptive equalizer. This technique used at 1200 and 2400 bps gives approximately 3 dB *S/N* advantage, as compared to an exclusive use of fixed compromise equalizers, as in most other modems, including the original Bell 212A modem.

An adaptive equalizer, often referred to as a transversal filter, adjusts itself during the handshake sequence sent by the originating modem. The equalizer behaves like a tunable filter, which corrects for the transmission channel attenuation and delay distortion by producing a complementary response. The flattening of the combined attenuation and delay characteristic reduces the intersymbol interference during data transmission. Figure 10.8 shows a more detailed block diagram of the adaptive equalizer with the individual delay and

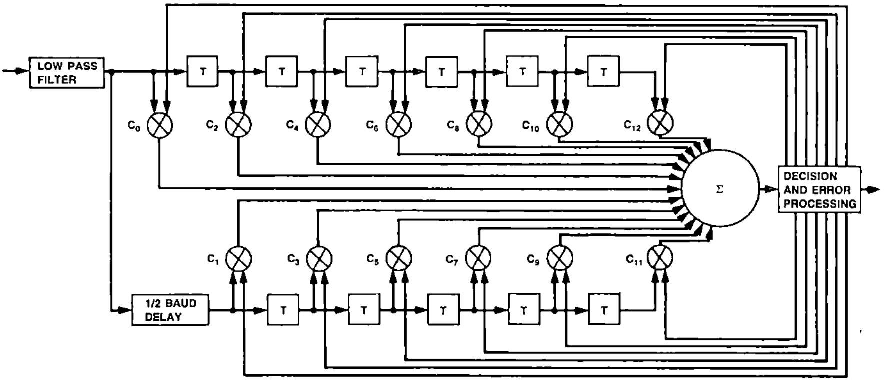

Figure 10.8 **Adaptive Equalizer**

gain blocks. A signal passes through a series of delay blocks, each of *T*/2 duration, where *T* is the time between signal elements. Part of the signal after phase reversal is then fed back into each block to optimize the final shape. The variable gain blocks C0 through C12, associated with each delay block, are adjusted by the decision logic circuit, which tries to optimize the equalizer while receiving a known sequence of bits before the actual data is transmitted. The gain adjustments made during this handshake period at the beginning of the transmission remain set for the remainder of the call.

Tone Dialer

The tone dialer shown in more detail in Figure 10.9 sends the standard dual frequencies as follows:

Digit	Frequency Pairs (Hz)	
0	941	1336
1	697	1209

Digit	Frequency Pairs (Hz)	
2	697	1336
3	697	1477
4	770	1209
5	770	1336
6	770	1477
7	852	1209
8	852	1336
9	852	1477
*	941	1209
#	941	1477

The tones are generated first as pairs of 8-bit numbers and then are changed into analog tones by the D/A converter.

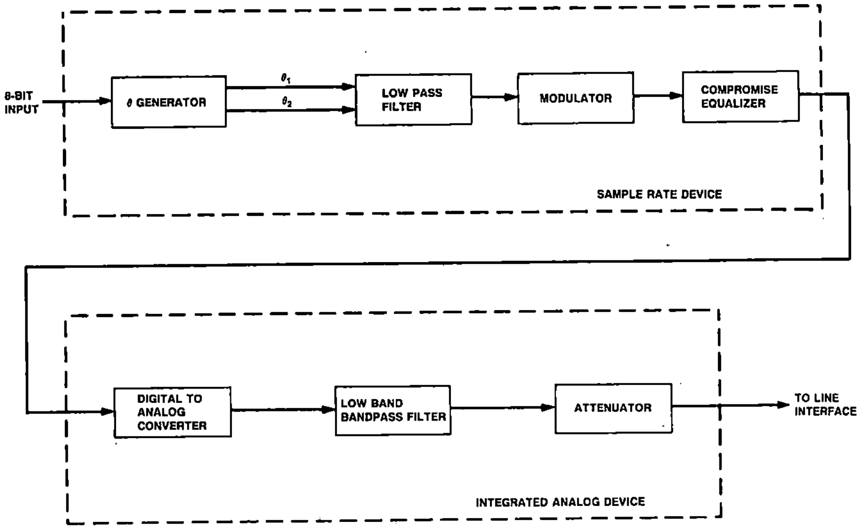

Figure 10.9 **Touch-Tone Dialer**

Call Progress Tone Detector

The circuit shown in Figure 10.10 detects the Ringing and Busy signals; this information is then relayed via communications software to the terminal or computer. The information would be required for starting a new dialing attempt, if the phone was busy. The main components of the tone detector circuit are an automatic gain control block and a low pass filter, which detects signals between 345 and 635 Hz, where the call progress tones are located. The smoothing low pass filter averages the energy in the passband while the output control circuit writes a "1" to an internal register, if energy is detected, and a "0" if no energy is detected

COMPLETE MODEM

The three chips comprising the RS2424DS set and a few external components form a high-quality 300/1200/2400 bps modem. Thanks to digital design, the modems based on these chips do not differ from each other in basic characteristics, such as the minimum signal-to-noise ratio required for

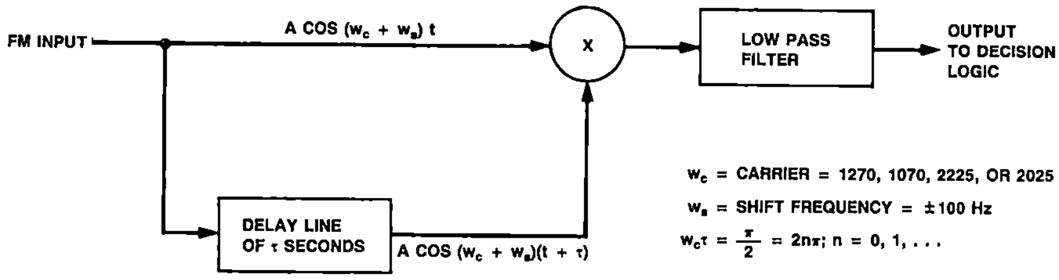

Block diagram of the modem receiver configured for call progress tone detection. The receiver analog input bypasses the integrated analog filters and is input to the variable gain stage which increases the amplitude of low level signals to keep the receiver circuits operating near their optimum point. The 10-bit analog to digital converter outputs serial data from the integrated analog device to the baud rate device. In the baud rate device, the automatic gain control logic determines the average power level of the signals at the IA output, and adjusts the variable gain stage for optimum performance. The presence of energy above -43 dBm is detected by the energy detect logic. The signal is sent to the bandpass filter which has a passband of 345 to 635 Hz. This is the band where call progress tones are located. The smoothing filter averages the energy over the band. The data output control writes a 1 to the TONE bit in the receiver while energy is detected and a 0 when no energy is detected.

Figure 10.10 Call Progress Tone Detector

errorless data transmission for a given type of transmission facility. Measurements of modem noise sensitivity described in Chapter 14 confirm the superiority of modems based on digital chip set design. Figure 10.11 shows a general block diagram of a modem using the R2424DS chip set; Figure 10.12 shows a nearly complete schematic of that modem. In addition to the three chips, a complete modem also requires a power supply capable of providing +5 V, +12 V, and –12 V. In this particular implementation, –12 V is derived from –5 V with a voltage regulator (VR1). The complete modem also needs a quartz crystal (Y1) for the master clock, a dual operational amplifier (Z1), a transformer (T1), a relay (K1), and other components for the Data Access Arrangement (DAA), as required by the FCC on a telephone line interface.

It should also be noted that the serial interface in the chip set is CCITT V.24, which is similar in many respects to the popular RS-232-C. Functionally, the two interfaces are equivalent for most applications, but the V.24 does not

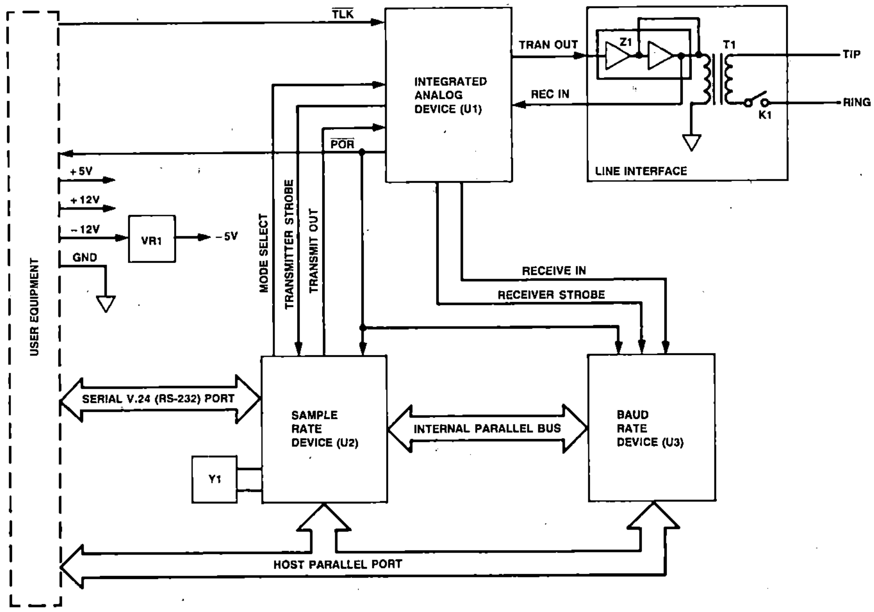

Figure 10.11 **Block Diagram of a Complete Modem**

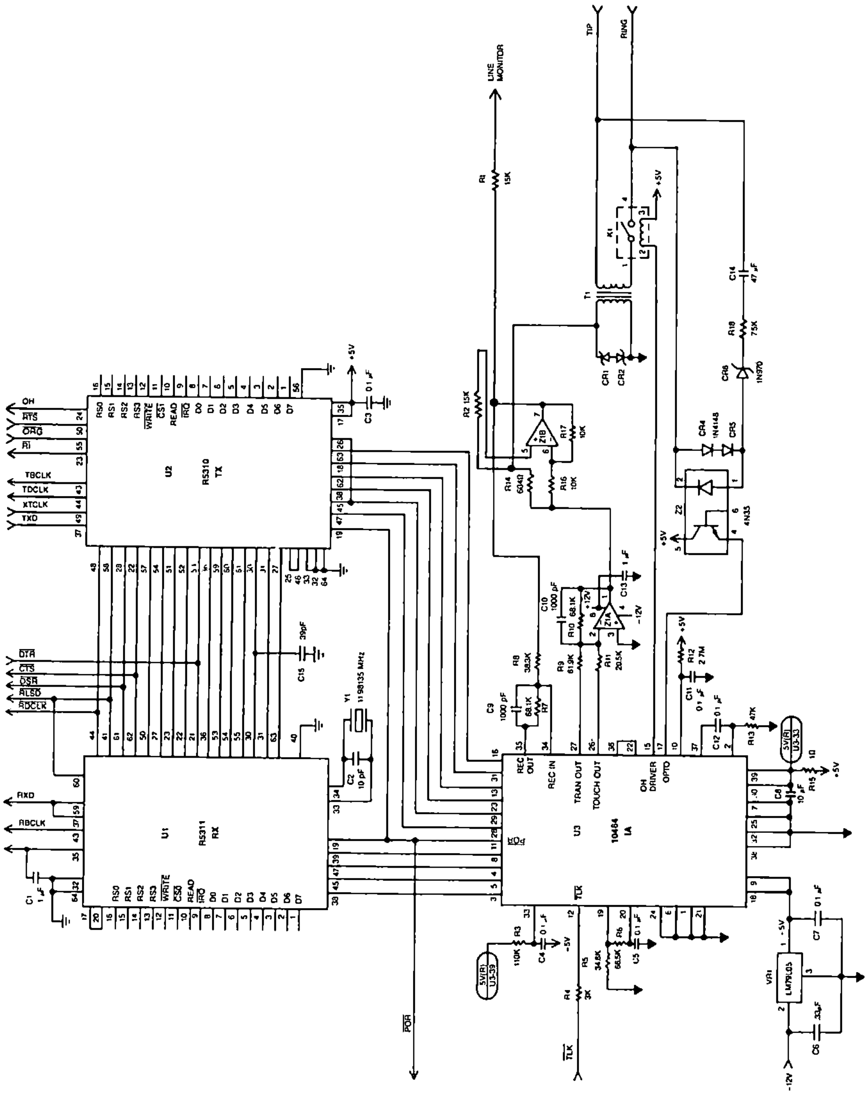

Figure 10.12 **Schematic Diagram of a Complete Modem**

specify the electrical interface and voltage levels. The R2424DS implementation of V.24 uses TTL voltage levels (0 V, +5 V) while RS-232-C uses bipolar levels, typically +12 V and −12 V. There are many commercial interface driver chips which translate voltage levels between the TTL and the RS-232-C interfaces and they would have to be included in a complete modem circuit.

Although data passing to and from the host computer is transferred via the serial V.24 interface, the modem also provides a parallel interface to the computer, which would be required in an internally mounted modem. The parallel interface gives the computer access to the scratch memory on the modem's signal processor, and gives it capability to set the modem configuration and to control assorted functions independent of the serial data path. The parallel interface would also allow the modem to interpret the AT commands, which are not interpreted by the R2424DS set. The commands and their interpretation could be stored either in the host computer or in a separate ROM chip.

Part Three Modems for the Commercial Market

There are many types of modems which are only available for the commercial market. They fulfill specific needs of corporations and universities by providing communication between micro, mini, and mainframe computers. Many of these modems require special leased or broadband transmission facilities, rather than the Public Switched Telephone Network.

Chapter 11 discusses the basic features and commercial implementations of low, medium and high speed modems, which operate over voice-band facilities. Chapter 12 describes the Limited Distance modems, which are frequently used for data exchange between near by locations. Chapter 13 covers specialized and less common modem applications, e.g., wide-band modems, multiplexers, modems with acoustic couplers and security modems.

11. Commercial Voice-Band Modems

As with the modem market for the personal computer, the commercial modem market is full of even more plentiful choices and options, albeit at a higher cost. Compared to only three transmission speeds available for modems used in personal computers — 300, 1200, and 2400 bps — in the commercial market there are transmission speeds available between 300 bps and many megabits per second. Even when one limits the field to voice-band modems, which will be discussed in this chapter, the range of transmission speeds is still between 300 bps and nearly 15 kbps. While all modems for personal computers communicate over the switched Public Telephone Network, some commercial modems require specially conditioned voice-band leased or private transmission facilities.

Commercial modems cover a whole gamut of applications. They range from the typical modem use, which is the exchange of data between terminals and computers, to such applications as facsimile, reading of utility meters, control of traffic lights, connection of point-of-sale terminals, money dispensers or vending machines. Many of these applications, e.g., facsimile, operate in half-duplex mode, use the whole bandwidth of a transmission channel, and can thus take advantage of higher transmission speeds. Development of inexpensive modem chip sets led to unobtrusive built-in designs, where the user is hardly aware of the presence of the modem, as it becomes the integral part of equipment. Unlike the personal computer modem market, which until recently was completely dominated by a single manufacturer, the Hayes Corporation, the commercial modem market supports approximately a dozen manufacturers, the major ones being AT&T, UDS, Codex, Rixon, Gandolf, Ven-tel, and US Robotics.

FEATURES AND PROTOCOLS

In the rest of this chapter we will cover the various choices and options determined by applicable standards available in the commercial voice-band modem market. The final selection will depend on many factors, the most important one being the compatibility with the existing equipment. Frequently the only solution for expanding an existing data network is to purchase equipment from the same manufacturer who supplied the previously installed devices.

Most commercial modems, except for a few, which use proprietary circuitry, follow one of the established standards. These standards are either the former Bell System de facto standards, or the recommendations of the world standards organization, the Comité Consultatif International de Télégraphie et Téléphonie, CCITT for short. The former Bell System de facto standards apply to many modem types manufactured and used in the United States, which were developed before the breakup of the Bell System. In addition, all modems follow interface standards of either the U.S. Electronics Industries Association (EIA) or the CCITT. These standards apply to electrical interfaces between computers, terminals, printers, modems, and other assorted devices, which are being attached to either of those. The prime example of an interface developed by the EIA is the popular serial RS-232-C standard. The corresponding CCITT equivalent is the V.24 recommendation. The CCITT standards apply to most newer modem designs in the United States and in the rest of the world, as well as to practically all modems used in Europe.

Adherence to standards is a necessary but not a sufficient requirement that a modem of one manufacturer can communicate with a modem made by another manufacturer. Adherence to a standard means only that a standard is not violated and that the manufacturer follows a certain subset of requirements expressed in the standard. To differentiate between modems following the same standard, manufacturers enhance their products to make them unique and still be able to communicate with other modems following the same standard. Many modems can follow several standards, which can be manually or automatically selected, when the data connection is established.

The few proprietary commercial modems, which do not follow established standards, can be found mostly in high-speed applications, and in the limited distance and in the specialized applications modem market, where they are used on private or leased transmission facilities. These last two categories will be discussed in the next two chapters. In addition, proprietary modems fill a certain small niche of high-speed, high-performance (and high-price) devices using techniques like multiplexing, data compression, specialized error correction, etc.When a proprietary modulation scheme not following a standard is used, all modems in a network have to come from the same manufacturer. As these devices are mostly used on point-to-point or multipoint connections over leased transmission facilities, compatibility with other modems is only of limited importance.

I will start this chapter with a short story of how a new modem standard is "born," followed by a discussion of advantages and disadvantages of low-, medium-, and high-speed voice-band modems. Next will come an outline of the most common commercial modem standards and modem options, and a discussion of commercial communications software. I will then continue with commercial implementations of modem hardware by major manufacturers and conclude it with a description of commercial voice-band modems using proprietary designs.

BIRTH OF A STANDARD

Development of a new standard or recommendation is a slow, painful, and circuitous procedure. The following is a description of the development of the V.22 bis 2400 bps standard extracted from a report by one of the CCITT delegates, Dale Walsh of U.S. Robotics, Incorporated.

"The 1200 bps V.22 recommendation was completed during the April 1980 meeting in Geneva. The session was particularly tough for U.S. manufacturers because of several hot issues — would the standard be compatible with Bell 212A or with Vadic 3400 modems? The 212A scheme won, but Vadic extracted an 'Alternative C' recommendation, which shares some of the features of Vadic 3400 but is neither compatible with Vadic 3400 nor with Bell 212A. An 'Alternative B', compatible with Bell 212A was then also adopted.

At the same time groundwork began on 2400 bps full-duplex two-wire modem and was given a tentative name FDX 2400. The echo cancellation scheme was proposed to lower the cost of the modem. Two groups then started working on specifications — one on the low priced echo cancellation scheme and the other one on a more expensive frequency division solution. The two groups with totally different approaches became firmly entrenched. The frequency division group also split into two subgroups suggesting different modulation/coding schemes, one using a modulation rate of 600 Baud, the other 800 Baud. During 1981 the US Modem Working Party met periodically and agreed on the 600 Baud approach, which became the V.22 bis Recommendation, the current world-wide standard. To satisfy the first group, working on the echo cancellation scheme, that approach became the V.22 ter Recommendation. Both recommendations were formally adopted at the Plenary Assembly meeting of CCITT in October 1984."

TRANSMISSION SPEED VERSUS COST OF OPERATION

The cost of a phone call does not depend on how much information is being transmitted. Therefore there is a strong incentive to speed up the information flow, in particular for file transfers. Current software, even in the personal computer field, is always memory hungry and files of 2 Mbytes or more are common. Table 11.1 shows how long it takes to transmit a 2-Mbyte file and how much the file transfer will cost at 40 cents/minute, at typical daytime telephone rates between New York and Los Angeles, at various transmission speeds. To help in comparisons, it should be remembered that a 2-Mbyte file corresponds to approximately 800 pages of text, or to six 5.25 in. diskettes.

Table 11.1 **Time Required and Cost of Transferring a 2 Mbyte File**

Trans. Speed (bps)	**Transmission Time** (minutes)	**Cost** $
300	111	$44.45
1200	28	11.10
2400	14	5.55
4800	7	2.75
9600	3.5	1.40

Note: Table 11.1 assumes no time loss due to error correction, block retransmission, etc. The actual data throughput, in particular at higher transmission speeds, can be considerably less due to those factors.

Until 1975 the most common "high" speed on the switched telephone network was 300 bps, frequently implemented with acoustically coupled modems. Between 1975 and 1985 the Bell 212A 1200-bps modem and its derivatives were most popular on the switched network, with higher speeds available on leased, conditioned point-to-point lines. Since 1985 the 2400-bps modem based on the CCITT V.22 bis recommendation has become very popular as its price dropped to the $200—$300 range.

With the current state of technology, transmission speeds of up to 14400 bps on the switched network are possible, but the cost of such modems is still high, mostly above $2000, and they involve certain compromises. Several seconds may be required to synchronize the transmitting and receiving terminals, and many modems can only operate in half-duplex mode at higher speed. Still, as a 9600-bps full-duplex standard for the Public Telephone Network already exists (CCITT V.32), and many manufacturers implement it, V.32 will probably become a common standard in the near future. In general, a high-speed modem will automatically adjust its speed downward depending on the line condition, as determined during the handshake period. The lower fallback speeds are compatible with the 300/1200/2400 bps standards.

Half-duplex operation at high speed is acceptable for file transfer, where a minimum of interactive communication is required. However, if a block error correction scheme is used, occasional two-way communication is required, which slows down the data transfer.

The upper limit for modems operating over leased, conditioned voice lines is currently 19200 bps. Several manufacturers also make 14400-bps and 16800-bps modems. These modems use either the "trellis" coding or other advanced methods of error detection and correction. The trellis coding scheme was discussed in Chapter 4 and is described in detail in the CCITT recommendations V.29 and V.32. It consists of sending four consecutive data bits, followed by a derived fifth bit in each data signal. Other proprietary designs use multiple carrier frequencies, which are spread across the voice-band. At higher transmission speeds error detection and correction is necessary. Error detection consists of checking one or more parity bits transmitted with each block of data against the parity computed from the data stream at the destination. When errors are detected a request goes out to the transmitting modem to retransmit a block of data. If there is enough redundancy in the received information then some error correcting schemes will make an educated guess what the data should be. Error correcting schemes work well as long as the line disturbances, such as bursts of noise, are infrequent. Otherwise, constant retransmission of blocks of data may slow the transmission rate to be below that achieved by a slower modem. Thus a 9600-bps modem operating over a noisy line with frequent block retransmission may have a slower effective transmission rate than a 2400-bps modem.

Table 11.2 shows advantages and disadvantages of various types of voiceband modems according to their speeds.

Table 11.2 **Advantages and Disadvantages of Modems at Various Speeds**

1. Low-Speed Modems (up to 1200 bps)

Advantages:

- Low cost
- Operates over the Public Telephone Network with its inherent flexibility and reliability.
- Auto-Answer capability.
- Wide user community.

Disadvantages:

- Inherent high transmission cost.
- Slowness, long time to transmit a file.

2. Medium-Speed Modems (1200 bps up to 4800 bps)

Advantages:

- Faster data transmission, reduced cost.
- Dedicated lines (if used) give fewer errors.

Disadvantages:

- Higher cost for hardware.
- If used on Public Telephone Network, may require special error correction schemes.
- Smaller user community.

3. High-Speed Modems (4800 bps and higher)

Advantages:

- High transmission speed frees computers and terminals.
- Multiplexing capabilities (when available) further reduce costs.
- High data integrity on leased, conditioned facilities.

Disadvantages:

- High cost when used infrequently.
- In general requires use of expensive leased transmission facilities, though

certain models can also be used in full-duplex mode at up to 9600 bps on the Public Telephone Network.
Most modems in this category use proprietary designs.

BELL AND CCITT MODEM STANDARDS

Table 11.3 and the following paragraphs summarize the most common Bell and CCITT modem standards implemented by many modem manufacturers. The latest version of the CCITT Book of Recommendations, which was issued in 1985 and is based on the VIII Plenary Assembly meeting of the International Telegraph and Telephone Consultative Committee in Malaga, Spain in October 1984, lists over 30 modem and interface standards, all starting with the letter V, e.g., V.22, V.35, etc. Not all of these standards have actually been implemented. Though generally referred to as standards, the document lists them as V. Recommendations.

Table 11.3 **Voice-Band Modem Standards**

Standard	Speed in bps	Remarks
Bell 103/108/113	300	U.S. Standard
Bell 202	1200	U.S. Standard
Bell 212A	1200	U.S. Standard, very common
Bell 201	2400	U.S. Standard
Bell 208	4800	U.S. Standard
Bell 209	9600	U.S. Standard
CCITT V.21	300	European low speed
CCITT V.22	1200	European medium speed
CCITT V.22 bis	2400	Current world standard
CCITT V.23	1200	Old European standard
CCITT V.26	2400	Old European standard
CCITT V.27	2400/4800	Fallback mode of V.29
CCITT V.29	9600	Four-wire standard for leased and private lines
CCITT V.32	9600	Highest speed standard for Public Telephone Network
CCITT V.33	14400	Leased or private lines only

Table 11.4 shows the approximate equivalents between Bell and CCITT modem standards. It should be remembered that although Bell and CCITT modems may use the same modulation scheme and bit rates, they may differ in other parameters, such as timing of handshake sequence, fallback transmission speeds, etc.

Table 11.4 **Equivalent Bell and CCITT Voice-Band Modems**

Speed	Bell Standard	CCITT	Mode
300	103	V.21	Full-duplex
300/1200	212A	V.22	Full-duplex
1200	202	V.23	Half-duplex
2400	201	V.26	Half-duplex
2400	none	V.22 bis	Full-duplex
4800	208	V.27	Half-duplex
9600	209	V.29	Half-duplex

As can be seen from the above tables, Bell and CCITT standards, which are implemented in the commercial modem market, also include personal modem standards, namely, Bell 103, Bell 212, and CCITT V.22 bis. Commercial modems using these standards should be able to communicate with personal modems, if the software discrepancies, if any, are resolved and the proper subset of requirements is selected in both cases. A commercial modem may not be able, for example, to interpret the Hayes AT command set, or its fallback transmission speed may be different from a corresponding personal modem. Also, commercial modems often provide a wider array of options and higher reliability standards than their personal counterparts. These features are of course reflected in a wide price differential between personal and commercial modems.

The following is a short description of the Bell and CCITT standards, which were not described in Chapters 4 and 7. The remainder of this chapter describes examples of commercial implementations of these standards.

Bell 103/108/113

The 300-bps asynchronous, full-duplex modem, using Frequency Shift Keying (FSK) modulation, can be found in many older installations. Though still in wide use in the United States, it is obsolete by current standards. The FSK modulation scheme used by this modem is described in Chapter 4. The assorted versions of this modem, such as 103J, 108F, 113B, differ by providing specific implementation for the switched Public Telephone Network, TELEX, TWX, or for two- or four-wire leased facilities. Most modems are equipped with voice/data switches, automatic answer capability, and can work with the standard 500/2500 type telephone sets. The 103-type modem is basically transparent to the computer/terminal and it can operate at any asynchronous speed not exceeding 300 bps.

Bell 202

The success of the Bell 103/108/113 type 300 bps full-duplex modems in the 1960s led to development of a faster, asynchronous 1200-bps modem using similar technology, the Frequency Shift Keying (FSK) modulation, but capable of only simplex (one-way) high-speed operation on two-wire circuits. However, on four-wire leased circuits the same modem can operate in full-duplex mode. When operating on two-wire circuits, the Bell 202 type modem can send data at 1200 bps in one direction of transmission in half-duplex mode on the so-called primary channel and, as an option, it can send data in the opposite direction of transmission on the so-called reverse channel at a slow speed of only 5 bps. Though the primary channel uses the simple and inexpensive circuitry required for the FSK modulation method, as in the Bell 103/108/113 type modems, the carrier frequencies used in the 300-bps and in the 1200-bps modem types are different. In the 202 type modems the frequency of 1200 Hz is assigned to binary "1", and 2200 Hz is assigned to binary "0". Because of the simple modulation scheme the modem encodes only 1 bit of information for each signal element. Its modulation rate in Baud is thus equal to its transmission speed in bps.

The optional reverse channel uses an even simpler modulation method, the On/Off Keying (OOK), which consists of sending a tone of 387 Hz to indicate a binary "1" and being silent to indicate a binary "0". The reverse channel, when provided, can be used to confirm transmission of a data block on a

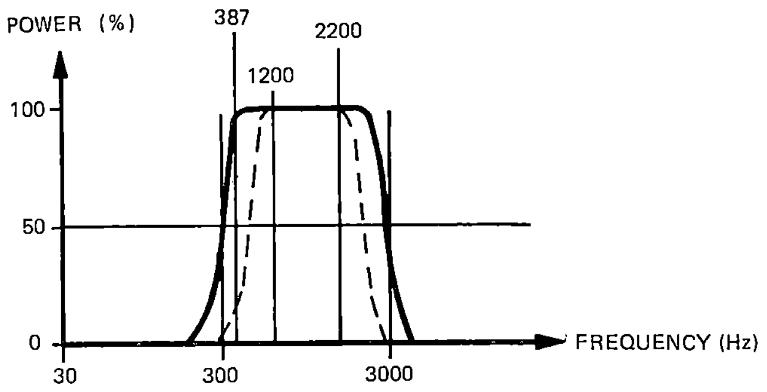

Figure 11.1 **Frequency Assignments for Bell 202 Modem**

primary channel, or it can request retransmission of a block of data in case of a detected error. The reverse channel would also be used to request change of direction of transmission for the primary and secondary channels. The terminal or computer has to recognize a request for a change of direction of transmission. The command would normally be sent from the computer to the modem via the RTS lead of the serial interface and would be confirmed by the CTS lead. Figure 11.1 shows the frequency assignments for the primary and secondary channels of the Bell 202 type modems.

Although the Bell 202 type modem is obsolete by today's standards, it is still being manufactured and it can be found in many data centers, in particular in four-wire leased line applications. Its cost is comparatively low and it was either purchased many years ago, or its performance is still adequate for the particular application.

Bell 212A

The Bell 212A type modems follow one of the most popular standards in the United States for both commercial and personal computer modems. The modem operates in full-duplex mode over Public Telephone Network facilities. Though the Bell modem standards are not used in Europe, a Bell 212A or a compatible modem should be able to communicate with a European V.22 type modem operating at 1200 bps.

The 212A type modems feature 300/1200 bps transmission speed and are the current standard of the personal computer industry. When operating at 300 bps the 212A modems are equivalent to Bell 103/108/113 standard. At 1200 bps they use Differential Phase Shift Keying (DPSK) modulation, which provides excellent results on the switched Public Telephone Network. Two bits are encoded in each signal element resulting in a modulation rate of 600 Baud in full-duplex mode. Separate carriers are used for both directions of transmission, 1200 Hz for the originating and 2400 Hz for the answering modem.

At 1200 bps the 212A type modem can operate in either synchronous or in asynchronous mode. At 300 bps, and at slower transmission speeds the modem operates only in asynchronous mode. In asynchronous mode of operation the modem can use any character format with an arbitrary number of data, start and stop bits per character. In synchronous mode, usually between 8 and 11 bits per character, the number of bits is selected with a software, jumper, or strapping option.

The 212A type modems used in the personal computing field are all equipped with pulse and touch-tone dialers, which can be operated by sending appropriate ASCII commands from the computer or terminal. An automatic dialer saves the computer operator the effort of manually dialing and redialing and saves the cost of a telephone set.

Modems without dialers are usually provided with voice/data switches and RJ11C jacks for a telephone set connection. The 212A type modems operate in the Originate mode, until a ring signal is detected. As the ring signal is usually not provided on leased two-wire lines, an option switch would be required for such an operation to force the receiving modem into Answer mode. Only some 212A type modems are therefore capable to operate on two-wire leased lines. For further description of the 212A modem see also Chapters 4 and 7.

Bell 201

The 2400-bps synchronous modem is widely used on four-wire leased lines and it finds occasional application on the Public Telephone Network. It operates in two-wire half-duplex, or in four-wire full-duplex mode. Although frequently equipped with auto-dialing features, it does not follow the Hayes AT standard popular in the personal computer field. The modem uses DPSK modulation, similar to the 212A modem, and it also assigns 2 bits to each relative phase change. Its modulation rate is 1200 Baud. The 201 type modem can operate on a 3002 unconditioned leased line without adaptive equalizers. Therefore, it can respond to a "polling" carrier within only 15 ms, which makes it an ideal candidate for multipoint private networks. The phase assignments of the Bell 201 type modems are shown in Table 11.5. They differ from phase assignments of the 212A modem. The 201 type modem uses a single carrier frequency of 1800 Hz.

Table 11.5 **Bell 201 Relative Phase Assignments**

Dibit	Relative Phase Change (deg)
00	45
10	135
11	225
01	315

Bell 208

The 4800 bps synchronous modem can be used on the Public Telephone Network and on private two-wire and four-wire private line circuits. Modulation method is DPSK with 3 bits assigned to each signal level. The modulation rate of the modem is 1600 Baud. The carrier frequency is 1800 Hz. The modem operates in half-duplex mode on the Public Telephone Network or on a two-wire private line; it operates in full-duplex mode on a four-wire private line. The relative phase assignments of the Bell 208 type modems are shown in Table 11.6. They differ from those of the CCITT V.27 modems. Although the two modem types are similar, they cannot communicate with each other.

Table 11.6 **Bell 208 Relative Phase Assignments**

Tribit	Relative Phase Change (deg)
001	22.5
000	67.5
010	112.5
011	157.5
111	202.5
110	247.5
100	292.5
101	337.5

The 208 demodulator multiplies the carrier frequency by 8 and derives the phase information by comparing the interval between zero crossings of the demodulated signal with the stored phase change values from the above table. A feedback signal is then created related to the difference between the actually measured values and the values from the above table. This difference signal affects the decision points, where a decision is made whether the signal is, e.g., a 00 or a 01. The circuit performs a function similar to an adaptive equalizer. The basic handshake time of the 208 type modem is 50 ms but can be changed for longer circuits to 150 ms by internal strappings.

Bell 209

This 9600-bps standard has been largely supplanted by the CCITT V.29 standard. It provides for operation on leased and private four-wire circuits.

CCITT V.21

The 300-bps full-duplex modem is standardized for use on the Public Telephone Network. The modem uses the same modulation scheme (FSK) and carrier frequencies as the Bell 103/113 modem. It is being replaced by faster modems in most applications.

CCITT V.22

This 1200-bps modem standard covers a whole family of full-duplex devices standardized for use on the Public Telephone Network and on two-wire private line circuits. The standard is very similar to the Bell System 212A and, in general a V.22 and a Bell 212A modems can exchange data. However, the Bell 212A modem cannot be officially sold in Europe. The principal characteristics of the V.22 modems are channel separation by frequency division, with carrier frequencies at 1200 Hz and 2400 Hz, inclusion of a scrambler, DPSK modulation at 600 Baud (2 bits/transmitted signal). The V.22 (but not the 212A) modem is also capable of transmitting a "guard" tone of 1800 Hz used for echo suppression on many European telephone networks. The two major versions of this modem are V.22A for synchronous operation and V.22B for synchronous or for asynchronous operation. The CCITT Recommendation also mentions a V.22C modem similar to V.22B, which has not yet been implemented.

CCITT V.22 bis

The standard is similar to V.22, in that it is designed for use in full-duplex mode on the Public Telephone Network and on two-wire private line circuits. The principal characteristics of the V.22 bis modem are channel separation by frequency division, with carrier frequencies at 1200 Hz and 2400 Hz, inclusion of a scrambler, QAM modulation at 600 Baud (4 bits/transmitted signal), inclusion of self-test facilities, inclusion of an adaptive and a compromise equalizer, and 1200/2400 bps operation in synchronous or asynchronous mode. The V.22 bis standard and its various subsets are becoming the leading modem standard in the personal computer field.

CCITT V.23

The 1200-bps medium speed modem has similar characteristics to the Bell 202 modem. It is used on the Public Telephone Network in half-duplex mode. The modem uses FSK modulation at 1200 bps for its main channel and the ON/OFF Keying (OOK) modulation for the slow speed reverse channel. The modem has two modes of operation. Mode 1 uses modulation rates of up to 600 Baud with mark/space carrier frequencies of 1300 Hz and 1700 Hz. In Mode 2, which corresponds to higher modulation rates, of up to 1200 Baud, the corresponding carrier frequencies are 1300 Hz and 2100 Hz. The ability to operate at lower frequencies in Mode 1 is helpful on connections equipped with loading coils, which would otherwise interfere with higher carrier frequencies.

CCITT V.26

The 2400-bps modem is designed to operate in full-duplex mode over four-wire leased telephone lines. The modem is similar to the Bell 201 modem. It uses differential four-phase modulation (DPSK) and encodes 2 bits for each phase change. The modulation rate is 1200 Baud. There are two Alternatives, A and B, which assign different coding schemes to a specific dibit-to-phase translation. Before setting up a connection using V.26 modems at both ends, it should be ascertained that all modems on the data network use the same Alternative.

CCITT V.27 bis and V.27 ter

The V.27 standard is a European equivalent of Bell 208. It is frequently implemented as a fallback mode of 9600-bps V.29 standard, though some modems, e.g., the Penril Datalink 4800, use V.27 4800-bps standards exclusively. The V.27-bis standard is optimized for leased lines, while V.27 ter can be used on the Public Telephone Network. The carrier frequency is 1800 Hz and 3 bits are assigned to each signal element. Thus the modulation rate is 1600 Baud. The standard also provides for a fallback mode of 2400 bps.

CCITT V.29

This 9600-bps modem is one of the most popular standards for new designs on four-wire leased and private line circuits. The main characteristics of the V.29 modems are fallback rates of 7200 bps and 4800 bps, capability to operate in full-duplex or in half-duplex mode depending on transmission rate, combined amplitude and phase modulation, synchronous operation, provision of an automatic adaptive equalizer, and optional inclusion of a multiplexer to combine 2400-bps, 4800-bps, and 7200-bps data streams. The carrier frequency is 1700 Hz. Each signal element consists of 4 bits; thus the modem operates at 9600/4 = 2400 Baud. Some manufacturers have adopted the standard to operate over Public Telephone Network by using various proprietary measures including error correction schemes. Modems using this standard may also operate over two two-wire lines on the Public Telephone Network. In general, the V.29 modems are less expensive than the V.32 modems described in the following paragraph.

CCITT V.32

The 9600-bps standard provides for synchronous operation at 4800 bps and at 9600 bps. It is the highest transmission speed standard designed for operation over two-wire switched Public Telephone Network. A V.32 type modem can operate in half-duplex or in full-duplex mode with a single carrier frequency located in the middle of the voice-band. The full-duplex operation is similar to voice conversation on a two-wire circuit, where a hybrid coil separates the two directions of transmission, both using the same frequency spectrum. An important adjunct circuit for full-duplex operation of a V.32 type modem is an echo canceller, which partially cancels both the high-amplitude near-end echo, and the delayed low-amplitude far-end echo, which would otherwise be returned to the transmitting modem and be treated as a received data stream.

The method of echo cancellation is not described in the V.32 standard and is left to the individual manufacturer. The methods used are proprietary and make modems from different manufacturers exhibit different bit error rates on the same call. The carrier frequency is 1800 Hz for both directions of transmission and each signal element consists of 4 bits. The modulation rate is 2400 Baud. At 9600 bps the V.32 standard mentions two alternative modulation methods, one using 16 carrier states and one using trellis coding and modulation with 32 carrier states. As both modes are usually implemented in commercial modems, care should be taken that the receiving and the transmitting modem follow the same modulation scheme. In the last mode of operation, the V.32 modem uses trellis modulation, an error correcting scheme, which generates a fifth parity bit from each 4 data bits using a special algorithm. The trellis modulation or coding scheme gives the extra performance edge to the V.32 standard, so that modems equipped with it can satisfactorily operate at 9600 bps over the Public Telephone Network. Echo cancellation and trellis circuits make the V.32 type modem more expensive than an equivalent V.29 modem, with prices in the order of $2500.

CCITT V.33

The V.33 recommendation does not appear in the latest 1984 version of the CCITT standards, but it has met with a preliminary approval of the international committee. Several manufacturers make modems following this recommendation. The modem can operate at multiple transmission rates, namely at 14.4 kbps, 12.0 kbps, and 9.6 kbps, which are user selectable. At 9.6 kbps the modem complies with the V.29 standard. The modem uses QAM modulation method with 6 bits assigned to each signal sample and a seventh bit used for trellis encoding. Thus at its highest speed the modem signaling rate is 2400 Baud. Though the V.33 standard is only specified for private four-wire transmission facilities, some half-duplex versions of V.33 modems exist, which can operate over the two-wire Public Telephone Network.

SETTING OF MODEM OPTIONS

Setting up a commercial modem, in particular a high-speed modem, requires selection of many options far exceeding the choices required for personal modems. The number of options increases when the modem is used on a leased point-to-point or multipoint private network. It is particularly important that all modems involved in a data connection use the same options. Here are some of the selectable options, which may be chosen with jumper or switch settings, or with software commands. These options have to be chosen in addition to the standard options such as transmission speed, parity, synchronous or asynchronous operation. For details of specific options applicable to your modem consult the appropriate manual.

Wire/Carrier Option

There are usually three configurations for which the modem can be set. The first choice, the four-wire constant carrier option, is chosen when the modem is a master station on a four-wire multipoint network, or when it is used on a point-to-point four-wire connection. The second choice, the switched four-wire option, is used when the modem is a remote station or is a slave station on a multipoint connection. The third choice, the two-wire switched option, is selected when the modem is used on a two-wire dialed or on a leased connection.

Fallback Option

This option gives a choice of various standards at which the modem will communicate at lower speeds if it cannot operate satisfactorily at its nominal high speed. A typical choice for a 9600-bps modem would be 4800-bps transmission speed as fallback. The choice would be between the 4800-bps Bell 208 or CCITT V.27 bis/ter standards. It is evidently important that all modems on the network use the same fallback options.

Transmit Level

The transmission level should be set for regular dial-up lines on the Public Telephone Network to –10 dBm +/–1 dB. A higher transmission level is in general not allowed, since it could interfere with other users. On leased or on private lines the transmission level can typically be set between –15 dBm and –1 dBm. The level should be set to the lowest value at which error-free transmission can be achieved.

Carrier Detect Level

The carrier detect level is normally set between –20 dBm and –45 dBm. Choosing a lower carrier detect threshold will make the modem more sensitive, but will cause occasional false readings due to noise. Again, the detect level should be chosen as low as possible while assuring error-free transmission.

Anti Stream Timer

This option prevents a modem on a multipoint private network from shutting down the whole network by putting the Request to Send (RTS) signal on permanently. This is a similar situation to a "stuck" microphone on a Fire Alarm or other Public Safety radio network. The timer will turn the RTS signal off, when its duration exceeds the preset time.

Echo Suppressor Disabler

A modem can usually generate tones, which disable echo suppressors on a dialed connection exceeding 2400 km (1500 miles) in length. This option should be selected if full-duplex mode of operation over long dialed-up connections is used. A working echo suppressor would otherwise block transmission in one direction, thus making a full-duplex modem effectively a half-duplex modem.

Signal Quality Option

Many high-speed modems produce a signal on pin 21 of the serial interface jack indicating when a certain error rate is exceeded. The signal quality option sets the threshold for this indication. The typical choices are one error in 1000 or one error in 100,000.

Dial Backup Option

Some recently introduced modems, e.g., IBM 5866 and AJ 2441-1, sense line quality and, if the connection is not satisfactory, will redial. The user can also select an alternate number to call, if the primary connection is interrupted. The modem can also dial, if a leased line breaks down. The phone numbers to dial and timeout periods have to be preset before a connection is established.

Modem Address

When a modem is used in a private line multipoint application, each modem needs a specific address. The master unit usually has a letter M in its address; other units use numerical codes.

SOFTWARE FOR COMMERCIAL MODEMS

The large variety of commercial modem types and adherence to many different Bell, CCITT or proprietary standards makes it difficult to obtain support from the major communications software houses. Many of the software programs mentioned in Chapter 9 will work with commercial modems although some modifications may be required to take advantage of additional features. Because of the need to communicate with main-frame computers, programs like Kermit or Blast are frequently used in the commercial environment. In general, a modem manufacturer will also provide a software package to support a specific modem. An example of such a hardware/software combination is the SyncUp SNA 3770 modem card, manufactured by the Universal Data Systems Corporation, which is supplied with its own software package. The program supports all modem features, except for asynchronous low-speed operation. When operated in asynchronous mode, the modem can use any of the standard personal communications programs described in Chapter 9.

The modem card plugs into any IBM PC, XT, AT or compatible computer and works in Bell 201, 212, or 208 mode. Depending on the mode which was selected, the modem will operate over two-wire Public Telephone Network or over two- or four-wire leased circuits. The modem card emulates, as far as the main-frame computer is concerned, a 3770, a 3777-3, or a 3776 terminal. The modem will operate in accordance with the SDLC synchronous data link control protocol at 2400, 480, 7200, or 9600 bps. It can also operate in asynchronous mode at 300 bps. The modem provides automatic dialing and automatic answer capability. This feature allows the personal computer equipped with this modem to operate as an attended or as an unattended Remote Job Entry (RJE) terminal to a main-frame computer.

EXAMPLES OF VOICE-BAND COMMERCIAL MODEMS

The standards and recommendations for voice-band modems described in the previous paragraphs have been implemented by many manufacturers. A number of commercial implementations of Bell and CCITT standards and a few special application modems using proprietary standards will be described here. Some of these modems can be used on the Public Telephone

Network and some require voice-band leased or private transmission facilities.

In the 1970s, before the breakup of the Bell System, Bell Laboratories developed a family of low-, medium-, and high-speed modems. These modems were manufactured by a Bell System subsidiary, the Western Electric Company. Today, after the breakup of the Bell System, many independent companies have taken over the manufacturing of modems based on the former Bell System standards in addition to manufacturing modems based on the newer standards developed by the CCITT. The Bell standards are used in the U.S. replacement market; both Bell and CCITT modems are also used for new installations.

Table 11.7 shows a selection chart of commercial modems, developed by Universal Data Systems, a subsidiary of Motorola Corporation, a major U.S. manufacturer of data communications equipment. Other modem manufacturers, e.g., Codex and Gandolf, have similar product lines. These modems are based on the former Bell System designs and on the CCITT recommendations. Table 11.7 is followed with a more detailed description of selected modems.

LOW SPEED MODEMS

The low speed modems are based on the Bell 103/108/113 type designs featuring FSK modulation, full-duplex operation over the Public Telephone Network, and 0—300 bps asynchronous transmission speed. All modems provide the RS-232-C serial interface. The following is a list of features differentiating several closely related products:

UDS 103JLP Modem

The 300-bps asynchronous modem derives its power from the telephone line. It is equipped with a manual Talk/Data switch. The modem has a manual originate mode and a manual/automatic answer mode.

Table 11.7 **UDS Modem Selection Chart**

Model	0-300 bps	1200 bps	0-1800 bps	2400 bps	4800 bps	7200 bps	9600 bps	12000 bps	14400 bps	Asynchronous	Synchronous	Half Duplex - 2 Wire	Full Duplex - 2 Wire	Full Duplex - 4 Wire	PSTN	Private Line - 2 Wire	Private Line - 4 Wire	Auto Answer	Auto Dial	Call Progress Detection	Comm. Software Included	Error Control	Telephone Line Powered	3270 BSC host dial-up support	Antistreaming	Multiplexer Included	Standalone	IBM PC Compatible	Rack Mountable	Universal Data Shelf™ Compatible	Test Features Included
1406T							I	I	I	I	I			I			I									I	I				I
1408S								I	I		I			I			I					I				I	I				I
14.4 Trellis A/B							I	I	I		I	I		I	I	I	I	I									I		I		I
V.33							I	I	I		I			I			I										I		I	I	I
9600FP					I	I	I				I			I			I								I		I		I	I	I
9600 Trellis A/B					I		I				I	I		I	I	I	I	I									I		I		I
9600A/B					I	I	I				I	I		I	I	I	I	I									I		I		I
9600					I	I	I				I			I			I										I		I		I
Sync-Up 208A/B					I						I	I		I	I	I	I	I	I	I	I							I	I		I
208B/LS					I						I	I			I	I		I						I			I		I	I	I
208B/D					I						I	I			I			I	I	I							I		I	I	I
208AB/AS					I					I	I	I		I	I	I	I	I									I		I	I	I
208A/B					I						I	I		I	I	I	I	I							I		I		I	I	I
EC224A/D	I	I		I						I			I		I			I	I	I		I					I		I	I	I
224A/D	I	I		I						I	I		I		I	I		I	I	I							I		I	I	I
224A	I	I		I						I	I		I		I	I		I									I		I	I	I
FasTalk 2400	I	I		I						I	I		I		I	I		I	I	I	I						I	I			I
Sync-Up201C/212A	I	I		I						I	I	I			I			I	I	I	I							I			I
Sync-Up 201C				I							I	I			I			I	I	I	I							I			I
201C/LS				I							I	I			I			I						I			I		I	I	I
201C/D				I							I	I			I			I	I	I							I		I	I	I
201B/C				I							I	I		I	I	I	I	I									I		I	I	I
201B				I						I	I	I		I		I	I										I		I	I	I
EC212A/D	I	I								I			I		I			I	I	I		I					I		I		I
212A/D	I	I								I	I		I		I	I		I	I	I							I		I	I	I
212A	I	I								I	I		I		I	I		I									I		I	I	I
FasTalk 1200	I	I								I			I		I			I	I	I	I						I	I			I
212A LP	I	I								I			I		I			I									I				
202T		I	I							I		I		I		I	I								I		I		I	I	I
202S/D		I								I	I	I			I			I	I	I							I		I	I	I
202S/T-R		I								I		I		I	I	I	I	I									I		I	I	I
202S/T		I								I		I		I	I	I	I	I									I		I	I	I
108	I									I			I	I		I	I										I		I	I	I
103J	I									I			I		I			I									I		I		I
103J LP	I									I			I		I			I					I				I				

UDS 103J Modem

The modem has the same basic features as UDS 103JLP but it requires an external power supply. The modem is equipped with analog and digital loopback test capability. It also has a manual Talk/Data/Test switch.

UDS 108 Modem

The modem is specifically designed for private line two- or four-wire operation. The modem requires a 600-Ohm or a high-impedance interface. It has self-test features with analog and digital loopback capability. It can also perform end-to-end self-tests. The modem has selectable CTS delay.

MEDIUM-SPEED MODEMS

The medium speed modems are based on the previously described Bell 201, 202, and 212A designs featuring FSK and DPSK modulation, full or half-duplex operation, and 1200- or 2400-bps transmission speed. All modems are equipped with an RS-232-C serial interface. The 212A Bell standard became the de facto standard of the personal computer industry, while other modems found their niche in various areas of the commercial market. Following is a list of these products manufactured by the UDS Corporation.

UDS 201B/C Modem

The modem features 2400-bps synchronous operation over four-wire private lines. It provides RS-232-C and CCITT V.24 interface. It has a full complement of test features. An 8-position switch is used for feature selection. The modem uses DPSK modulation. It operates in half-duplex mode over two-wire public Telephone or leased transmission facilities.

UDS 201C/D Modem

The 201C/D modem has all the features of the 201B/C. In addition, it can detect call progress tones, like busy, ringing, or dial. Automatic detection of IBM's EBCIDIC and ASCII characters is also provided. The modem can also auto-dial.

UDS 201C/LS Modem

The 201C/LS modem has all the features of UDS 201B/C. In addition it supports IBM's 3270 terminal communication protocols with main-frame computers.

202 Type Modems

Following are several examples of 202 type modems manufactured by the UDS Corporation.

UDS 202S/T Modem

The 202S/T modem has all the basic features of 202 type modems, namely, 1200-bps asynchronous half-duplex operation on a two-wire facility on the switched Public Telephone Network or full-duplex operation over four-wire private lines. Self- and remote-test capability Data/Talk switch to alternate between voice and data transmission are provided.

UDS 202S/D Modem

The modem is similar to the 202S/T, except for provision of an automatic dialer and a call progress tone detector. The modem is also compatible with certain parts of the CCITT V.23 protocol so that it can be used on a European connection.

UDS 202T Modem

This modem is specifically designed for private line operation. It has antistreaming capability to prevent network hang-up. It has a full complement of internal tests.

212A Type Modems

The following modems manufactured by UDS are based on Bell 212A de facto standard.

UDS 212A LP Modem

The modem has all the standard features of a Bell 212A type modem, the DPSK modulation and capability to operate in full-duplex mode at 1200 bps over two-wire switched Public Telephone Network. In addition it derives its power from the telephone line, so that no external power connection is required. Like many other modems it requires only a subset of the RS-232-C signals, namely, pins #2 (TD), #3 (RD), #5 (CTS), #6 (DSR), #8 (CD), #20 (DTR), #22 (RI), and #7 (GND).

UDS EC212A/D Modem

This is an auto-dial modem with special error control. Data is framed in groups of up to 128 bytes per frame. Each frame contains also parity bytes computed with the CRC polynomial from the frame data (see also description of error protocols in Chapter 9). A detected error causes retransmission of the defective block of data. The auto-dial feature of the modem allows storing of 5 numbers of up to 30 digits each. The numbers are stored in non-volatile memory and are not lost when power fails.

HIGH-SPEED MODEMS

These modems operate at transmission speeds between 4800 bps and 14400 bps. They are based on CCITT V.29 and V.32 recommendations and on the Bell 208A and 208B de facto standard. Depending on the specific implementation the modems can operate over the Public Telephone Network or over leased voice-band transmission facilities.

UDS 208A/B Modem

The 4800-bps synchronous modem combines Bell 208A and 208B standards. It is equipped with an adaptive equalizer on the receive side and a compromise equalizer with selectable characteristics on the transmit side. The modem includes an antistreaming feature, which prevents one modem from disabling all other modems on a multipoint network. The Clear-to-Send delay is selectable between 8.5, 50, and 150 ms depending on the polling characteristics of the network. The modem can operate in half-duplex mode on the Public Telephone Network or in full-duplex mode on a four-wire private circuit. Modulation used is 8-phase DPSK and the modulation rate is 2400 Baud. The carrier frequency is 1800 Hz located in the middle of the voice-band. The modem provides an Answer-Back tone of 3 seconds duration at 2025 Hz. The transmitter output level is adjustable. There is an internal version of this modem available under the designation Sync-Up 208A/B. The internal modem fits into a standard full-size slot of a personal computer. UDS provides a software package called Sync-Up BSC, which allows a personal computer with the internal 208A/B modem to emulate various IBM terminals, in particular the IBM 2780/3780 and the IBM 3270.

UDS 9600 Modem

The 9600-bps modem is based on the CCITT V.29 recommendations. The modem is designed primarily for four-wire operation in point-to-point applications. The modem operates in synchronous mode over unconditioned 3002 or equivalent voice-band transmission facilities. The modem has fall-back transmission rates of 7200 bps and 4800 bps. Its modulation rate is 2400 Baud at each of these three speeds, encoding 4 bits per signal element at 9600 bps, 3 bits per signal element at 7200 bps, and 2 bits per signal element at 4800 bps. To set its adaptable equalizer, the modem sends a training sequence of 253.5-ms duration. The equalizer is then continuously updated during the entire transmission. The RTS-CTS delay is 15 ms when no equalization is required; otherwise it is equal to the duration of the training sequence. The carrier frequency is 1700 Hz and the modulation mode is 8-phase QAM with four amplitude levels. The modem has an assortment of testing modes with indicator lights showing its status.

UDS 9600FP Modem

The main difference between this and the previous modem is that the 9600FP modem has an extremely short response time, the RTS-CTS delay, of only 8 ms. The short response time assumes that no training time for adaptive equalizers is required; otherwise the response time is the same as for the UDS 9600. The short delay is of importance on multipoint networks, when several modems are polled in succession.

UDS 9600 Trellis A/B Modem

The special feature of this modem is error detection and correction by means of trellis coding. Use of trellis coding and of adaptive equalizers makes it a better choice for data transmission in half-duplex mode over the Public Telephone Network than the previous two modems.

UDS V.32 Trellis Modem

This recently introduced 9600-bps modem is the highest speed modem operating in full-duplex mode over two-wire switched telephone circuits. The modem operates in synchronous mode at 9600 bps and at 4800 bps or at slower speeds in asynchronous mode. The modem follows the Hayes AT command set. It can store in its nonvolatile memory up to 10 telephone numbers. The modem is equipped with an LCD screen on which prompts and error messages are displayed. The prompts are "answered" by pressing a "YES/NO" key on the front panel. The modem uses adaptive equalizers and adaptive echo cancellers for both the near-end and the far-end echo. The equalizers and echo cancellers adjust themselves during the handshake sequence and during data transmission.

UDS 14.4 A/B Trellis Modem

The 14.4-kbps modem with trellis coding is the fastest modem to operate in half-duplex mode over the Public Telephone Network or in full-duplex mode over four-wire voice-band 3002 unconditioned private or leased lines. At 14.4 kbps, its highest speed, and at 12.0 kbps, when operating in full-duplex mode, the modem is based on the CCITT V.33 preliminary recommendation. It operates on a subset of V.29, when operating over a switched two-wire facility. When in half-duplex mode the modem recognizes carrier loss and reverses the direction of transmission. The modem has several fallback modes, which are either automatically or manually selected depending on the line quality, namely, 14.4 kbps, 12.0 kbps, or 9.6 kbps. At 9.6 kbps the modem complies with the V.29 standard.

PROPRIETARY HIGH SPEED MODEMS

A number of proprietary designs exist to satisfy certain applications requiring high-speed transmission over voice-band lines. A user is then willing to accept the limitations of a proprietary design, namely, a necessity for the same kind of modem at both ends of the transmission path, in return for higher speed.

An example of such high-speed design is the Trailblazer modem from the Telebit Corporation. The modem adjusts its modulation rate to the line quality and typically transmits at a modulation rate of only 7.5 baud using a large number (up to 512) of carrier frequencies. Each carrier frequency is continuously monitored and 0, 2, 4, or 6 bits are assigned to each frequency depending on the line condition. The modem can achieve transmission rates of up to 10 kbps without any data compression. Figure 11.2 shows different constellations assigned to each carrier depending on the condition of the transmission line (low or high distortion and noise). Figure 11.3 shows the spectrum of frequencies carrying the Trailblazer signals.

Another example of a proprietary modem is the HF144 modem made by the Emulex Corporation. The HF144 modem can be used for facsimile transmission at 14400 bps in half-duplex mode. Depending on the condition of the transmission line, the modem automatically chooses or is manually switched to operate at an optimum transmission speed anywhere between 14400 bps and 300 bps. The modem can also operate in V.29 and in V.33 mode. The modem has a built-in Eye Quality Monitor, which can be used for deciding at which transmission speed to operate.

FACSIMILE MODEMS

A major application for high-speed voice-band modems is facsimile, the transmission of pictures or text in graphics mode, between remote locations. A light scanning device in a facsimile machine scans each line of material to be sent and transfers the information to an attached computer or directly to a modem for transmission to a remote terminal. Some facsimile modems are built into the facsimile machines; others consist of a card mounted in a PC with connections to a facsimile machine and to a phone jack. A standard facsimile connection without PCs and a typical connection through serial ports for a PC-based facsimile modem are shown in Figure 11.4. It is also possible to compose text and pictures on a PC using desktop publishing programs such as PageMaker or Ventura Publisher, store the completed pages (including graphics) on disk, and then send them to a remote computer by means of a facsimile modem, even without access to a facsimile machine. Software provided for PC-based facsimile modems includes drivers for the popular laser printers and frequently allows one to translate text files, like those generated by a word processor, into their graphics equivalents.

Facsimile modems generally operate in half-duplex mode over the switched Public Telephone Network at transmission speeds of up to 9600 bps. The majority of facsimile modems are based on a special Rockwell three-chip set called R96FAX. The modem chip set satisfies the CCITT Group 2 and Group 3 requirements and follows the V.29 Recommendation at 9600, 7200, or 4800 bps, V.27 at 4800 or 2400 bps, or FSK at 300 bps. Table 11.8 shows the

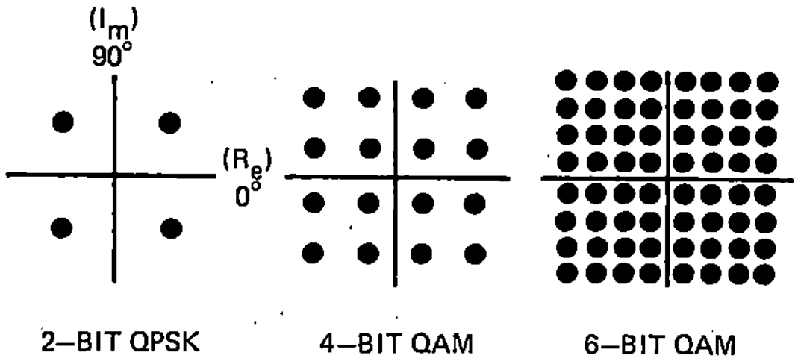

Figure 11.2 **Trailblazer Modem Constellation Diagrams**

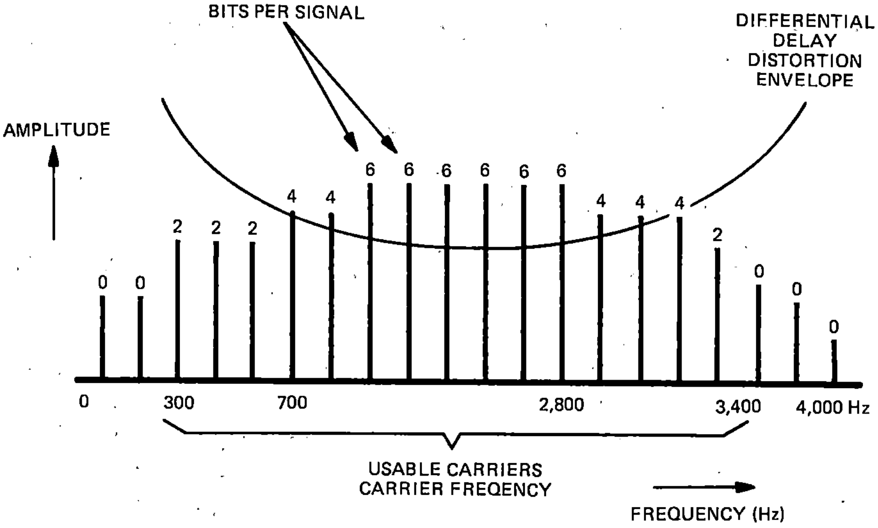

Figure 11.3 **Trailblazer Modem Spectrum**

line signal-to-noise requirements to achieve an error rate of 1 in 100,000 for these transmission speeds and standards. Most facsimile modems follow one of four design standards called groups. A Group 1 modem can work with another Group 1 modem, a Group 2 can work with another Group 2 modem, etc. Some Group 3modems are also downward compatible and can operate, e.g., with either Group 1, 2, or 3 modems. Group 1 and 2 modems are older analog designs, developed in the mid 1960s and in 1976 and find only limited use.

Table 11.8 **S/N Ratios in dB for R96FAX Based Modems**

(Bit Error Rate: 1 Error in 100,000 Bits)

Standard	Transmission Speed (bps)	S/N (dB)
V.29	9600	23
V.29	7200	20
V.27	4800	18
V.29	4800	15
V.27	2400	11
103A (FSK)	300	5

The most popular Group 3, adopted by CCITT in 1980; and the more recent Group 4 modems, adopted in 1984, are strictly digital designs and can produce high-resolution output. Both use data compression algorithms, which reduce the amount of transmitted data by a factor between 5 and 10. A typical transmission time for Group 3 is 30—60 seconds per page. The Group 3 resolution is selectable, and is either 100 vertical by 200 horizontal dots per inch (dpi), or it is 200 × 200 dpi. Group 4 facsimile modems are capable of 400 × 400 dpi resolution, but cannot operate on the switched Public Telephone Network.

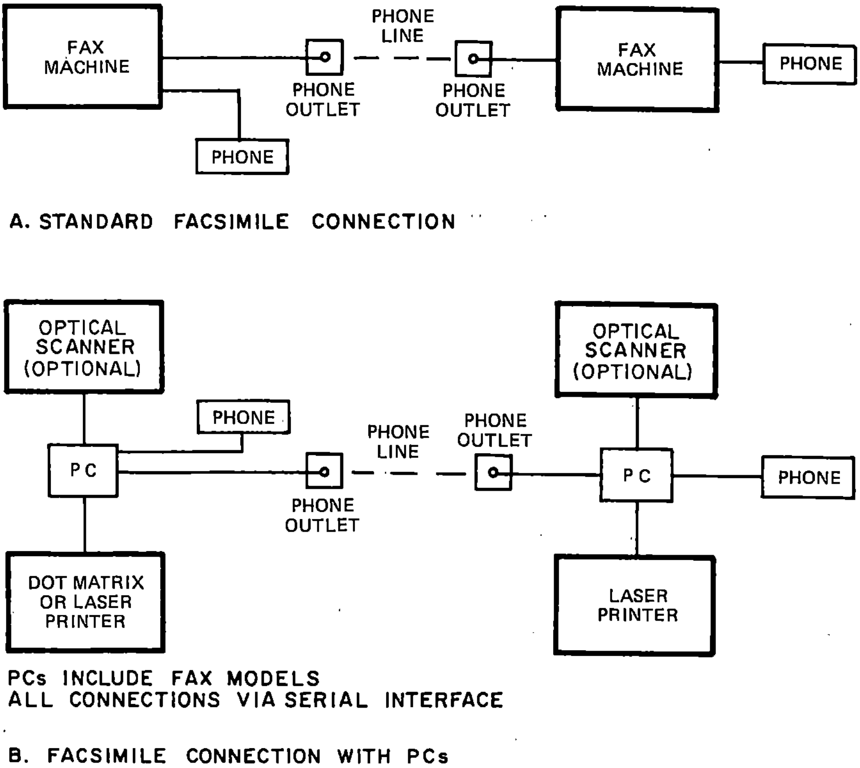

Figure 11.4 **Connection of a Facsimile Modem**

12. Limited Distance Modems

A limited distance modem is a special type of modem which provides an inexpensive alternative for data transmission between permanent nearby locations at distances generally not exceeding 25 km (16 miles). Typical applications are in linking various manufacturing plants belonging to the same complex or a university campus spread over a limited geographical area. To take advantage of limited distance modems, such nearby locations should be connected with privately owned twisted-pair copper wires, coaxial cable, or with optical fibers which are not a part of the Public Telephone Network. To be able to use limited distance modems the cables (except for glass fibers) should have DC continuity between modems. Cables with DC continuity are often referred to as metallic lines. A leased telephone circuit or a circuit on the Public Telephone Network will, in general, have no DC continuity, unless it is within the same exchange.

A limited distance modem extends the permissible distance between two RS-232-C interfaces which is otherwise, according to specifications, only guaranteed for distances of up to 16 m (50 ft). The connecting copper wires or coaxial cable, depending on the particular modem, should not have any embedded loading coils of the type commonly found on long telephone loops. Loading coils of typically 88 mH each are installed by the telephone company every 1.7 km (6000 ft) to improve the voice frequency response of telephone cable. The inductance of the coils combines with the internal capacitance of the cable to form a low-pass filter out of the telephone cable. The result is flat frequency response in the voice-band, up to about 2500 Hz, but high attenuation at frequencies above the voice-band. High attenuation above 2500 Hz would be disastrous for higher data transmission rates. Similarly, if an out-of-service telephone cable is being used for a limited distance modem, bridged taps left from previous telephone subscribers should be removed. A bridged tap appears when telephone service is discontinued and the telephone loop leading to the subscriber's premises is left bridged across the line. The added capacitance causes phase distortion which affects data transmission.

A limited distance modem typically consists of a box equipped with a 25-pin D-shell connector for the RS-232-C interface at the terminal/computer side, and a screw-down terminal block to connect the cable leading to the remote location. A limited distance modem using a glass fiber as transmission medium would have a special fiber connector instead of screw-down terminals. There is a variety of limited distance modems to accommodate other interfaces than RS-232-C at a wide range of transmission rates.

Limited distance modems do not use intermediate repeaters on the transmission line and the maximum cable length, maximum transmission rate and the type of cable used (gauge and capacity) are closely interrelated. A limited distance modem can be usually configured by setting certain switchesto appear as a DTE (Data Terminal Equipment) or as a DCE (Data Communications Equipment), so that no "null" modems will be required to complete the connection. Installation for an RS-232-C limited distance modem consists of attaching at one end a 25-pin DB-25 connector to the terminal/computer either directly or through a short cable, and attaching the copper cable to screw terminals at the other end as shown in Figure 12.1. To decide whether to configure the modem as DTE or DCE, if it is not known in advance, one can observe LED indicators provided on most limited distance modems. In the "stand-by" condition both transmit and receive LEDs should be in the OFF

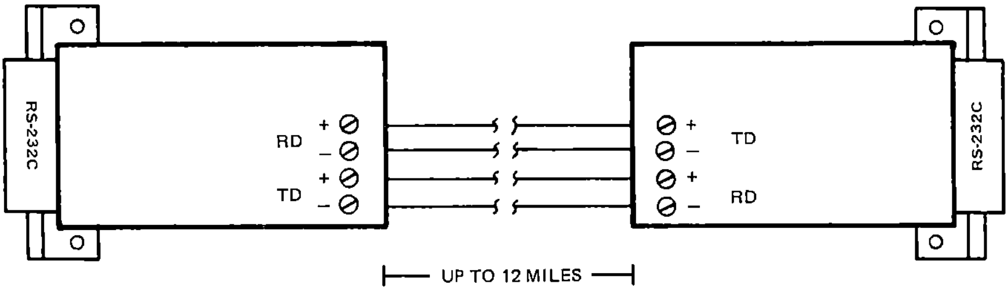

Figure 12.1 **Limited Distance Modem Hook-Up**

condition if the modem is correctly connected. If the indicators are lighted, then change the position of the DTE/DCE switch.

An important feature to look for, when selecting a limited distance modem, is to ascertain for safety reasons that the modem provides electrical insulation between computer/terminal and the transmission line by featuring either line insulation transformers or opto-couplers. Lack of these safety features may lead to destruction of both the modem and computer in case of a power surge. High-voltage transients caused by lightning in the vicinity of the transmission line and other electrical disturbances can easily destroy the delicate semiconductors. The induced voltage is primarily caused by the sharp rise of voltage associated with lightning. A typical leading edge of a transient caused by lightning bolt is of the order of kilovolts per microsecond.

Separate over-voltage protecting devices can also be connected between the limited distance modem and the transmission line. These devices provide additional protection beyond the insulation normally found in limited distance modems. The so-called Lighting Sponge manufactured by the General Semiconductor Industries is an example of such a device. The protection scheme includes two to three separate stages which limit high-voltage transients. These are high-speed gas tubes, semiconductor devices, and metal oxide varistors (MOV). Each successive stage is slower than the previous one but can handle higher energy. The protecting device would be normally installed at both ends of a transmission line. Specialized voltage protecting devices can also be installed on dial-up telephone circuits, where they protect the tip and ring line at different levels. The cost of voltage protecting devices is usually under $100.

A minor disadvantage of using limited distance modems is that there is currently no standardization in the modem design, and that the modems use proprietary circuitry. Therefore modems at both ends of a communication link have to be of the same model and be made by the same manufacturer.

Most limited distance modems are current drivers, i.e., the modem sends a current of typically 20 mA over a two-wire metallic line, similar to an old-time telegraph circuit. Considering a typical DC resistance limitation of a limited distance modem of 1500 Ohms, one can see that the voltage imposed by this type of modem on the metallic line can be up to $0.020 \times 1500 = 30$ V. This is much higher than the signal voltage on a telephone line, which is on the order of 100 mV. It is one of the reasons why a limited distance modem cannot operate on the Public Telephone Network, as the high voltage would interfere with adjacent circuits causing crosstalk and introducing distortion. The FCC limits on signal amplitudes at various transmission rates for data transmitted over the Public Telephone Network are listed in the AT&T Publication 43401 and are shown in Table 12.1. These limits apply to circuits leased from Common Carriers, but do not apply to private metallic circuits, which are outside the FCC jurisdiction.

Table 12.1 **Maximum Power Levels Permitted by AT&T 43401**

Transmission Speed (bps)	Power Level (dBm)
2400	-4
4800	-11
9600	-18
19200	-25

The reason that a current driver can transmit over longer distances than the RS-232-C bi-directional voltage signals is that the twisted cable exhibits at baseband frequencies a fairly low impedance, more suitable to current transmission.

In addition to limited distance modems using current drivers, there are also limited distance modems using modulation methods similar to those found in standard modems. The advantage of such units is that they can operate at lower voltages, so that they will not interfere with regular voice circuits carried in adjacent cables. The disadvantage is higher cost. An example of such top-of-the-line modems would be the Model 8250 LDSU from the Codex Corporation. The modem operates at distances of up to 40 km (23 miles) at 2400, 4800, 7200, 9600, and 19,200 bps in synchronous mode on point-to-point or multipoint circuits. The modem uses differential phase modulation somewhat similar to Bell 212A. The modem is equipped with an adaptive equalizer, so that individual adjustments for the transmission facility are not required. Local and remote unattended diagnostic capability is also provided. Table 12.2 shows the maximum distances obtainable with the modem as function of transmission speed, type of cable and output transmission level in dBm (0 dBm = 1 mW).

A set of two modem chips for limited distance modems has recently been developed by the Signetics Corporation. The NE5080 transmitter and the NE5081 receiver provide transmission rates as high as 8 Mbps over 75-Ohm coaxial cable. The maximum transmission rate decreases with increase in distance, but even at 30 km (19 miles) the modem can still operate at 500 kbps. The modem which can be built from the two chips and a few external components uses FSK modulation, the simple scheme found in the 300-bps Bell compatible 103 type modems. The transmit and receive frequencies of the modem can be set by external resistors. Thus it is comparatively easy to design

Table 12.2

8250 Synchronous LDSU

Data Rate (bps)	0 dBm Transmitted Power AWG 19	AWG 22	AWG 24	AWG 26	Telco Restricted Mode AWG 19	AWG 22	AWG 24	AWG 26	Transmitted Power Level in Telco Restricted Mode
2400	23	15	12	9	23	15	12	9	0
4800	17	12	8	6	15	9	7	5	−6
7200	15	9	7	5	12	7	5	4	−12
9600	14	8	6	4	9	5	4	3	−16
19,200	10	6	4	3	6	4	3	2	−20

NOTE: AWG = American Wire Gauge

a multichannel limited distance modem system by selecting different center frequencies for each modem pair and combining the modem outputs on the same coaxial cable. Figures 12.2 and 12.3 show the block diagrams of the two modem chips. Figure 12.4 shows the connection of the chips to coaxial cable for a full-duplex operation.

Fiber optics technology is also reaching into the domain of limited distance modems. Transmission over optical fibers has a number of advantages, and a few disadvantages over using metallic conductors. The advantages are a tremendous available bandwidth of the order of hundreds of MHz, low loss, freedom from environmental electromagnetic interference, invulnerability to surreptitious tapping, and last but not least, savings on scarce resources such as copper. The disadvantages are the relatively high cost, specialized installation equipment, and need for experienced personnel to install and maintain it. Figure 12.5 compares the effective loss of two kinds of glass fiber with a pair of 22-gauge copper wires and with coaxial cable as a function of frequency. A lot of work has been done by the telephone companies to facilitate glass fiber installation. Special splicing connectors have been developed, which precisely align two ends of a glass fiber. The glass fiber ends are secured in a plug with epoxy, while an elastic boot limits the bending radius of the fiber at the connectors entrance. A modem glass fiber connector can be installed in less than 15 minutes.

Examples of limited distance modems using fiber optics are models 2280

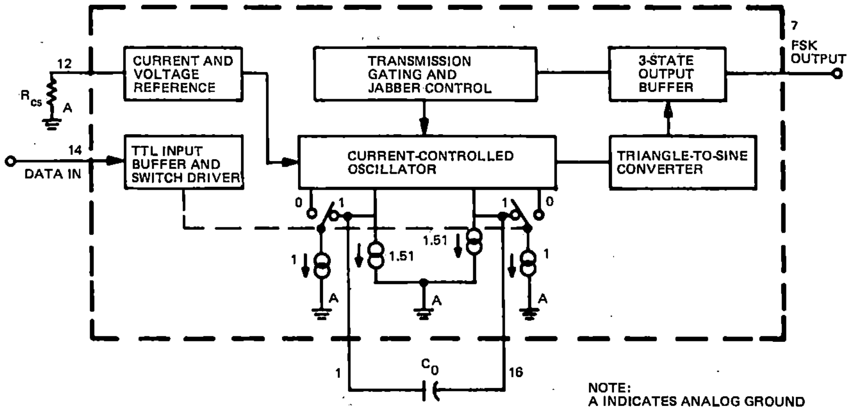

Figure 12.2 **Diagram of the NE5081 Transmitter**

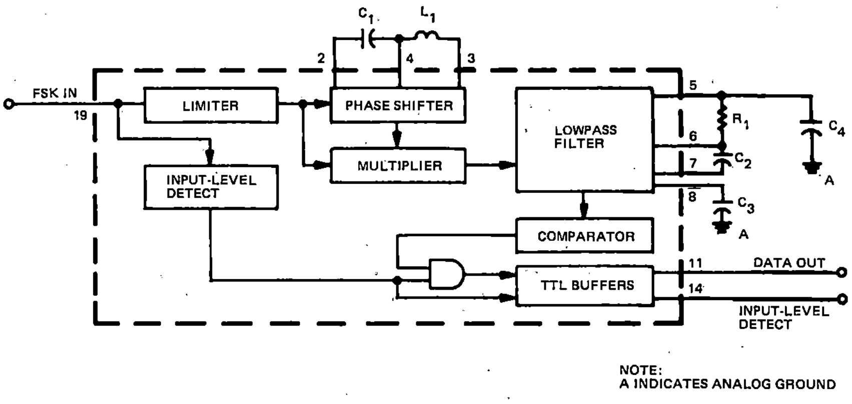

Figure 12.3 **Diagram of the NE5081 Receiver**

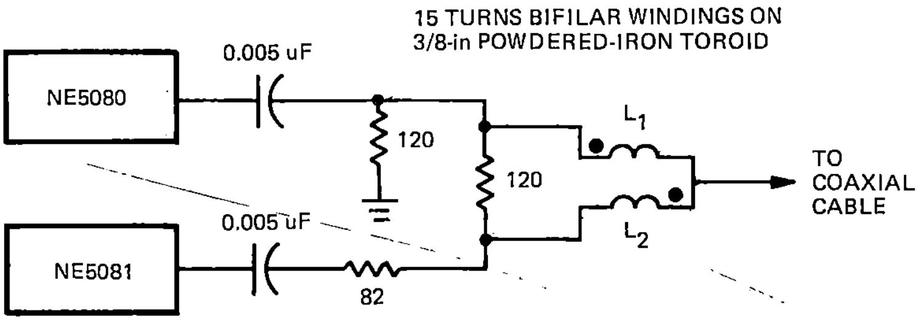

Figure 12.4 Full Duplex Operation for NE5080/81 Modem

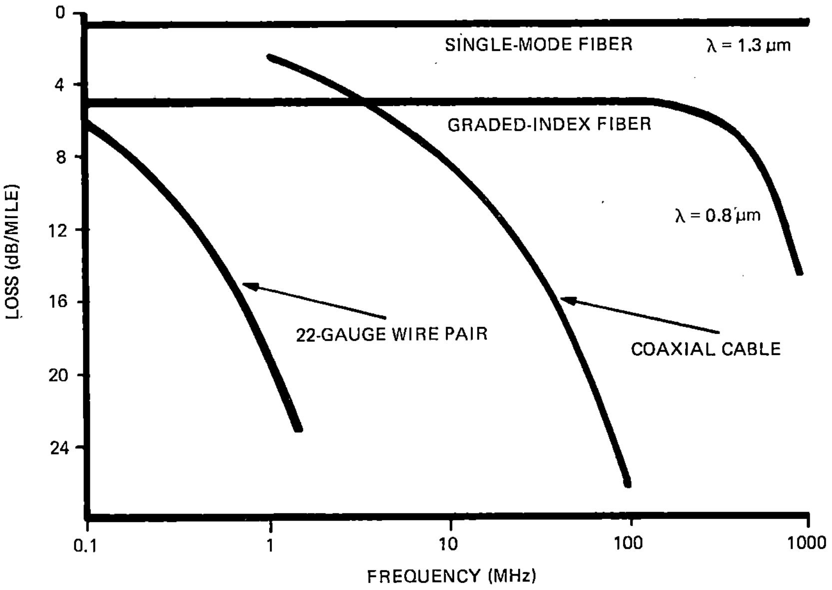

Figure 12.5 Glass Fiber Loss Vs. Frequency

and 2290 manufactured by the Canoga Perkins Corporation of Canoga Park, California. The 2290 modem operates at transmission speeds of up to 6.312 Mbps; the 2280 modem operates at speeds of up to 12 Mbps. Both modems have V.35, RS-422, RS-423, T1, TTL, and DMR11/DMC11 interfaces. The transmitter is a light emitting diode (LED), the receiver is a PIN diode. PIN diodes are special high frequency silicon semiconductors consisting of p- and n- doped regions separated by an intrinsic section. Both modems use proprietary coding schemes. The maximum distance between modems is 2.5 km for standard configuration and 6 km with a Long Distance option.

Typical applications which can profit from the high transmission speed of these two modems are satellite downlinks, T1 multiplex extensions, high-speed graphics devices, and CPU to CPU data transfers.

Power to the limited distance modem is either provided by an external power source, typically an AC outlet, or in some modem designs it is derived directly from the RS-232-C interface.

Prices of limited distance modems range between $100 and $200 for current drivers and $500 to $1000 for units using internal modulators. Prices of fiber optics modems are in the $2000—$3000 range. The prices depend on the number of features like internal diagnostics and flexibility of use. As the limited distance modems are nearly always used on privately owned circuits, there are usually no other recurring charges in operation of such data links. Due to low marginal cost a limited distance modem can pay for itself in a few months.

LIMITED DISTANCE MODEMS USING AC POWER LINES

Signetics Corporation produces an inexpensive limited distance modem integrated circuit, the NE5050, which can be used to build a modem to transmit data at up to 1200 bps over power lines. This method of communication is somewhat similar to appliance controllers which also operate over power lines. A typical connection of the modem to a power line in a three-node industrial application is shown in Figure 12.6. As would be the case with any communication network using power lines as transmission medium, all nodes would have to be served by the same utility power transformer. This would normally limit the system to a single building or to adjacent buildings. Depending on the number of modems on the network, each NE5050 modem

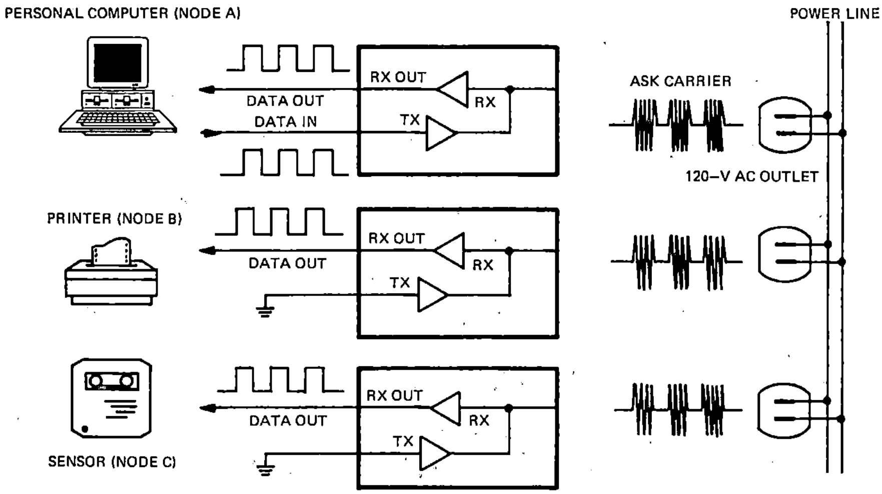

Figure 12.6 **Application of the NE5050 AC Modem**

can operate with either Amplitude Shift Keying (ASK) or with the Frequency Shift Keying (FSK) modulation. The modem can operate at one or two frequencies in either half- or in full-duplex mode. The carrier can be preset to a specific frequency, typically of the order of 100 kHz.

A power line modem on a board, using a different approach, has been recently introduced by the Adaptive Networks Inc. located in Cambridge, Massachusetts. The AN192 modem uses a proprietary spread-spectrum technology with carrier frequencies between 50 kHz and 400 kHz. Use of this wideband approach and of an error correction scheme make the modem adaptable to higher transmission speeds than would be the case with a standard narrowband modem. The modem accepts data transmission rates between 300 and 19200 bps in either synchhronous or in asynchronous mode. The modem has a standard RS-232-C interface and its operation should be transparent to the user. The modem supports a multipoint or a master/slave arrangement with as many as 255 units connected to the power line Each unit can broadcast messages to all others and is equipped with a "watchdog" timer to prevent interference from an unattended unit, which has gone "off-hook." Figure 12.7 shows the modem board. Because of its small size and low cost, this modem

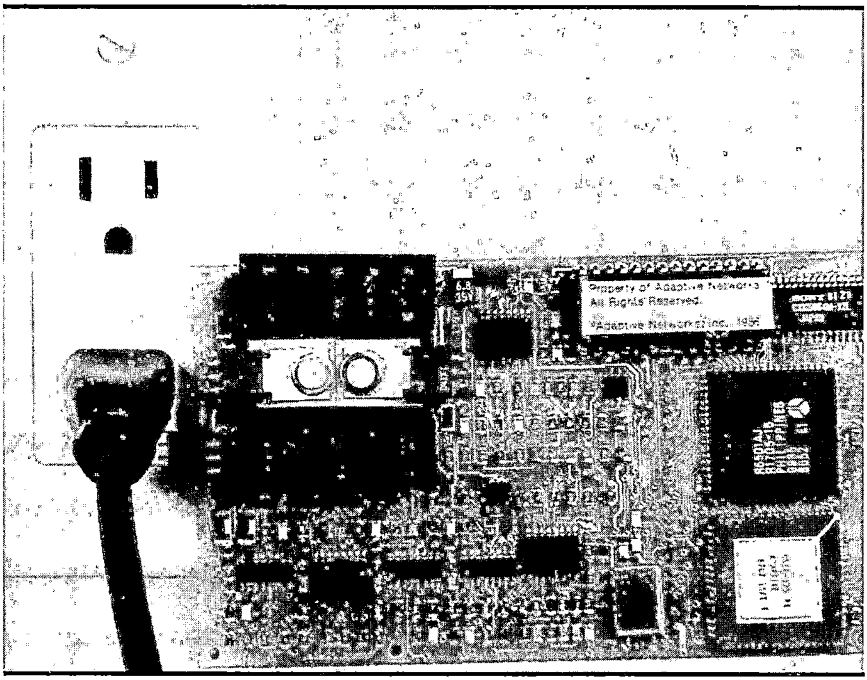

Figure 12.7 **Modem Board with the AN192 Chip**

may find all kinds of new applications. For example, it could be used for sharing high-speed printers between various PCs located throughout a building.

13. Specialized Modem Applications

The general purpose personal and commercial modems described in the previous chapters may not satisfy certain specialized applications. In this chapter I will discuss wideband modems used for high-speed transmission over wideband facilities, acoustic modems known for their portability, security modems with special features for protecting the data and multiplexing modems, which combine multiple data streams into a single data path.

WIDEBAND MODEMS

Wideband modems combine certain features of limited distance modems, namely, the wide range of transmission speeds and requirements for specialized transmission facilities, with features of regular modems, namely, the ability to operate over long distances, albeit not over the Public Telephone Network. The transmission medium for wideband modems is typically coaxial cable with intermediate repeaters. Use of coaxial cable has a number of advantages over the twisted-pair cable. Coaxial cable has wider bandwidth than twisted-pair cable and it allows for flexible architecture. A typical application for a wideband modem is a data distribution system using a Cable TV (CATV) network as its backbone transmission system. The disadvantage is higher installation cost, in particular if it can not be "piggy-backed" on an existing system.

Fairchild M505 Wideband Modem

An example of a wideband modem is the Fairchild model M505. The modem has field changeable data transmission rates between 56 kbps and 10 Mbps. Its required bandwidth is 0.7 × transmission rate in bps. Transmission of the contents of a 24-channel T1 group of 1.554 Mbps thus requires a bandwidth of 1.1 MHz. The carrier frequencies of M505 are programmable within a range of 5 to 400 MHz. By proper selection of carrier frequencies, it becomes possible to piggy-back data transmission on a working CATV distribution network. Because of the joint use, the amount of harmonics has to be strictly controlled, since spurious harmonics of a data signal may fall within the passband of another service. The modem specifications call for a minimum of 50 dB signal-to-harmonic ratio. The modem can be equipped with RS-442/449, MIL- STD-188/114, T1 (DS1), T2 (DS2), or CCITT V.35 interfaces. The modem uses QPSK modulation.

Figure 13.1 illustrates a block diagram of the modem while Figure 13.2 shows a typical LAN application of the M505 using CATV coaxial cable as the transmission medium. The application shown in Figure 13.2 involves three buildings in a manufacturing complex separated by several kilometers. The application requires voice and data communications.

In this particular application, a CATV system is installed between buildings and bi-directional amplifiers in the system take care of signal losses. Four standard low-cost CATV taps supply the physical interface. The PBX switchboards are connected at T1 transmission rates of 1.544 Mbps with two M505 modems, one in the main plant and one in the engineering annex. Six additional modems provide three data links, one to the warehouse and two to the engineering annex from the main plant. Eight carrier frequencies are used in this example, one for each transmitter and one for each receiver. The whole system uses only a minor portion of the CATV system capacity, since all four data links will fit into a single 6-MHz channel. One pair of frequencies is used each for the PBX, the warehouse, the terminal controller in the engineering annex and for the CAD/CAM graphics terminal. Since a CATV system may have up to 59 channels, there is plenty of available frequency space left for additional data and graphics terminals, PBX switchboards, closed circuit TV for surveillance and conference purposes, paging and background music.

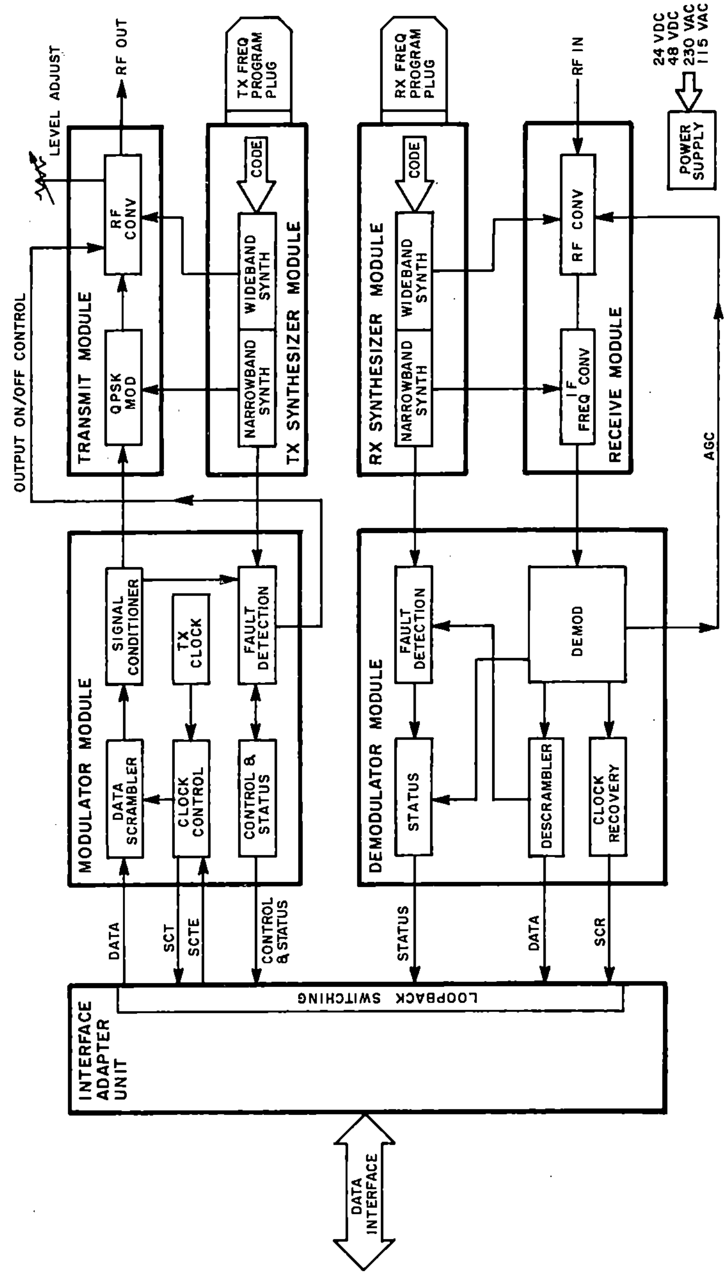

Figure 13.1 **Block Diagram of an M505 Wide-Band Modem**

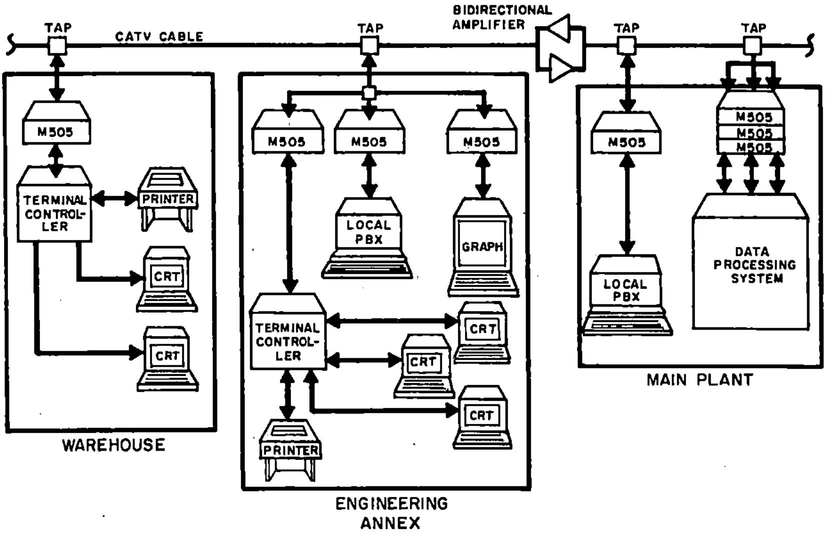

Figure 13.2 **Typical Application of an M505 Wide-Band Modem**

ACOUSTIC MODEMS

Modems using acoustic couplers as interfaces to the telephone network are no more than a footnote in the development of data communications. The main reason for their development was to make portable data terminals free from early restrictions related to attachment of "foreign" devices to the telephone network. At the intermediate stage of deregulation in the United States, when Data Access Arrangement (DAA) devices were required for electrical connection to the network, an acoustically coupled modem was allowed to operate without a DAA. Today, the acoustically coupled modems occupy just a small market niche and are being used mainly by traveling salespeople, reporters, or field engineers, who can capture data on their portable or even pocket-sized computers and transfer the data to the central location from any phone booth, key telephone having a 50-pin jack, or any foreign location, where the RJ11C jacks are not being used. Even some of these niches may disappear since some telephone companies, e.g., the U.S. West and its subsidiary, Mountain Bell, are now introducing pay phones, at airports initially, specifically designed for direct modem connection. Such

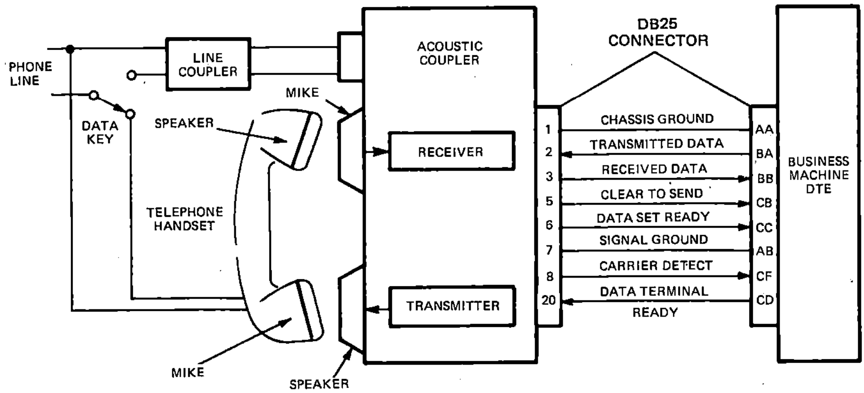

Figure 13.3 **An Acoustically Coupled Modem**

phones, called the Touchbase Universal Voice/Data phones, come equipped with an RJ11C telephone jack to connect the modem, and they have a slot for a credit card to collect charges. Dialing can be performed directly by the customer's modem. Each of these phones contains two separate communication lines, so that users can talk and send data simultaneously.

The acoustic telephone set coupler was first developed at the Stanford Research Institute in the 1960s by John Van Geer, who needed a portable data terminal with functions equivalent to the then common teletypewriter, such as the Bell System TTY 33. A diagram of a terminal coupled with an acoustic modem to a telephone handset is shown in Figure 13.3. The obvious problem inherent to acoustic coupling is that the telephone handset, to which the acoustic coupler is attached, was designed to transmit voice and not data. The human ear is much more forgiving to noise and nonlinear distortion than a data set would be. A short burst of acoustic noise, e.g., a spoon dropping from a dish, will hardly be noticed in a telephone conversation, but it will destroy hundreds of bits of information in an acoustically coupled modem.

One of the weakest links in an acoustically coupled modem is the microphone in the mouthpiece of a telephone handset. Developed by early pioneers of telephony, and still basically unchanged in standard telephone sets, it consists of closely packed carbon granules kept in a tight enclosure exposed to the sound waves of the talker. When a sound wave hits the carbon granules, they compress, causing the resistance of the microphone to decrease. Although adequate for voice communication, the sensitivity of the carbon microphone changes with age. Knocking a telephone handset against a hard surface will greatly affect the carbon microphone sensitivity. To make things even worse for data transmission, the nonlinear resistance of the carbon microphone generates a strong second harmonic frequency, which may interfere with the opposite direction of transmission on a full-duplex data circuit. Other factors affecting transmission besides harmonic distortion are vibration and ambient noise.

In spite of all these potential problems, many 300-bps Bell 103A type equivalent acoustically coupled modems were developed during the 1970s. The advantage of the 103A type modem is that, besides operating at relatively slow speed, its receiving and transmitting frequencies (1070 Hz, 1270 Hz, 2025 Hz, and 2225 Hz) are not exact multiples of each other and thus are not harmonically related. Therefore, the second harmonic distortion can be filtered out more easily. The 300-bps acoustically coupled modems were either designed as an integral part of a data terminal like in the popular Texas Instruments 700 series, or were made into attachments pluggable into portable computers like in the TANDY Model 100/200.

A few 1200-bps acoustically coupled modems were also developed by Racal-Vadic and by Anderson-Jacobson as medium-sized units equipped with an RS-232-C connector. The earlier 1200 bps-modems operated in half-duplex mode compatible with the Bell System 202A standard. In 1973, Racal-Vadic developed the first 1200-bps full-duplex modem for the switched Public Telephone Network. The acoustically coupled VA3400 modem was put on the market one year before Bell introduced the 212A type modem. The VA3400 frequency assignments were optimized for low harmonic distortion by choosing a higher Originate frequency of 2250 Hz and a lower Receive frequency of 1150 Hz. Thus the second harmonic of the high-power Originate frequency (4500 Hz) would fall outside the voice frequency band and would not interfere with the low-power Receive frequency. The 212A modem uses an Originate frequency of 1200 Hz and a Receive frequency of 2400 Hz, the exact second harmonic of the Originate frequency, which makes it quite unsuitable for an acoustic modem. Therefore, though the 212A and the VA3400 modems use the same kind of modulation (DPSK), they are incompatible with each other. Subsequently, the Anderson Jacobson Corporation designed a line of 1200 bps acoustically coupled modems, e.g., Model 1232, which is compatible with 212A, but can only operate in the Originate mode. Thus a 212A type acoustically coupled modem cannot communicate with another acoustically coupled modem. Because of limited interest in acoustically coupled modems, there is no further work in this area being pursued by other modem manufacturers.

SECURITY MODEMS

Much of the data which is stored in computer files and can be accessed through a modem may be valuable to a third party. In addition, care is necessary to avoid tampering with data with or without a criminal intent. Well-publicized stories about "hackers" getting access to classified information, or criminals transferring money to their own accounts, caused many sleepless nights for corporate data managers. The anonymity of the telephone network currently makes tracing of incoming calls difficult, if not impossible.

Securing information which can be accessed through an anonymous phone call via modem can be done at many levels. The first level of security can be achieved by embedding the security aspects in software by assigning passwords to users. As many communications managers have found out, this method is only partially successful. People leave passwords written next to their terminals or on blackboards. Self-assigned passwords are frequently short and easy to crack. Somebody with a good knowledge of a system may even find an uncoded file listing all passwords. Passwords and other information can also be obtained from archived information or from a physical circuit tap. Hackers frequently use a program, which guesses the most common passwords, like nicknames, first names, and various programming terms.

To alleviate this situation, combined hardware/software security measures have been developed. A popular method of protection is to have the called modem hang up after the initial identification of the calling party and then call back, when it has determined that the calling number is in the authorized file stored in modem's memory. For improved security, two lines should be assigned to a call-back system, one for the incoming calls, and the other for outgoing calls. The reason why a second telephone line is often recommended is that on a single line system it is comparatively easy for the caller to confuse the call-back system. The called security modem is then under the impression that the calling modem has hung up and that the return call was already made, while the modem is actually still connected to the original caller.

A good example of a commercial security modem implementation is the ITT Security Modem. When an access call is made, the modem prompts the caller to enter the user's ID password. If the password is in the modem's memory and is valid, then the modem instructs the caller to hang up and wait to be called back. The modem will then call the number linked in its memory with the password. This feature prevents people, who somehow get hold of the passwords, from calling from a phone booth, but it also limits the legitimate user to a single calling location. The ITT Security Modem can store up to 25 user passwords and phone numbers in its nonvolatile CMOS memory. When the caller is legitimate, other calls are locked out until the "call-back" call is made. The modem comes equipped with two jacks so that it can be set up to accept calls on one phone line and make call-backs on a second line, whose number may be kept secret. Access security can be set at four different levels: no security, password only, password acceptance and call-back on one line, or password acceptance and call-back on a different security line. The modem provides a security audit trail of valid and invalid access attempts to the host computer. The modem can also be set to require a password to allow the user to dial out. In addition, a physical key has to be turned in a lock to be able to access the security software and to change the security options, passwords, or the call-back numbers. Security stickers seal the modem case to disclose any physical tampering.

Another security modem, the Ven-Tel MD212, similar to the ITT Security Modem, requires a supervisory password to examine, modify, or delete any of the telephone numbers, passwords, account numbers, or other information stored in the modem. The user password limits the user to dialing any of the nine stored telephone numbers. When dialing with the restricted password, the phone numbers and log-ins are blanked from the terminal. An integral timer resets the modem after 5 minutes of inactivity to prevent compromise of an unattended system. A log-on controller monitors line activity and terminates a call automatically, when it detects an improper response of the caller.

There is no question that a security modem makes establishment of a data call more complicated and gives the user a feeling of the Big Brother watching. Still it is a preferable solution, where tampering with data can be disastrous.

MULTIPLEXING MODEMS

A special kind of modem, which combines several data channels from multiple sources before sending the combined data stream to the remote location, is called a multiplexer. Multiplexers, similar to modems, always work in pairs and there will be a similar unit at the remote location. At the remote location the receiving multiplexer separates the data stream into individual channels and distributes them to the proper users. A multiplexer is of value, when the cost of transmission facility is relatively high, e.g., a full-time leased circuit between two cities over buried coaxial cable, transatlantic cable, or over a satellite. Analog and digital multiplexing has long been used in carrier telephony, where hundreds or even thousands of voice channels are multiplexed into adjacent frequency bands (FDM — Frequency Division Multiplex) or are combined into adjacent time slots in a high-capacity channel (TDM — Time Division Multiplex), before the combined data stream is sent via a coaxial or a microwave broadband circuit. The analog L5 carrier system introduced by AT&T a few years ago carries 10,800 frequency-modulated voice circuits on a pair of coaxial cables; the digital carrier multiplexers range from a 24-channel T1 to FT3, which can carry 96,768 voice channels on a pair of glass fibers. For the last few years multiplexing has become available to commercial and private data communications users with a typical cost of $5,000 to $10,000 for a 9600-bps device combining 2—16 data channels.

There are two kinds of multiplexers. The simpler kind combines several channels without regard to channel traffic by assigning a fixed bandwidth to each channel. The combined bandwidth of a data channel put out by the multiplexer is then equal to the sum of the bandwidths of individual channels. A more elaborate device, the so-called statistical multiplexer, provides data compression by swapping idle time of one channel for busy time of another channel. Compared with straight time division multiplexing or compared with the frequency division multiplexing, where bandwidth is allocated regardless of activity, statistical multiplexing allows several terminals to be connected simultaneously, resulting in an equivalent transmission speed greater than the sum of the transmission speeds of the connected terminals. The bandwidth in a statistical multiplexer is dynamically allocated to active terminals only, and is thus less than the combined bandwidth of its input channels. In order not to lose any data during peak traffic periods, a statistical multiplexer always provides buffering of incoming data.

A good example of a statistical multiplexer is the Model 6005 manufactured by Codex Corporation. The multiplexer supports both synchronous and asynchronous terminals. Computer equipment operating at various speeds in synchronous and asynchronous mode can be combined in a single high-speed transmission facility carrying data between terminals, printers, facsimile machines, and micro- and minicomputers. The maximum transmission speed for the combined data stream is 9600 bps in full-duplex or in half-duplex mode. Figure 13.4 shows the architecture and typical applications for the multiplexer, specifically two point-to-point network configurations. Figure 13.5 shows potential savings, which can be obtained by the statistical multiplexer,

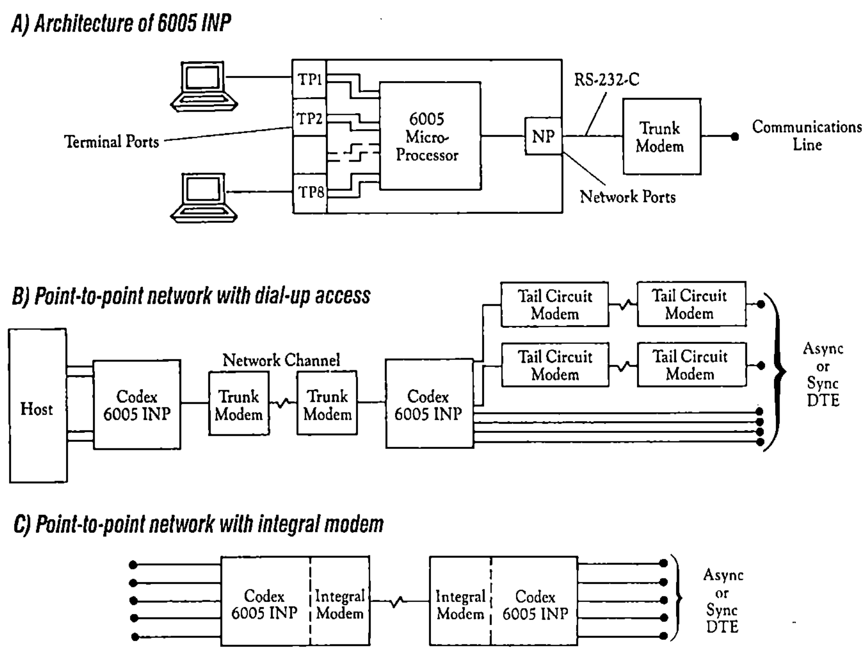

Figure 13.4 **Architecture and Typical Applications of a Codex 6005 Modem/Multiplexing**

as compared with individual circuits for each terminal. The comparisons assume leased full-time transmission facilities for each case; they would not be valid for occasional use on the switched Public Telephone Network.

An example of a straight, nonstatistical multiplexer, is the UDS Model 1406T TDM Modem. The modem/multiplexer has six input ports, which can accept data at 2400 bps, 4800 bps, 7200 bps, 9600 bps, 12,000 bps, or 14,400 bps in synchronous or in asynchronous mode. The port interface is RS-232-C. On the transmitting side, the modem operates at 9600 bps, 12,000 bps, or 14,400 bps. At the two higher speeds, the modem follows the preliminary CCITT V.33 recommendations; at 9600 bps it follows CCITT V.29 with op-

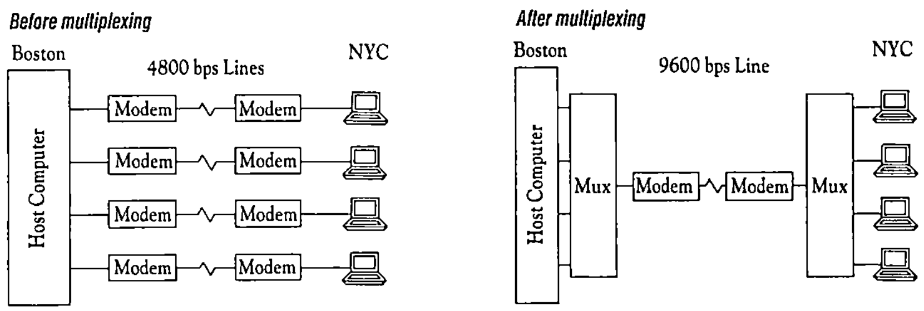

Monthly Telephone Charges (4@ $350)	$1,400
Monthly Modem Charges (8@ $50)	$ 400
Total Monthly Charges	$1,800

Note: Prices used are estimated. Modem and multiplexer costs are calculated on a three-year lease, representing typical equipment.

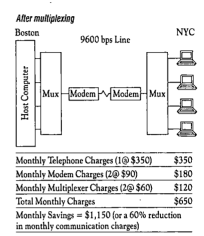

Monthly Telephone Charges (1@ $350)	$350
Monthly Modem Charges (2@ $90)	$180
Monthly Multiplexer Charges (2@ $60)	$120
Total Monthly Charges	$650

Monthly Savings = $1,150 (or a 60% reduction in monthly communication charges)

Figure 13.5 **Potential Savings in Transmission Cost Due to Multiplexing**

tional Trellis coding. The modem operates in full-duplex mode over private or leased voice-band unconditioned (3002) four-wire lines. The modem comes with the usual assortment of testing features and LED indicators. In addition, a front panel LCD display shows the status and configuration of the multiplexer and the status of the device obtained as the result of internal tests.

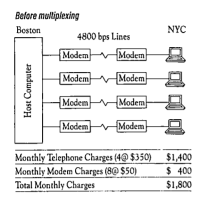

Part Four
Diagnostics and Testing

In this part of the book the reader will find out what to do if the data gets lost or becomes garbled somewhere between the source computer or terminal and its destination. Chapter 14 discusses built-in facilities for modem testing, testing of interfaces between modems and computers, and testing of stand-alone modems. The final Chapter 15 covers testing of transmission facilities, in particular those leased from the Common Carriers.

14. Testing Modems and Interfaces

Before deregulation of the United States telephone industry, if a data connection failed for some reason, the solution was to call the local telephone company and have the problem fixed. Not any more — since most of the data communications equipment is now user owned and operated, and jurisdiction over various data links is often fuzzy, it is the responsibility of the user to make at least the initial diagnosis of the problem. Otherwise, the local telephone company, the long distance carrier, and the equipment supplier will often all announce that their equipment is not at fault, leaving the user holding the bag. In fact, if the problem can be traced to the user's premises, calling the local telephone company will not only not solve the problem, but to add insult to injury, will often result in unnecessary service charges.

When data transmission fails, the failure is caused by one or more of the following components of the data communications system:

1. Local human operator
2. Local computer
3. Local communication software
4. Local cabling
5. Local interface
6. Local modem
7. Telephone loop between user and local end office
8. Toll connecting trunk to the toll office
9. Toll trunks between toll offices
10. Toll connecting trunk to the remote end office

11. Telephone loop between remote end office and user
12. Remote modem
13. Remote interface
14. Remote cabling
15. Remote communication software
16. Remote computer
17. Remote human operator

Methods for diagnosing the problem, localizing it to one of the 17 components listed above, and then fixing it, are the subject of this and of the following chapter. The methods range from sending the famous telegraph phrase exercising every uppercase letter and digit, "THE QUICK BROWN FOX JUMPS OVER LAZY DOG 0123456789," to the use of the most sophisticated test equipment. Much of the testing and diagnosis can also be done by means of test circuits built into many top-of-the-line modems and even by proper interpretation of indicator lights provided on most external modems.

In case of trouble the first checks are obvious, but are often overlooked: Are the power and all signal cables plugged in and connected, are power indicator lights on, are transmission parameters on the transmitting and receiving terminals, in particular the bit rate and parity, the same? If the answer is yes, then as the next step, one should try to interpret the trouble itself and try to find possible explanations. In fact, no fully automatic instrument or procedure will ever replace the power of logical deduction based on observation aided by instrument readings. For example, transmission errors on only a few calls, even between the same two locations, are probably caused by the switched section of the telephone network (culprits 8 through 10) over which the communications user has very little control. A lower transmission rate, use of error detecting and correcting protocols, or selection of a less noise-susceptible modem may be the best solution. On the other hand, if the trouble only occurs on calls to a certain location, then the remote end of the communication path (11—17) may have to be further investigated.

What follows in the rest of this chapter is a review of assorted instruments, indicators, and tests, which should help to localize and then hopefully fix most data communications problems not related to the transmission facility. Chapter 15 then covers diagnostic measurements of the transmission facility itself. We will start with an explanation of indicator lights found on many external modems, then continue with self-test procedures and tests of interface signals.

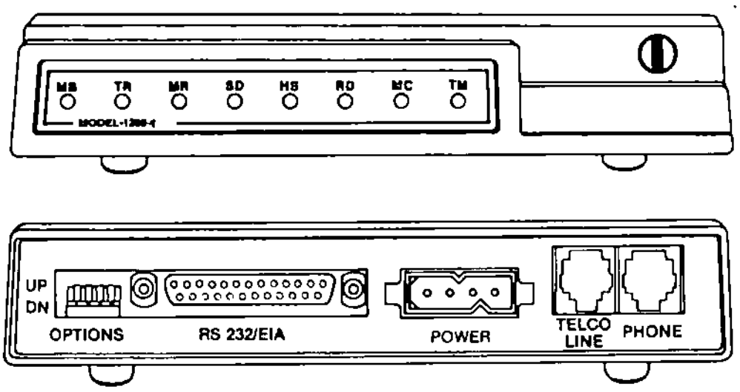

Figure 14.1 **Front and Back Panels of an External Modem**

INDICATOR LIGHTS

All external modems, except for those which are at the bottom of the manufacturer's product line, will have a row of indicator lights on the front panel as shown in Figure 14.1. Proper interpretation of these lights will help in localizing many problems one may encounter. As these indicators vary from modem to modem, your specific modem will probably just have a subset of the indicator lights mentioned here. They may also be called by slightly different but similar names. Many commercial modems will also have, in addition, or as replacement of simple indicators, LED or LCD screens which display messages and prompt for answers.

Modem Ready (MR)

This indicator lights up when power is applied to the modem. If a modem self-test feature is provided, as discussed later in this chapter, the MR indicator will flash in the self-test and in the diagnostic mode. On some modems, the test modes use a separate Test Mode (TM) rather than the MR indicator. The MR light is the first indicator to check before starting any data transmission.

Terminal Ready (TR)

The interpretation of this indicator depends on certain configuration settings of switches or jumpers. In general, the TR indicator shows the condition of the Data Terminal Ready (DTR) lead on the RS-232-C interface. The Data Terminal designation applies in this case to the computer or to the terminal, whichever is connected to the modem and which has proclaimed by setting the DTR lead ON that it is ready to start sending data. The next step in the handshake sequence between the modem and the computer is setting the Data Set Ready (DSR) lead ON by the modem to indicate that the modem is ready to receive data from the computer or from the terminal. If the DTR indicator is not ON, then most of the modem features will be disabled and the modem will not operate. If that happens, then try a different modem, or consult the specific modem manual for further details.

Send Data (SD) or Transmit Data (TD)

This indicator monitors the TD lead of the serial interface and flashes on and off as data is being transmitted from the local computer/terminal to the modem. By observing the flashing rate, one can deduce the approximate transmission speed, e.g., whether the terminal is sending at 300-bps, rather than at the 1200-bps rate. The SD/TD and the RD indicators described in the following paragraph are important diagnostic tools, since they show if any data is being exchanged between the computer and modem, if both directions of data transmission are operating properly, and if the modem operates at the correct transmission speed.

Receive Data (RD)

This indicator monitors the RD lead of the serial interface and flashes on and off as data is being received from the remote device. By observing the flashing rate, one can also deduce the approximate transmission speed of the received data, which in general should be the same as that of the transmitted data.

High Speed (HS)

On multiple-speed modems this indicator lights up when the highest speed mode is in operation. The light may be controlled by a switch setting, or it may derive its status from the status of one of the serial interface leads, which is set depending on the transmission rate of data being transmitted. On some 300/1200/2400 bps modems the light remains dark at 300 bps, turns green at 1200 bps, and turns red at 2400 bps. On 300/1200 bps modems the light is ON only at 1200 bps.

Modem Check (MC)

The MC indicator lights up when the modem is off-line. The light goes off when a connection has been established through successful handshake and the modem is ready to send or receive data. On most modems, this indicator will flash to show an error during an automatic test.

Make Busy (MB)

This indicator is usually associated with self-tests. The light will be ON during the analog loopback self-test, for example. During that test, the modem sends a test pattern through the modem's transmitter, which is then returned to the modem receiver. The Make Busy prevents the modem from transmitting the pattern on the phone line while the test is being performed.

Carrier Detect (CD)

The CD indicator lights up to indicate reception of a valid data carrier from the remote terminal. If in the middle of transmission, suddenly nothing happens, and the screen goes "dead," a look at this indicator will show whether the connection is still "alive." When dialing a bulletin board, or another computer, the CD light being ON is the first indication that a connection has been established.

Auto Answer (AA)

The AA indicator lights up when the modem is configured to automatically answer incoming calls. This is one of the indicators, which should always be checked when leaving the house. If it is ON, all incoming callers will be greeted by a happy beep, which they may not know how to interpret. On the other hand, if a data call is expected, then the indicator should be left ON. When the modem is configured to be in the Auto Answer and Originate mode and it detects an incoming call, it will turn the AA light ON during the ring. If it is configured for Auto Answer and Call mode, then the AA light will be OFF during the ring.

Off-Hook (OH)

This indicator lights up, when the modem is directly connected to the phone line. The indicator is quite useful because most data communications software packages turn off the modem speaker, when a call is in progress. Watching the OH and CD indicators helps in assuring the user that the modem is still on-line. The light goes out when the modem hangs up. Only then should one pick up the phone to establish a voice connection.

SELF-TEST FEATURES

Many modems, in particular those in the middle and upper price range, have various self-test features which should further aid in diagnosing many data transmission problems. This is particularly true for higher speed 2400-bps modems. Some of these features are similar to, or are the same as those found in test instruments costing thousands of dollars. The most common test features found in modems are the self-test, the local analog loopback test, the local digital loopback test and the remote digital loopback test. These tests will be discussed in the following paragraphs.

Self-Test

This test varies from modem to modem. It usually consists of a check that supply voltages are within acceptable range and that there is continuity between the major components. Passing this test means that the basic modem circuit is operating. The test is normally automatically activated every time, when the modem is powered up and can also be activated by the user.

Loopback Tests

These tests are based on CCITT recommendation V.54 and consist of selectively connecting back-to-back various sections of a data transmission path. The tests check the local and the remote modems, the local terminal, and the connecting telephone lines. The loopback tests are activated in Hayes compatible modems by AT&Tx commands, where x can be 0 through 8. Each test can be manually terminated by means of the AT&T0 command, or it can be timed for 1 to 255 seconds by the timer resident in the internal modem register S18. The following is a list of the common loopback-test commands according to the Hayes AT command set:

&T0 — Terminate any test in progress
&T1 — Initiate local analog loopback test
&T2 — Initiate end-to-end self-test with internal pattern generators at both ends
&T3 — Initiate local digital loopback test
&T4 — Enable response to remote digital loopback test request
&T5 — Disable response to remote digital loopback test request
&T6 — Initiate remote digital loopback test
&T7 — Initiate remote digital loopback self-test with internal pattern enerator

&T8 — Initiate local analog loopback self-test with internal pattern generator

For example, sending the command ATS18=15&T8 to the modem will start the local analog loopback self-test with the internal pattern generator (typically an alternating string of 1's and 0's) and will finish the test after 15 seconds. This and other tests return result codes, "000" followed by "OK" if the test was passed successfully, or a three-digit number showing the number of errors followed by "OK." We will now describe the self-tests in order in which they become increasingly comprehensive.

Local Analog Loopback Test (&T1)

This is the first test to try. The test configuration is shown in Figure 14.2. The test checks the local terminal/computer and the local modem. The modem "loops back" the data to the screen of the local terminal. To start the test, disconnect the phone line and type AT&T1 <CR> while in local command mode. A panel test indicator light, if provided, should now be ON and the modem should change to on-line mode. Type "THE QUICK BROWN FOX JUMPS OVER LAZY DOG" and see whether the message appears correctly on the screen. To end the test, type "+++" to put the modem back into local command mode, upon which the modem should respond "OK." Then type AT&T0 <CR> to end the test.

If the typed text does not appear correctly on the screen, or not at all, first check all connections and the DIP switch/jumper settings. In particular, the Echo ON/OFF switch should be in the position which echoes to the terminal in the command mode. Next, check the cable between the serial jacks on the terminal and the modem. The pin configuration may be incorrect, the terminal may be configured as DCE instead of DTE, and pins 2 and 3 in the cable may be reversed (see description of the "null" modem in Chapter 6). Check also that the Data Terminal Ready (DTR) lead in the serial interface is ON (the appropriate indicator light should light up). If the terminal/computer does not provide the DTR signal to the modem, which may be the case, then there should be a switch or a jumper on the modem to force the DTR lead to the ON mode. As a last resort, if the problem of not being able to see one's own typing on the terminal screen still persists, substitute another modem.

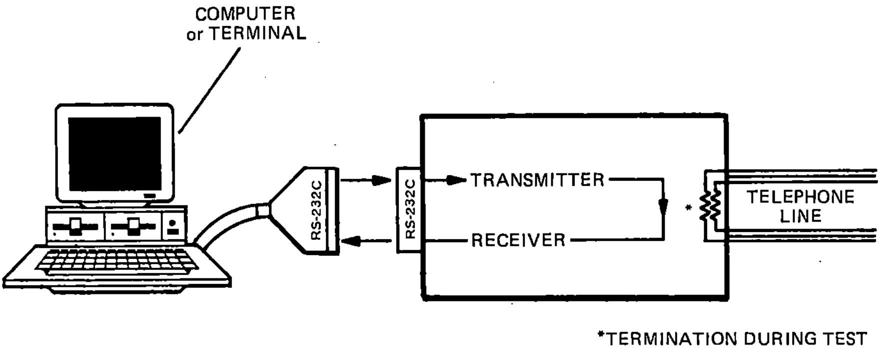

Figure 14.2 Local Analog Loopback Test

Local Analog Loopback Self-Test (&T8)

This test checks the ability of the local modem to send and receive data and should be performed if the previous (&T1) test failed. Figure 14.3 shows the test configuration. The internal test generator sends a test pattern; the internal counter counts errors, if any, and sends the count to the terminal. The test can be initiated in the command mode, e.g., by the command ATS18=15&T8 <CR>. After 15 seconds the message

000
OK

should appear on the screen to indicate no errors, or

xxx
OK

to indicate xxx errors. Failure of this test usually points to a defective modem.

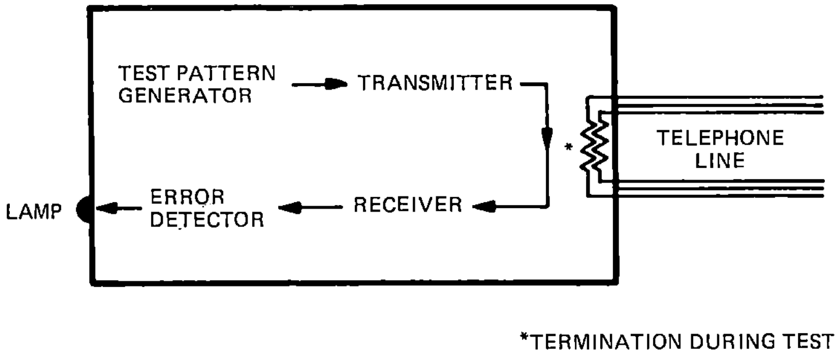

Figure 14.3 **Local Analog Loophole Self-Test With pattern Generator**

Remote Digital Loopback Test (&T6)

This test is an extension of the Local Analog Loopback test but it also includes the telephone transmission facility and the remote modem. The test configuration is shown in Figure 14.4. The test is initiated by first establishing a connection to the remote modem, then going into the command mode by typing the escape sequence "+++", and then typing the AT&T6 command. Typing "THE QUICK BROWN FOX ... " should result in the same sentence appearing on the terminal screen. Problems showing up during this test, which did not show up in the previous tests, are most likely caused by either the telephone line or by the remote modem.

Remote Digital Loopback Self-Test (&T7)

This test is similar to the Remote Digital Loopback test except that it uses the internal test pattern generator instead of the terminal. The test configuration is shown in Figure 14.5. By excluding the local terminal from the overall test, it focuses more on problems related to the telephone line or to the remote modem.

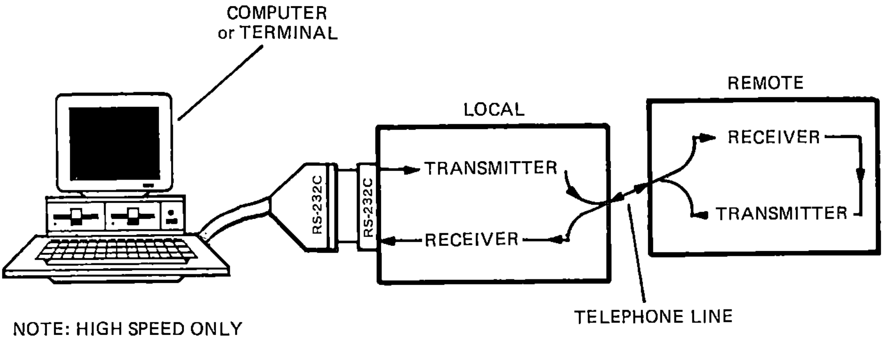

Figure 14.4 **Remote Digital Loopback Test**

Local Digital Loopback Test (&T3)

This test is initiated by the remote terminal or by the remote modem. The test may require an additional telephone voice line to be set up. The test configuration is shown in Figure 14.6. The local modem loops back all data received from the remote modem. The remote modem can then compare the

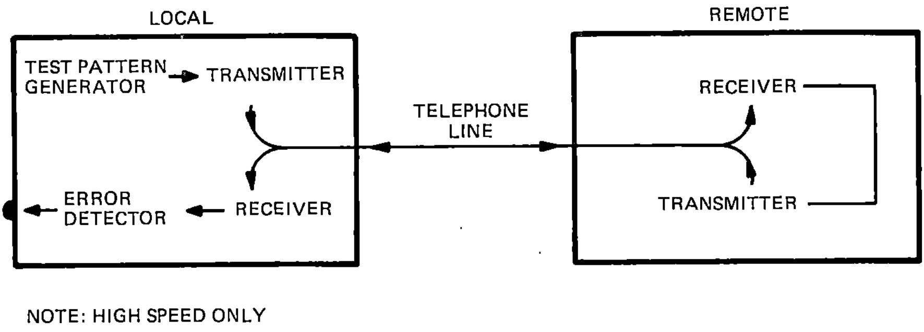

Figure 14.5 **Remote Digital Loopback Self-Test With Pattern Generator**

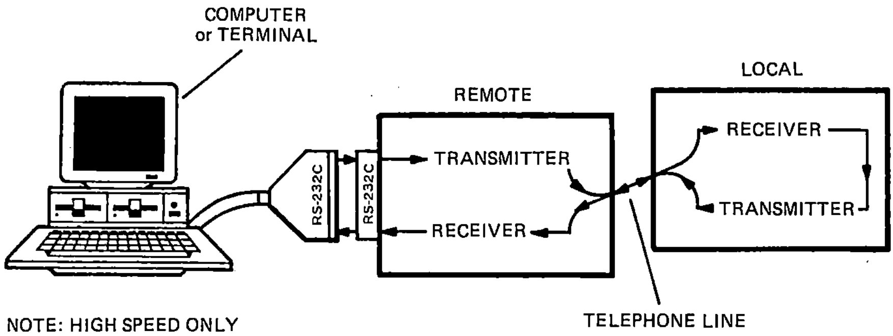

Figure 14.6 **Local Digital Loopback Test**

data sent with the data received. This test is used primarily to allow a remote modem not equipped with a digital loopback to perform such a test. The test is started from the local modem by first establishing a connection, going into the command mode by typing "+++", then typing the command AT&T3. The remote terminal can now start sending "THE QUICK BROWN FOX .... " and look for the correct sequence appearing on the remote terminal. The test is concluded by typing AT&T0 <CR> at the local terminal.

End-to-End Self-Test (&T2)

This test requires coordination between the local and the remote terminals, since the remote modem has to be instructed by means of the same AT&T2 command to send a test pattern and check for errors in the test pattern received from the local modem. As shown in Figure 14.7, both modems are sending test patterns, which are checked by their counterparts. Of course this test assumes that both the local and the remote modems have the capability

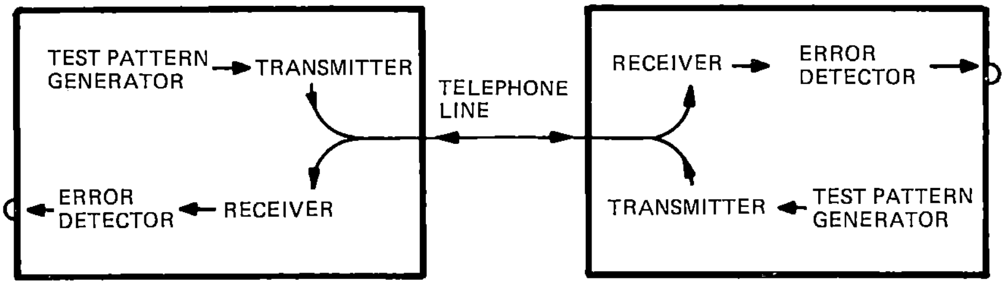

Figure 14.7 **End-to-End Loopback Self-Test With Pattern Generator**

for sending such a pattern. This test is passed if both modems report no errors.

MODEM NOISE SENSITIVITY TESTING

If the initial tests point to the modem as the probable cause of data errors, it may be advisable to test the modem by itself without any additional data channel components. The basic test which measures the sensitivity of the modem to the signal-to-noise (*S/N*) ratio on the transmission facility, is the same kind of test as the one performed in modem surveys. Such surveys, which are periodically conducted by independent organizations, such as the PC Magazine, compare performance of modems made by various manufacturers. The main problem in evaluating the noise sensitivity test conducted on a single modem is its interpretation. The test can only be compared to a similar test performed earlier on the same modem or performed on the same kind of modem known to be in working condition. The reason is that modem manufacturers very seldom provide *S/N* sensitivity in their specification sheets.

The basic layout of the modem sensitivity test is shown in Figure 14.8. The layout simulates a realistic data connection, but the variable components, such as line noise and distortion, are replaced by commercially available reproducible line simulators and impairment generators. A line simulator introduces attenuation and delay distortion corresponding to an average switched

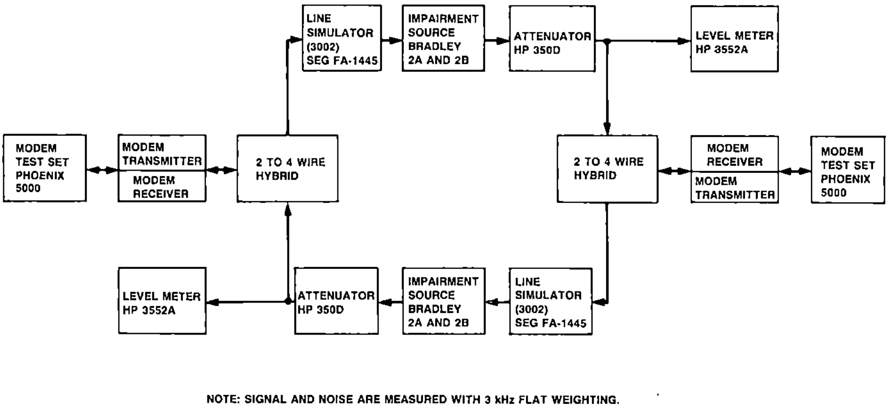

Figure 14.8 **Modem Noise Sensitivity Test Set-Up**

telephone line; an impairment generator introduces steady and impulse noise. The modem test sets shown at both ends of the connection exercise all modem functions starting with the handshake protocols and continue with transmission of pseudorandom sequences of data. The final result recorded by the modem test set is the bit error rate for a given *S/N* ratio adjusted with the impairment generator. Signal and noise levels are monitored with the level meters shown in the same figure.

TESTS OF THE RS-232-C INTERFACE SIGNALS

The modem indicator lights, though helpful, are not provided on built-in modems and cover only a few selected signals out of the total of up to 25 leads constituting the RS-232-C interface. To be able to diagnose modem related problems in the serial interface, it may therefore be necessary to acquire a so-called break-out box. A break-out box is one of the basic tools for testing the RS-232-C interface between the computer and the modem and to help in localizing an interface related problem. A break-out box has built-in male and female DB-25 jacks, into which serial cables can be inserted. Each of the 25 leads can now be patched through, opened up, or bridged for observation. Many break-out boxes also feature a row of LED indicators, so that the status of any lead can be continuously monitored. On data leads (#2 and #3) there will frequently be a green and a red LED or one LED which can turn either red or green, to indicate lead polarity. When the polarity changes, as during transmission of data, then the LED will flash and turn orange.

A break-out box is also equipped with a row of small jacks associated with each of the 25 leads. By means of jumpers plugged into those jacks, one can reconfigure a serial cable or in a few minutes one can make an experimental cable with any nonstandard pin arrangement. To calm one's nerves, one should remember that the RS-232-C standard guarantees that no damage will result from an incorrect connection of leads in the serial cable. The complexity of break-out boxes ranges from a simple home-brewed device through a standard, commercially available "passive" break-out box, to a data analyzer storing received and transmitted data in memory or on disk and filtering the data in search of certain specific patterns. There are even break-out box software substitutes, programs which simulate some of the functions of the device and display on a computer screen the status of certain leads. What follows is a short description of the three levels of break-out box sophistication.

Simple, Self-built Break-out Box

Figure 14.9 shows a home-brewed break-out box, which helped the author in solving many serial interfacing problems. The circuit uses a red and a green LED to distinguish between the positive and negative signal polarities. Touching the alligator clip to control leads, one at a time, will indicate their status. The ON status, which is a positive voltage, should turn the green LED on; the OFF status which is a negative voltage, should turn the red LED on. Similarly, attaching the alligator clip to lead #2 (Transmitted Data) or to lead #3 (Received Data) should alternately flash both LEDs when data is being received or transmitted. By rearranging the jumper wires, the break-out box can also be made into a "null" modem or a "cheater" cord as discussed in Chapters 6 and 7.

Commercial Type Break-out Box

Figure 14.10 shows a commercial version of a break-out box. A big advantage of this type of device, as compared to the previous implementation, is that the status of several leads can be observed at once. Also, each of the

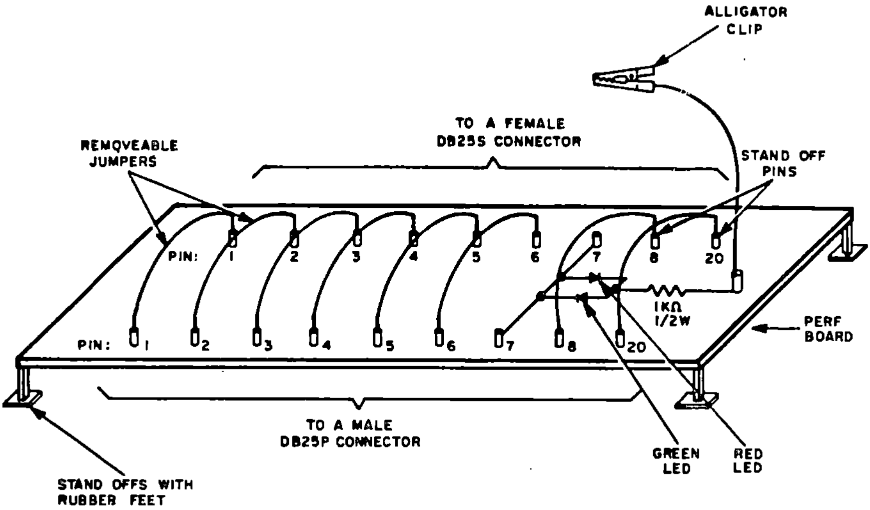

Figure 14.9 **Break-Out Box, Home-brewed Version**

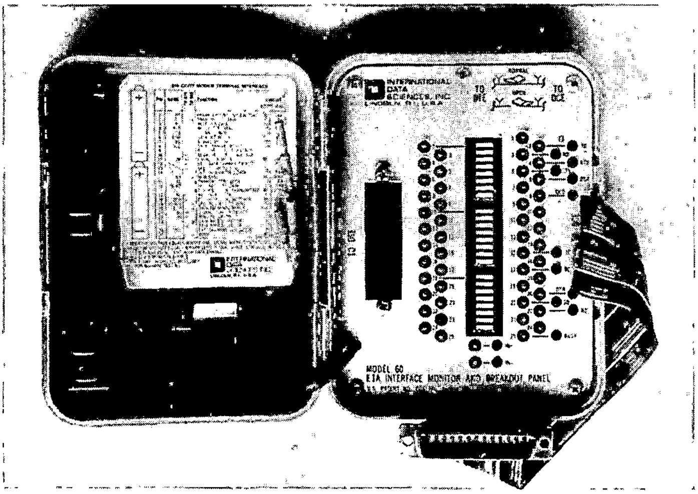

Figure 14.10 **Break-Out Box, Commercial Version**

25 leads can be patched through or can be opened up by means of miniature DIP switches. Short jumpers can be plugged into the panel to bridge a scope or a voltmeter on any of the leads, or the jumpers can be used for cross-connecting any of the leads. A battery is often included in the box, so that individual leads can also be forced to the ON or OFF state. In addition, LED indicators continuously monitor status of control and data leads #2 (TD), #3 (RD), #4 (RTS), #5 (CTS), #6 (DSR), #8 (CD), and #20 (DTR). A high impedance transistorized circuit powered by a built-in battery minimizes the load on the monitored leads, while still turning the LEDs at full brightness.

Observing the important indicators associated with leads #2 through #6, #8, and #20 should show the following results:

Condition A: Computer not powered, or computer powered, but communications software not loaded — all indicators should be dark.

Condition B: Communications program loaded, connection not yet established — the RTS, DSR, and DTR lights should now be on. At this point, one can press keys on the terminal and the TD light should blink.

Condition C: Connection to the remote terminal established — the RTS, CTS, DSR, CD and DTR lights should be ON permanently, the RD light should blink on incoming messages, and the TD light should blink on outgoing messages.

When the observed indicators do not agree with condition A, B, or C, then one can make the initial diagnosis of the serial interface problem by consulting Table 6.1, which shows the sequence of events and signals occurring on the serial port between the computer and the modem. The first event taking place is the DTR, Data Terminal Ready, lead going high. If the DTR is not ON, then the problem is on the computer side. When DTR is ON and everything is working properly, then the next signal to go high is DSR, Data Set Ready. Again, the DSR light being OFF may indicate a defective modem or a broken lead. The next lead to go high is RTS, the Ready to Send lead from the computer. At this point, the connection should be established and the remote terminal should start sending a carrier signal. The successful reception of the carrier should turn the CD light to ON. If it is not lit, it may indicate that the connection was not established or that the local or remote modems are defective.

After successfully establishing a connection with the remote terminal, the RTS, CTS, DSR, CD, and DTR lights should all be ON permanently, and the RD and TD lights should blink on incoming and outgoing messages, respectively. The blinking rate indicates the transmission speed. If the lights are blinking but nothing appears on the terminal screen, then the fault probably lies in the computer and not in the modem or the communication path.

A break-out box belongs in any organization that is involved in transfer of data so as to perform at least preliminary checks or diagnosis of a data transmission problem. It requires a certain amount of understanding and ingenuity for interpretation of results, but considering its low cost, it is an excellent investment.

Protocol Analyzer with a Break-out Box

A considerably more flexible, but also more expensive ($5,000—$10,000) test option is a protocol analyzer, which includes a break-out box. In fact, it could be called the ultimate break-out box. A protocol analyzer not only supervises all serial interface leads, but it also captures their status over a period of time and analyzes the data according to any given criteria. Some of this analysis occurs on-line by means of data "filters," by selecting only data fitting certain requirements, e.g., by looking only at the first 1024 bits following a certain flag pattern. The data is captured into the analyzer's memory and is then saved on a floppy or hard disk, where it can be analyzed off-line. Use of data filters is the only way to diagnose intermittent problems, since continuous recording of data over an extended period of time wouuld overflow any storage medium and mask the problem.

A good example of such an instrument is the Hewlett Packard HP4952A protocol analyzer. This portable instrument, when attached to a serial interface, will automatically determine all transmission parameters, such as transmission speed, number of bits or parity, and then analyze the data. Figure 14.11 shows the decision tree followed by the instrument to decide, how to interpret data captured at the serial interface. Operational options are displayed in a sequence of menus with simultaneous assignment of menu selections to the keyboard "soft" keys. The instrument will perform Bit Error Rate Testing, search for and display any given data pattern, show a side-by-side display of signals on various leads, and permanently store the data captured in its RAM capture buffer of 750 kbytes on a built-in floppy disk. The HP4952A protocol analyzer supports transmission rates between 50 bps and 64,000 bps. The data can be transmitted in ASCII, EBCDIC, Baudot, the airline reservation code IPARS, and in several other alphabets. Whatever the alphabet, it will be properly decoded by the instrument and displayed on the screen. The instrument supports several serial interfaces with different optional plug-in break-out boxes

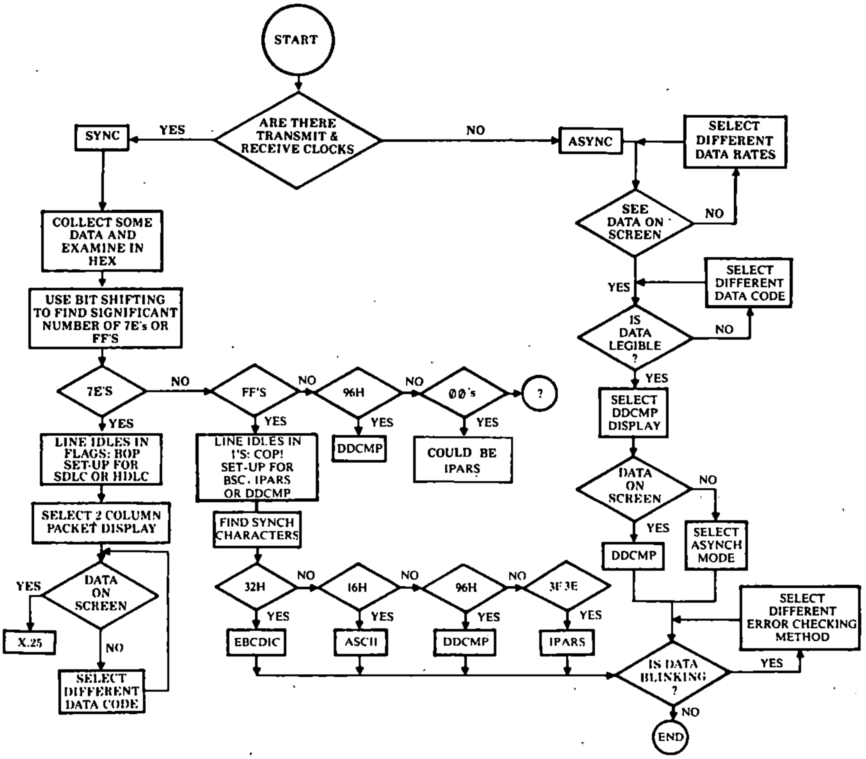

Figure 14.11 **Decision Tree of a Protocol Analyzer**

applicable to each interface. The interfaces supported by the manufacturer are RS-232-C/V.24, RS-449, RS-422-A, RS-423-A, and V.35.

The HP4952A protocol analyzer can be used in either the "immediate" mode, where all selections are made while the interface is being tested, or it can be used in the programmed mode. A program which controls all instrument settings, filters, and performs a preliminary analysis, can be written in advance and stored on the internal floppy. It can then be recalled and the instrument will start executing it when requested. This approach provides self-documenting results, which can be easily repeated. The following example shows a short program, written in a procedural language supplied with the analyzer, to time the delay between the time of the RTS lead being turned ON and the CTS lead being turned ON and display all control signals during that part of the handshake sequence.

```
BLOCK 1:
    START DISPLAY
    WHEN LEAD RTS GOES ON THEN GO TO BLOCK 2
BLOCK 2:
    BEEP
    AND THEN
    HIGHLIGHT
    AND THEN
    START TIMER 1
    WHEN LEAD CTS GOES ON THEN GOTO BLOCK 3
BLOCK 3:
    BEEP
    AND THEN
    HIGHLIGHT
    AND THEN
    STOP TIMER 1
    AND THEN
    STOP TEST
```

A protocol analyzer, as seen from this short description, is an instrument which belongs in any large organization involved in data transmission. Use of the instrument assumes a certain amount of training, but it will pinpoint hard-to-find, often intermittent problems, which could not be found by any other method.

15. Transmission Facility Testing

The typical conclusion of tests discussed in the previous chapter would be that there is a problem somewhere in the data path involving the terminal, modem, or the transmission facility. If all tests point to the transmission facility, that being a telephone line or a leased or privately owned circuit, then the transmission parameters of that facility should be tested. However, there is always the question as to what one can do with the results, in particular, if they put the blame for the poor data transmission on the switched telephone circuit. The telephone company does not guarantee any transmission parameters on such circuits. The only guarantee is that both parties in a telephone conversation can understand each other, and the only recourse is to ask for dropping of charges for a specific nonsatisfactory call. The only time that a privately conducted facility transmission test will help in convincing the common carrier to alleviate the situation is on a leased line circuit, where the telephone company actually guarantees specific requirements referring to attenuation and delay distortion, harmonic distortion, and noise, as discussed in Chapter 2.

The transmission parameters which affect data transmission can be measured individually with test instruments called Transmission Measuring Sets, which are made by all major instrument manufacturers. They come in a wide price range from a few hundred to several thousand dollars and with a large array of features. The tests may have to be done manually or automatically, with or without graphic output. Some instruments perform a single test, others perform several tests. Digital testers measure modem-channel-modem efficiency by determining the Bit Error Rate and the Block Error Rate. Analog testers measure various transmission parameters responsible for distortion of data. The interrelationship of these measurements is sometimes difficult to grasp, e.g., the relation between the amplitude distortion, the delay distortion, and the Bit Error Rate. In general, although such relations exist, they cannot be expressed quantitatively or explicitly. One just knows from the modem specifications that a certain combination of these parameters will provide satisfactory transmission, and improvement of any parameter by itself will result in additional improvement. In case of trouble, combined digital and analog testing should quickly pinpoint the problem by showing which transmission parameters meet or do not meet modem specifications.

ATTENUATION DISTORTION MEASUREMENTS

An attenuation tester is the most basic type of transmission measuring instrument. It consists of a variable frequency generator in the transmitting section and of a frequency selective or a "flat" voltmeter in the receiving section. The generator should cover frequencies of interest, typically 100 Hz to 10000 Hz; the output impedance should be selectable to fit typical transmission lines, namely, 150, 600, and 900 Ohms. The input impedance should be selectable in the same steps, or High (over 10 kOhms) for bridging. The output voltage should be stable within 0.1 dB over the frequency range and should be calibrated in dBm (decibels above 1 mW). Using Ohm's Law one can easily translate dBm, the units of electrical power, at a given impedance level into Volts.

Formula 15.1 **Units of Power**

Review of Units of Power

$$dB = 10\ LOG\ \frac{P2}{P1}$$

dB	Power Ratio
0	1.00
1	1.26
3	2.00
6	3.98
10	10.00
20	100.00

Units of Power

dB = A unit of relative measurement
dBm = A unit of absolute measurement
0 dBm = 1 milliwatt
dBrn = A unit of absolute measurement
0 dBrn = 1 picowatt = –90 dBm

Ohm's Law

$V = I \times R$
$P = V \times I = V^2/R$
$V = \sqrt{P \times R}$
e.g., Power = 0 dBm = 0.001 W
R = 600
$V = \sqrt{0.001 \times 600} = 0.775\ V$

where V = voltage, Volt
where I = current, Ampere
where R = resistance, Ohm
where P = power, Watt

Entering values in the above formulas shows that, e.g., a 0-dBm signal at 600 Ohms will result in a voltage of 0.775 V.

The receiving section of the attenuation tester should be a voltmeter with a frequency selectable filter, which can be adjusted to the received frequency. The reading scale should be in dBm and in Volts and the input impedance should be selectable to the same values as on the frequency generator.

A test is performed by either looping the transmission facility or placing another attended instrument at the other end of the transmission facility. If a one-way test is made, there should be voice communication between operators at both ends to coordinate their activities. A plot of measured attenuation at frequencies across the voice-band should give a good indication of the "health" of the circuit. Deviation from a flat line is called attenuation distortion. Comparison with the leased line characteristics shown in Chapter 2 will show any abnormalities.

DELAY DISTORTION MEASUREMENTS

Measurements of delay distortion are particularly important for data transmission. From the point of view of the operator, the delay distortion measuring set is somewhat similar to an attenuation tester. It has a variable frequency generator at the transmitting end, and it allows one to select input and output impedances and to select transmitting levels in dBm. The only visible difference to the user is that at the receiving end there is also a scale calibrated in microseconds. As shown in Figure 15.1, the transmitting section of a delay distortion measuring set sends a modulated wave, which is either looped back at the far end and returned and demodulated, or it is measured at the far end by another delay distortion measuring set. The zero crossings of the reference and the received signal after demodulation are then compared. The time difference will vary as the carrier frequency of the transmitted signal is changed. The time difference of the zero crossings is then plotted as function of carrier frequency and corresponds to the relative delay at those frequencies. If the plot is flat, there is no delay distortion. A typical curve of delay distortion versus frequency of a switched voice telephone channel is shown in Figure 15.2. Its minimum is in the middle of the voice-band between 1800 and 2000 Hz and it rises at low and high frequencies to several milliseconds.

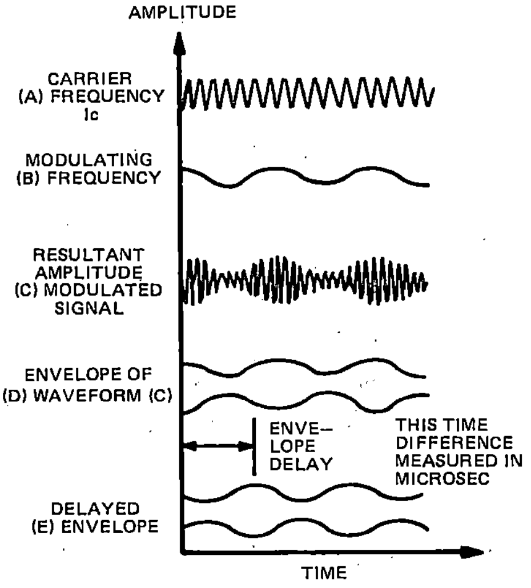

ENVELOPE/GROUP DELAY:

* BELL: REQUIRES 4-WIRE LINE
REQUIRES ONE OR 2 INSTRUMENTS
USES EITHER RETURN OR FORWARD REFERENCE

*CCITT: REQUIRES 2-WIRE LINE
REQUIRES 2 INSTRUMENTS
IS AN END-TO-END MEASUREMENT

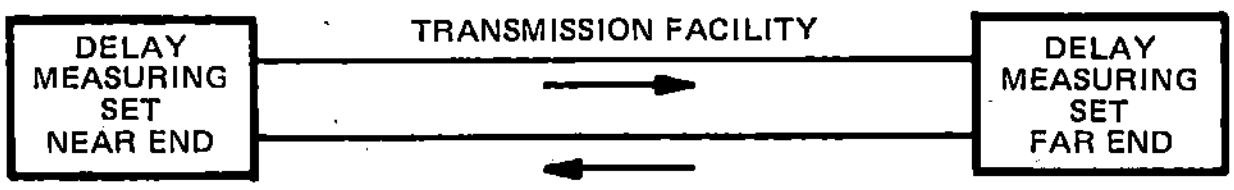

Figure 15.1 **Delay Distortion Measuring Set**

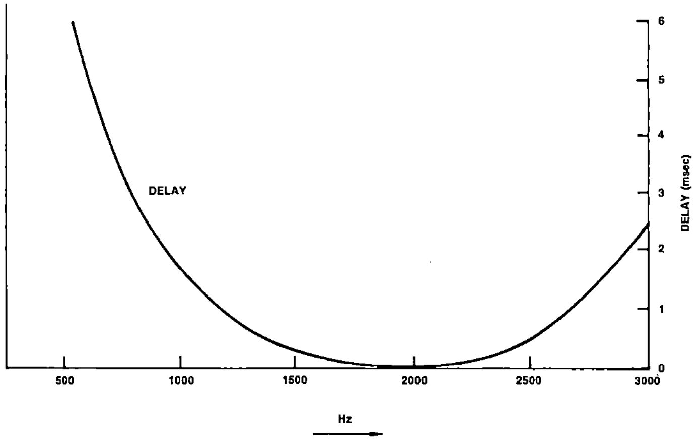

Figure 15.2 **Delay Distortion Versus Frequency**

NOISE MEASUREMENTS

There are two kinds of noise which affect data transmission, the steady noise and the impulse noise. The steady noise is determined by the characteristics of the transmitting and receiving equipment and by the modulation method. One of its components is the thermal noise associated with each resistor which is caused by the random movement of electrons. Steady noise can also be caused by interference from power lines. In general, the data communications user has no control over the steady noise, which ultimately determines the maximum data transmission speed.

The second type of noise is impulse noise, which consists of short bursts of noise, typically 10—15 dB above the floor of the steady noise. The impulse noise is caused by defective circuits, by crosstalk from other channels, and by nonlinearities in the modulation process or by atmospheric interference. The data transmission can live with the steady noise, since the design of transmitting and receiving modems takes this noise into consideration. However, impulse noise, being much higher than the steady noise, destroys the transmitted data during its brief occurrences. The solution to impulse noise is either improvement to the circuit or error detection and correction via block retransmission.

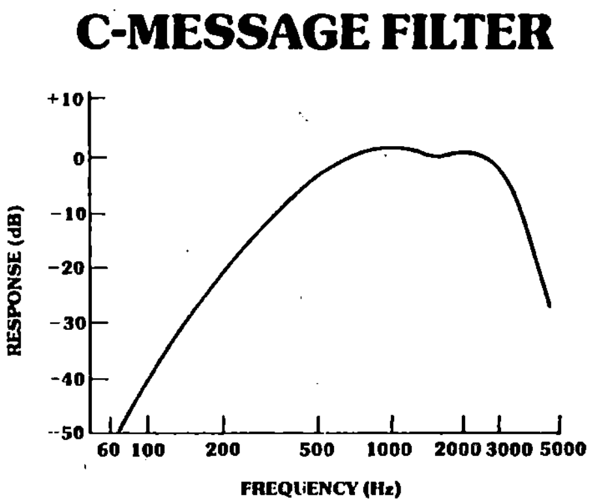

Figure 15.3 **C-Weighting For Noise Measurements**

The steady noise is measured with a voltmeter bridged on the line. The voltmeter should have flat frequency response along the voice-band. Some noise meters use the so-called C-weighting, shown in Figure 15.3, to measure noise on voice circuits. This weighting mimics the response of the human ear and should not be used on data circuits. Many telephone circuits include so-called companders and expanders. These circuits improve voice transmission by lowering circuit gain and thus the apparent noise during quiet intervals. The popular Dolby circuit used for many high-fidelity recordings follows the same principle. Therefore, to obtain a true noise reading the circuit should carry a signal of the same power as the expected data signal. The way to achieve this is to send a steady signal at, e.g., 1000 Hz over the transmission facility and filter it out with a sharp frequency discrimination filter at the receiving end.

The impulse noise is measured with a voltmeter attached to a counter over a certain time interval, typically 15—30 minutes. A counter counts each noise burst exceeding a specified level in dBm. In general, a row of counters preset to different noise levels, e.g., –15 dBm, –10 dBm, and –5 dBm are started at the same time. Over a period of, e.g., 30 minutes the –15-dBm counter may measure 35 counts, the –10-Bm counter may measure 10 counts, and the –5-dBm counter may measure 3 counts. From this distribution, one can then derive the expected bit error count. If it is found that the expected error count due to the impulse noise is much lower than the actual error count, then there has to be some other cause of errors.

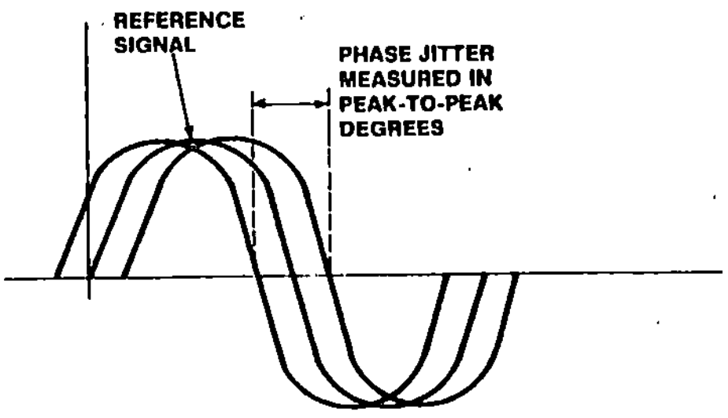

Figure 15.4 **Phase Jitter and How It Affects a Data Signal**

PHASE JITTER MEASUREMENTS

Phase jitter, as shown in Figure 15.4, affects bit error rates particularly in modems using differential phase modulation. Because bit values are determined by the relative phase of successive signal elements, phase jitter can affect signal recognition. This impairment is caused by "fading" of microwave signals and by changes in carrier frequencies in the common carrier multiplex terminals. Phase jitter can also be caused by defective modems. Phase jitter is measured by comparing the received signal with a steady signal generated by a local quartz-controlled clock. Phase difference between the received signal and the local signal is translated into voltage, which is then measured.

SPECIALIZED DATA TRANSMISSION IMPAIRMENT TESTERS

In addition to measurements of the basic transmission parameters such as attenuation and delay distortion, phase jitter and noise, there are instruments which make a single measurement related to data transmission quality. An instrument which was quite popular a number of years ago and can still be found in some telephone companies is the so-called Peak-to-Average Ratio or PAR meter.

The PAR signal is a complex waveform consisting of 16 harmonically unrelated sine waves at different amplitudes. The power spectrum of the signal is shown in Figure 15.5 and the periodic PAR signal as a function of time is shown in Figure 15.6. The receiver portion of the instrument computes the ratio of the received peak energy to average energy. This ratio is related to both attenuation and delay distortion and gives an indication of the circuit quality. The simple measurement is particularly useful for comparisons between similar circuits. The measured PAR value between 0 and 100 is a quick benchmark reading. The reading is most sensitive to envelope delay, noise, and attenuation distortion, but will not indicate which particular parameter is at fault. A PAR reading, which differs by at least 4 units from a previous reading, indicates some problem on the transmission line and should be followed by more detailed testing. This single reading of the PAR meter can thus detect a problem before it becomes serious.

TRANSMISSION IMPAIRMENT MEASURING SETS

The majority of the above described analog tests can frequently be performed with a single instrument. The so-called Transmission Measuring Sets measure attenuation and delay distortion, phase jitter, and noise. Many of the tests are performed automatically with results plotted, recorded, or printed. An example of such an instrument is the Hewlett Packard HP 4947A Transmission Impairment Measuring Set. The instrument measures attenuation and delay distortion, flat and C-message circuit noise, impulse noise, Peak-to-Average Ratio, gain and phase hits, phase jitter, and intermodulation distortion. Plots are generated on an attached standard printer showing distortion versus frequency plots.

Other transmission test sets like the HP 4948A can monitor the circuit while data is being transmitted. The HP 4948A test set is bridged on a two-wire data circuit and measures various transmission parameters while exchanging data with the remote modem. Thanks to the high-impedance input of the instrument, testing can continue without interrupting normal operation. The instrument can also simulate specific modems and measure modem signals. In this mode, the instrument will measure the amplitude and frequency of the modem output in dBm and Hz, the amplitude modulation and jitter in percent and phase, and phase jitter in degrees. The cost of this type of instruments is in the range of $5000 to $10,000.

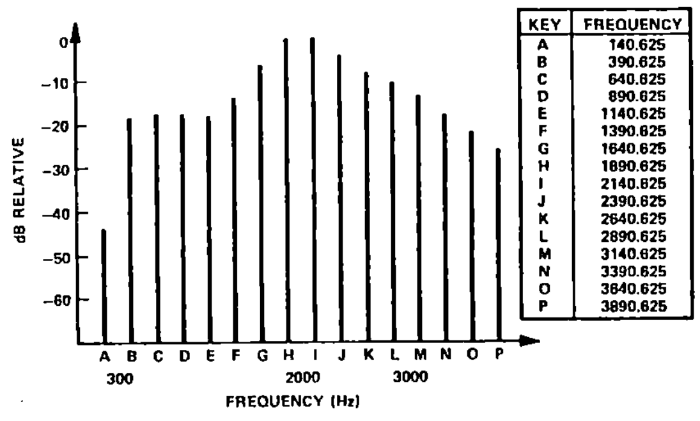

Figure 15.5 **PAR Power Spectrum**

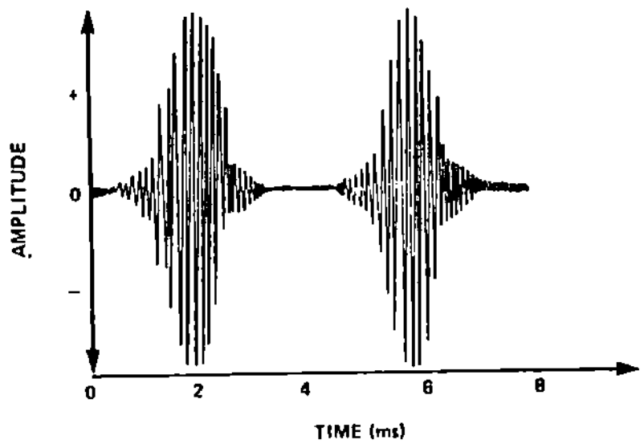

Figure 15.6 **PAR Signal**

BIT ERROR RATE TEST SETS

A Bit Error Rate Test set (BERT) sends a pseudorandom sequence of bits over a given period of time to the remote terminal. The data is then looped back and errors are counted. This test is particularly useful if the modem does not have a built-in error tester, as some do. Although there are some stand-alone BERT instruments on the market, the BERT function is usually included in most protocol analyzers, as in the previously mentioned HP4952A instrument.

This short review of test methods and test instruments should help in locating most data transmission problems. Understanding what went wrong and fixing it gives the user a feeling that he or she, and not a bunch of electronic circuits, is in control.

Conclusion: What The Future Will Bring

One hardly needs a crystal ball to anticipate many future developments in data transmission in general, and modem technology in particular. All one has to do is to extrapolate current trends toward lower prices, higher speeds, and further miniaturization. It is quite certain that the future generation of PCs will have built-in modems as just another standard interface. This trend was started in 1983 with the TANDY Model 100 portable and its built-in 300-bps modem. To help in component miniaturization, the current two- and three-chip modem sets will certainly shrink into single-chip modems. The difficulty that the digital section of a modem can be better implemented by the NMOS fabrication technology, while the analog section is easier to make using CMOS technology, will certainly be overcome.

As far as transmission speed is concerned, a few years ago the 300-bps modem was prevalent for data transmission over the Public Telephone Network. By 1987 the 1200-bps full-duplex modem became the prevalent standard with 2400-bps V.22 bis modem becoming more and more popular. The 9600-bps V.32 full-duplex modem will certainly be the prevalent standard by the year 1992 or even sooner. Improvements in long haul telephone circuits due to deregulation may result in wholesale replacement of analog telephone trunks by digital trunks. Should a strong demand for end-to-end digital connections develop, then the need for modems as we know them today would disappear and they would be replaced by other data communications devices, such as Data Service Units, Data Channel Units, and multiplexers. A multiplexer could combine data streams originated by computers, telephones, and assorted entertainment systems and send them over a fiber optics link to their proper destinations.

On a more prosaic tone, improvements in the local telephone offices, namely, replacement of compromise impedance matching circuits terminating each local loop, by active adaptive circuits, would provide a higher return loss on each line. This would result in much better echo performance and a lower circuit loss. Combined with use of low-noise long-haul facilities made of glass fiber there would be a dramatic improvement in the signal-to-noise ratios on both voice and data circuits. Higher transmission speeds and higher throughput due to fewer errors would then be possible.

Appendices

Glossary

The following terms are related to data communications in general and to modems in particular:

ACK, Acknowledgment - A communication control character transmitted by a receiver indicating that the message was received correctly.

Acoustic Coupler - A device converting electrical to audio signals and vice versa, allowing the connection of a modem to the Public Telephone Network by means of any telephone headset.

ASCII - The American Standard Code for Information Exchange is an 8-bit code accepted as a data communications standard in North America to achieve compatibility between data services. ASCII uses 7 bits for information and the 8th bit for parity.

Asynchronous Transmission - Transmission in which the time intervals between transmitted characters may be of unequal length. Transmission is controlled by the start and stop bits at the beginning and end of each character. Also referred to as start-stop transmission.

Attenuation - Decrease in the signal amplitude. If the decrease is a function of frequency than the attenuation relative to attenuation at 1000 Hz is called attenuation distortion.

Bandwidth - Range of frequencies which are subject to attenuation of typically less than 3 dB.

Baud - A unit of modulation rate. Equal to transmission speed divided by the number of bits per signal element. Frequently confused with bits per second (bps).

BCC - Block Check Character, is used for error checking and is the result of a transmission verification algorithm accumulated over a transmission block during synchronous transmission of data.

BERT - Bit error rate test set. An instrument used for checking quality of data transmission.

Bit - A binary digit, can be 0 or 1, the smallest unit of information.

Bit Rate - Unit of transmission speed in bits per second (bps).

Byte - A sequence of 8 bits, usually corresponding to a character.

Carrier - A high-frequency signal modulated by the data signal to carry it over telephone network or other transmission facilities.

CCITT - The International Telegraph and Telephone Consultative Committee, the international organization concerned with proposing standards related to telecommunication.

Command File - User-written program required by the communications software to make a data phone call. Contains parameters such as the phone number, transmission speed, number of data/stop bits, and parity.

Common Carrier - A public owner of transmission facilities which has the obligation to provide such facilities to the public on demand.

Conditioning - Special treatment of transmission facilities to reduce their attenuation and delay distortion.

CRC - Cyclic Redundancy Check, a checking method used to detect errors, in which the numeric binary value of a block of data is divided by a constant divisor. The quotient is discarded and the remainder serves as check sequence.

C-weighting - Frequency attenuation shaping of certain test instruments to simulate a frequency response of the human ear to various components of the audio spectrum.

Dataphone - A trademark of AT&T applied to various modems.

dB - Decibel - logarithmic ratio. Generally applied to powers, voltages or currents.

dBm - Decibel above 1 mW - unit of electrical power.

DCE - Data Communications Equipment, equipment which provides all functions required to establish, maintain and terminate a connection. It performs signal conversion and coding between the data terminal equipment and the common carrier's entry point. Typically a data set or a modem.

Delay Distortion - Characteristic of the transmission medium, affects the transmission speed of frequency components of a data signal. Results in signal distortion.

Dibit - A sequence of two bits associated with one signal element.

Differential Phase Shift Keying (DPSK) - Modulation method used by the Bell 212A modem based on detection of successive relative phase changes of the data signal.

DTE - Data Terminal Equipment, the box that DCE connects to. The term usually refers to a computer or a data terminal. Many devices, such as printers, are configured alternately as DTEs or DCEs.

EBCDIC - Extended Binary Coded Decimal Interchange Code, an 8-bit code used mostly by IBM. Enables representation of graphics and control code characters.

Echo - Data or voice reflected back to the transmitter by impedance mismatches along the transmission path.

EIA - Electronic Industries Association - a group of US manufacturers recognized as the standards writing agency for communications equipment, see also RS-232-C.

Emulation - Use of one system to imitate all functions of another system. The emulating system will operate under control of any software written for the emulated system.

Error Correcting System - A system employing error detection and correction. Correction is usually accomplished by retransmission of blocks of data.

Equalizer - Device to compensate for distortion introduced by transmission facilities

Facsimile - Transmission of pictures, maps, diagrams etc. The image is scanned on the transmitter, reconstructed at the receiving station and duplicated on paper or film. Also called FAX.

Frame - Transmission data segment. In synchronous protocols data is formatted in blocks or frames for transmission. Each frame consists of a start flag followed by an address field, control field, data field, frame check sequence and a stop flag.

Frequency Shift Keying (FSK) - Method of modulation, where a binary "0" generates one frequency and a binary "1" generates another frequency.

Full Duplex - A communication system or equipment capable of simultaneous transmission in both direction.

Half Duplex - A circuit which provides transmission in one direction at a time.

Handshake - Exchange of predetermined signals occurring when the data connection is first established.

HDLC - High Level Data Link Control. A link level bit oriented protocol used in synchronous transmission.

Hertz (Hz) - Unit of frequency, equal to cycles per second.

Hybrid Transformer - A special kind of transformer used to wire transmission systems to separate the two directions of transmission.

Interface - A shared boundary between two communications devices, e.g. a computer, a modem, a printer or a communication channel.

IPARS - International Passenger Airline Reservation System. Originally developed by IBM for its nominal purpose, but fast becoming a generic term for any airline protocol.

ISO - International Standards Organization responsible for development of general network protocols.

Leased Line - A telecommunication channel leased from the Common Carrier between two or more fixed locations. Charges are usually a fixed sum per month.

Light Emitting Diode (LED) - A semiconductor low current, low voltage lamp. Special LEDs are used as generators of light energy for lasers and for fiber optics transmission.

Limited Distance Modem - A device which permits data communications over short distances.

Link - A transmission path between two data sets, channels or switching offices.

Loading Coil - Inductance added to a telephone line to improve its frequency distortion at low frequencies. Not recommended for data transmission.

Local Loop - A pair of wires connecting the telephone subscriber to the local telephone office.

LRC - Longitudinal Redundancy Check, a simple parity check of a block of data.

Mark - A signal on a data circuit indicating a binary "one".

MIL-STD-188-C - A US military standard similar to RS-232-C, except that the voltage levels are different.

Modem - What this book is all about.

Modem Eliminator - Sometimes used to describe a limited distance modem, sometimes to describe a "null" modem.

Multiplexer - A device to combine several signals into a composite data stream for economic transmission. Techniques employed are frequency division (FDM) and time division (TDM)

NAK - Negative Acknowledgment, a communication control character indicating that some information was received incorrectly.

Network - A series of points interconnected by communications channels, often on a switched basis. Networks are either common to all users or are privately leased from common carriers for exclusive use by a customer.

Node - A point in a transmission system, where lines or trunks from many systems meet. Also the point in a network, where switching occurs.

Null Modem - A cable or dual-sided plug which allows the connection of two DCEs or two DTEs.

OOK - On/Off Keying, the simplest form of modulation consists of turning the signal on or off.

OSI - Open System Interconnection. Standardized procedures for exchange of information among terminal devices, computers, people, networks, processes, etc., that are "open" to one another for this purpose by virtue of their mutual use of these procedures. OSI is being developed by ISO and CCITT. It will provide a common basis for the coordination of standards development for the purpose of system interconnection within a seven layer model.

Packet - Data grouped for transmission through a public data network such as an X.25 network.

Packet Switching - Transfer of data by means of addressable packets, where a channel is only occupied for the duration of transmission of the packet. The channel is then available for transmission of other packets. In contrast with circuit switching, the data network determines routing during, rather then prior to, the transfer of a packet.

Parity Bit - An eighth bit added to the seven bits representing a character, so that the total of "one" or "mark" bits in a character including the parity bit, will be either even, for even parity, or odd, for odd parity.

PBX or PABX - Private Branch Exchange, telephone switching service usually at a customer's premises.

Phase Modulation - Method of modulation, where a binary "0" generates one phase value and the binary "1" generates another frequency. Phase values are frequently assigned to dibits or quadbits, rather than to single bits.

Post-Processing - The ability of a protocol analyzer to perform data analysis on data contained in a data capture buffer just as if the data were arriving in real time.

Protocol - A formal set of conventions governing the format and control of inputs and outputs between two communications devices or processes.

Protocol Converter - A device for translating output of one computer or terminal into formats which can be interpreted by another computer or terminal.

Public Telephone Network - Switched telephone network operated by the Common Carrier.

Quadrature Amplitude Modulation (QAM) - Modulation method used by high speed modems combining amplitude and phase modulation of the data signal.

Quadbit - A sequence of four bits associated with one signal element.

RAM - Random Access Memory, used to store temporary data in the computer.

ROM - Read Only Memory, used to store permanent data which can not be changed.

RS Standards - US Industry standards for interfacing computers to data communications equipment developed by EIA. The most popular interface standard in the US is RS-232-C.

Script File - User-written program required by the communications software to guide the data phone call after a connection has been established. Contains parameters such as the logon sequence, password, and menu selection.

SDLC - Synchronous Data Link Control, a synchronous data transmission protocol.

Space - A binary "zero", opposite of "mark".

Start/Stop Bits - Special character-delimiting bits used in asynchronous transmission.

Statistical Multiplexer - Multiplexer equipment, which dynamically allocates transmission capacity to only active channels, thus allowing better channel utilization than with regular multiplexers.

Store and Forward - A method of transmission in which messages received from one user are stored at intermediate points and retransmitted to other users whenever a transmission path is available. Used in packet switching networks.

Synchronous Transmission - Method of communication in which synchronization between the transmitter and receiver is achieved by sending timing signals independent of the transmitted characters. Timing can be common to all network stations or can be included in each block of data.

V. Standards - A series of voice grade recommendations (standards) developed by CCITT for interfacing and modem standards.

X. Standards - A series of CCITT recommendations for transmission of data over public data networks. The best known of these standards is X.25.

Directory of Manufacturers

*Audio Precision
P.O. Box 2209
Beaverton, OR 97075
(503) 297-4837

*Huntron, Inc.
15720 Mill Creek Blvd.
Mill Creek, WA 98012
(206) 743-3171

*National Instruments
12109 Technology Blvd.
Austin, TX 78727
(512) 259-9119

*NCI
6438 University Dr.
Huntsville, AL 35806
(205) 837-6667

*R.C. Electronics, Inc.
5386-D Hollister Ave.
Santa Barbara, CA 9311
(805) 964-6708

*Rapid Systems, Inc.
433 N. 34th St.
Seattle, WA 98103
(206) 547-8311

*Soltec Corp.
P.O. Box 792
San Fernando, CA 91341
(818) 767-0044

*Virtual Instruments Corp.
P.O. Box 668
Georgetown, CT 06829
(203) 544-8311

*Wayne Kerr, Inc.
600 West Cummings Park
Woburn, MA 01810
(617) 938-8390

* *Supplier of PC-based instruments*

Anritusu Corp.
5-10-27, Minamiazabu, Minato-ku
Tokoyo 106, Japan
03-446-1111

Ballantine Laboratories, Inc.
P.O. Box 97
Booton, NJ 07005
(201)335-0900

Beckman Industrial Corp.
630 Puente St.
Brea, CA 92621
(714) 773-8111

Booton Electronics Corp.
791 Route 10
Randolph, NJ 07869
(201) 584-1077

Cambridge Technology, Inc.
23 Elm St.
Watertown, MA 02172
(617) 923-1181

Coaxial Dynamics Inc.
15210 Industrial Pkwy.
Cleveland, OH 44135
(216) 267-2233

DATEL
General Electric Co.
11 Cabot Blvd.
Mansfield, MA 02048
(617) 339-9341

Dranetz Technologies, Inc.
P.O. Box 4019
Edison, NJ 08818
(201) 287-3680

Gould Inc.
Test & Measurement Group
19050 Pruneridge Ave.
Cupertino, CA 95-14
(408) 988-6800

Gould, Inc.
Recording Systems Division

3631 Perkins Ave.
Cleveland, OH 44114
(216) 361-3315

Hades Mfg. Corp.
151 Verdi St.
Farmingdale, NY 11735
(516) 249-1735

Hickok Electrical Instrument Co.
10514 Supont Ave.
Cleveland, OH 44108
(216) 541-8060

Hipotronics, Inc.
P.O. Drawer A
Brewster, NY 10509
(914) 279-8091

John Fluke Mfg. Co., Inc.
P.O. Box C9090
Everette, WA 98206
(206) 347-6100

Kyowa Dengyo Corp
10 Reuten Dr.
Closter, NJ 07624
(201) 784-0500

Leeds & Northrup Instruments
General Signal Corp.
*Numneytown Pike
North Wales, PA 19454
(216) 248-0040

Marconi Instruments Ltd.
3 Pearl Court
Allendale, NJ 07401
(201) 934 9050

Martel Electronics Corp.
373 Main St.
Salem, NH 03079
(603) 893-0886

Millivac Instruments, Inc.
P.O. Box 997
Schenectady, NY 12301
(518) 355-8300

Milwaukee Electronics Corp.
P.O. Box 23957
Milwaukee, WI 53223
(414) 358-4015

Multi-Amp Corp.
4271 Bronze Way
Dallas, TX 75237
(214) 333-3201

Non-Linear Systems, Inc.
P.O. Box N
Del Mar, CA 92014
(619) 481-3953

Optim Electronics
12401 Middlebrook Rd.
Germantown, MD 20874
(301) 428-7200

Panasonic Industrial Co.
Two Panasonic Way
Secaucus, NJ 07094
(201) 392-4050

Philips Test & Measuring Instruments, Inc.
85 McKee Drive
Mahwah, NJ 07430
(201) 529-3800

Preston Scientific
805 E. Cerritos Ave.
Anaheim, CA 92805

Quintek Test Solutions Ltd.
P.O. Box 6406
Nashau, NH 03063
(603) 889-0061

Racal-Dana Instruments Inc.
P.O. Box C-1954
Irvine, CA 92713
(714) 859-8999

RE Instruments Corp.
31029 Center Ridge Rd.
Westlake, OH 44145
(216) 871-7617

Simpson Electric Company
853 Dundee Ave.
Elgin, IL 60120
(312) 697-2260

Sycon-Weston
959 Cheney Ave.
Marion, OH 43302
(614) 382-5771

Tektronix, Inc.
P.O. Box 500
Beaverton, OR 97077
(503) 627-7111

Triplett Corp.
One Triplett Dr.
Bluffton, OH 45817
(419) 358-5015

Valhalla Scientific, Inc.
9955 Mesa Rim Rd.
San Diego, CA 91324
(619) 457-5576

Wavetek Corp.
9045 Balboa Ave.
San Diego, CA 92913
(619) 450-9971

Weinschel Engineering
One Weinschel La.
Gaithersburg, MD 20879
(301) 948-3434

Western Graphtec
12 Crysler St.
Irvine, CA 92718
(714) 770-6010

Yokogowa Corp. of America
200 Westpark Dr.
Peachtree City, GA 30269

List of CCITT V. Recommendations

Miscellaneous Definitions

V.1 - Equivalence between binary notation symbols and the significant conditions of a two-condition code.

V.2 - Power levels for data transmission over telephone lines.

V.4 - General structure of signals of Internationsl Alphabet No. 5 code for data transmission in the general switched telephone network.

V.5 - Standardization of data signalling rates for synchronous data transmission in the general switched telephone network

V.6 - Standardization of data signalling rates for synchronous data transmission on leased telephone-type circuits.

V.7 - Definitions of terms concerning data communication over the telephone network.

Interfaces and Voice-band Modems

V.10 - Electrical characteristics for unbalanced double-current interchange circuits for general use with integrated circuit equipment in the field of data communications.

V.11 - Electrical characteristics for unbalanced double-current interchange circuits for general use with integrated circuit equipment in the field of data communications.

V.15 - Use of acoustic coupling for data transmission.

V.16 - Medical analogue data transmission modems.

V.19 - Modems for parallel data transmission using telephone signalling frequencies.

V.20 - Parallel data transmission modems standardized for universal use in the general switched telephone network.

V.21 - 300 bits per second duplex modem standardized for use in the general switched telephone network.

V.22 - 1200 pits per second duplex modem standardized for use in the general switched telephone network and on point-to-point 2-wire leased telephone-type circuits.

V.22 *bis* - 2400 bits per second duplex modem using the frequency division technique standardized for use on the general switched telephone network and on point-to-point 2-wire leased telephone-type circuits.

V.23 - 600/1200-baud modem standardized for use in the general switched telephone network.

V.24 - List of definitions for interchange circuits between data terminal equipment and data circuit-terminating equipment.

V.25 - Automatic answering equipment and/or parallel automatic calling equipment on the general switched telephone network including procedures for disabling of echo control devices for both manually and automatically established calls.

V.25 *bis* - Automatic calling and/or answering equipment on the general switched telephone network (GSTN) using the 100-series interchange circuits.

V.26 - 2400 bits per second modem standardized for use on 4-wire leased telephone-type circuits.

V.26 *bis* - 2400/1200 bits per second modem standardized for use in the general switched telephone network.

V.26 *ter* - 4800/24 bits per second modem standardized for use in the general switched telephone network.

V.28 - Electrical characteristics for unbalanced double-current interchange circuits.

V.29 - 9600 bits per second modem standardized for use on point-to-point 4-wire leased telephone-type circuits.

V.31 - Electrical characteristics for single-current interchange circuits controlled by contact closure.

V.31 *bis* - Electrical characteristics for single-current interchange circuits using optocouplers.

V.32 - A family of 2-wire, duplex modems operating at data signalling rates of up to 9600 bit/s for use on the general switched telephone network and on leased telephone-type circuits.

Wideband Modems

V.35 - Data transmission at 48 kilobits per second using 60-108 kHz group band circuits.

V.36 - Modems for synchronous data transmission using 60-108 kHz ;group band circuits.

V.37 - Synchronous data transmission at a data signalling rate higher than 72 kbit/s using 60-108 kHz group band circuits.

Error Control

V.40 - Error indication with electromechanical equipment.

V.41 - Code-independent error-control system.

Transmission Quality and Maintenance

V.50 - Standard limits for transmission quality of data transmission.

V.51 - Organization of the maintenance of international telephone-type circuits used for data transmission.

V.52 - Characteristics of distortion and error-rate measuring apparatus for data transmission.

V.53 - Limits for the maintenance of telephone-type circuits used for data transmission.

V 54 - Loop test devices for modems.

V.55 - Specification for an impulsive noise measuring instrument for telephone-type circuits.

V.56 - Comparative tests of modems for use over telephone-type circuits.

V.57 - Comprehensive data test set for high data signalling rates.

Interworking with Other Networks

V.100 - Interconnection between public data networks (PDNs) and the public switched telephone network (PSTN).

V.110 - Support of data terminal equipments (DTEs) with V-series type interfaces by an integrated services digital network (ISDN).

Standards Organizations

American National Standards Institute (ANSI)
1430 Broadway
New York, NY 10018

Electronic Industries Association (EIA)
Standards Sales
2001 I Street N.W.
Washington, D.C. 20006

IEEE Standards Office
345 E. 47th Street
New York, NY 10017

GSA - Federal Standards
General Services Administration
Bldg. 197, (Washington Navy Yard)
Washington, D.C. 20407

International Organization for Standardization (ISC)
Central Secretariat
1, Rue de Varembe
CH-1211 Geneva, Switzerland

CCITT, General Secretariat
International Telecommunications Union
Place des Nations
1211 Geneva 20, Switzerland

Bell Communications
Research (BELLCORE)
Information Documentation
25 Lindsley Drive
Morristown, NJ 07960

Note:
CCITT standards may also be purchased from:

US Department of Commerce
National Technical Information Service (NTIS)
5285 Port Royal Road
Springfield, VA 22161

Additional information about the OSI model may be obtained from:

OMNICOM, Inc.
501 Church Street N.E., Suite 206
Vienna, VA 22180

ASCII Codes

THE AMERICAN STANDARD CODE FOR INFORMATION INTERCHANGE (ASCII)								
Binary	*Hex*	*Char*	*Binary*	*Hex*	*Char*	*Binary*	*Hex*	*Char*
0000000	00H		0100001	21H	!	1000010	42H	B
0000001	01H		0100010	22H	"	1000011	43H	C
0000010	02H		0100011	23H	#	1000100	44H	D
0000011	03H		0100100	24H	$	1000101	45H	E
0000100	04H		0100101	25H	%	1000110	46H	F
0000101	05H		0100110	26H	&	1000111	47H	G
0000110	06H		0100111	27H	'	1001000	48H	H
0000111	07H	<BELL>	0101000	28H	(	1001001	49H	I
0001000	08H	<BKSP>	0101001	29H	)	1001010	4AH	J
0001001	09H	<TAB>	0101010	2AH	*	1001011	4BH	K
0001010	0AH	<LF>	0101011	2BH	+	1001100	4CH	L
0001011	0BH		0101100	2CH	,	1001101	4DH	M
0001100	0CH		0101101	2DH	-	1001110	4EH	N
0001101	0DH	<CR>	0101110	2EH	.	1001111	4FH	O
0001110	0EH		0101111	2FH	/	1010000	50H	P
0001111	0FH		0110000	30H	0	1010001	51H	Q
0010000	10H		0110001	31H	1	1010010	52H	R
0010001	11H		0110010	32H	2	1010011	53H	S
0010010	12H		0110011	33H	3	1010100	54H	T
0010011	13H		0110100	34H	4	1010101	55H	U
0010100	14H		0110101	35H	5	1010110	56H	V
0010101	15H		0110110	36H	6	1010111	57H	W
0010110	16H		0110111	37H	7	1011000	58H	X
0010111	17H		0111000	38H	8	1011001	59H	Y
0011000	18H		0111001	39H	9	1011010	5AH	Z
0011001	19H		0111010	3AH	:	1011011	5BH	[
0011010	1AH		0111011	3BH	;	1011100	5CH	\
0011011	1BH		0111100	3CH	<	1011101	5DH	]
0011100	1CH		0111101	3DH	=	1011110	5EH	Λ
0011101	1DH		0111110	3EH	>	1011111	5FH	—
0011110	1EH		0111111	3FH	?	1100000	60H	'
0011111	1FH		1000000	40H	@	1100001	61H	a
0100000	20H	space	1000001	41H	A	1100010	62H	b
1100011	63H	c	1101101	6DH	m	1110111	77H	w
1100100	64H	d	1101110	6EH	n	1111000	78H	x
1100101	65H	e	1101111	6FH	o	1111001	79H	y
1100110	66H	f	1110000	70H	p	1111010	7AH	z
1100111	67H	g	1110001	71H	q	1111011	7BH	{
1101000	68H	h	1110010	72H	r	1111100	7CH	|
1101001	69H	i	1110011	73H	s	1111101	7DH	}
1101010	6AH	j	1110100	74H	t	1111110	7EH	~
1101011	6BH	k	1110101	75H	u	1111111	7FH	Δ
1101100	6CH	l	1110110	76H	v			

Note. Control codes denoted by < > (BKSP = backspace, TAB = tabulate, LF = line feed, CR = carriage return.)

Voice Grade DDD Modems

Company Model	Data rate (bps)	Modulation method	Transmission mode	Synchronization	Calling mode	Price $ (quantity)	Notes, features
ANCHOR AUTOMATION INC. 6913 Valjean Ave., Van Nuys, CA 91406, (818) 997-7758							
Express I	300, 1200	FSK, DSK, DPSK	half, full duplex	asynch	auto dial/ auto answer	299(Q1)	Bell 212A, Hayes compatible; plugs into IBM PC/AT/XT; includes LYNC software
Lightning 24	300, 1200, 2400	FSK, PSK, DPSK, QAM	half, full duplex	asynch, synch	auto dial/ auto answer	499(Q1)	Bell 212A, 1224, CCITT, V.22 bis compatible
Volksmodem 12	300, 1200	FSK, PSK, DPSK	half, full duplex	asynch	auto dial/ auto answer	199(Q1)	Bell 212A, Hayes compatible
ANDERSON JACOBSON INC. 521 Charcot Ave., San Jose, CA 95131, (408) 435-8520							
AJ 2412-STH	300, 1200, 2400	FSK, QAM	half, full duplex	asynch, synch	auto dial/ auto answer	395(Q1)	Bell 103, 212A, CCITT V.22, V.22 bis, Hayes compatible
AJ 2441-1	300, 1200, 2400	FSK, QAM	half, full duplex	asynch, synch	auto dial/ auto answer	695(Q1)	Bell 103, 212A, CCITT V.21, V.22, V.22 bis compatible; rackmount or standalone
AJ 9631-5	4800, 9600	QAM, TCM	full duplex	synch	auto dial/ auto answer	2,995(Q1)	CCITT V.32 compatible, rackmount or standalone
ASHER TECHNOLOGIES INC. 1009 Mansell Rd., Roswell, GA 30076, (404) 993-4590							
Quadmodem II	300, 1200, 2400		half, full duplex	asynch	auto dial/ auto answer	425-695(Q1); 276-452(Q100)	Bell 103, 212A, CCITT V.22 bis compatible; plugs into IBM bus compatible; includes CROSSTALK XVI software
AT&T INFORMATION SYSTEMS One Speedwell Ave., Morristown, NJ 07960, (800) 247-1212							
4024	2400	FSK, QAM	half, full duplex	asynch, synch	auto dial/ auto answer	750(Q1)	Bell 103, 212, CCITT V.22 bis compatible
4112	1200	FSK	full duplex	asynch	auto dial/ auto answer	489(Q1)	Bell 103, 212, CCITT V.22 bis compatible; plugs into PC 6300, IBM PC bus compatible; includes SoftCall software
4112V	1200	FSK	full duplex	asynch	auto dial/ auto answer	599(Q1)	Bell 103, 212, CCITT V.22 bis compatible; plugs into PC 6300, IBM PC bus compatible; includes Communications Manager software
BIZCOMP CORP. 532 Mercury Dr., Sunnyvale, CA 94086, (408) 733-7800							
2110	300, 1200	FSK, PSK, DPSK	half, full duplex	asynch	auto dial/ auto answer	449(Q1); 225(Q100)	Bell 212, Hayes compatible; plugs into IBM PC or compatible
4120	300, 1200	FSK, PSK, DPSK	half, full duplex	asynch	auto dial/ auto answer	499(Q1); 249(Q100)	Bell 212, Hayes compatible
4124	300, 1200, 2400	FSK, PSK, DPSK, QAM	half, full duplex	asynch	auto dial/ auto answer	599(Q1); 349(Q100)	Bell 212, CCITT V.22 bis compatible
BYTCOM INC. 2169 Francisco Blvd., San Rafael, CA 94901, (415) 485-0700							
24/12 CONTAC PLUS	300, 1200, 2400	FSK, PSK, QAM	half, full duplex	asynch, synch	auto dial/ auto answer	389(Q1)	Bell 103, 113, 212, CCITT V.22 bis compatible; plugs into IBM PC or compatible
24/72 FASTLINK	300, 1200, 2400, 7200	FSK, PSK, QAM	half, full duplex	asynch, synch	auto dial/ auto answer	899(Q1)	Bell 103, 113, 212, CCITT V.22 bis compatible
212PC CONTAC	300, 1200	FSK, PSK	half, full duplex	asynch	auto dial/ auto answer	299(Q1)	Bell 103, 113, 212 compatible; plugs into IBM PC or compatible
CERMETEK MICROELECTRONICS INC. 1308 Borregas Ave., Sunnyvale, CA 94088-3565, (408) 752-5000							
1200SM	300, 1200	FSK, PSK	full duplex	asynch	auto dial/ auto answer	595(Q1)	Bell 103, 212A compatible
1200SPC	300, 1200	FSK, PSK	full duplex	asynch	auto dial/ auto answer	345(Q1)	Bell 103, 212A compatible; includes software
2400 SPC	300, 1200, 2400	FSK, PSK, QAM	full duplex	asynch	auto dial/ auto answer	445(Q1)	Bell 103, 212A compatible; includes software

Company, Model	Data rate (bps)	Modulation method	Transmission mode	Synchronization	Calling mode	Price $ (quantity)	Notes, features
CODEX CORP. Maresfield Farm, 7 Blue Hill River Rd., Canton, MA 02021-1097, (800) 426-1212							
224 Series	300, 1200, 2400	QAM	full duplex	asynch, synch	auto dial/ auto answer		Bell 103, 212, CCITT V.22, V.25 compatible
2300 Series	4800, 9600	QAM	full duplex	synch			
2600 Series	4800-19.2K	QAM, TCM	full duplex	synch	auto dial/ auto answer		CCITT V.27 bis, V.29 compatible; point-to-point
COMDATA CORP. 7900 N. Nagle Ave., Morton Grove, IL 60053, (312) 470-9600							
212E2-32	1200	PSK	full duplex	asynch	manual orig./ manual answer		Bell 212A compatible
224	300, 1200, 2400	FSK, PSK	full duplex	asynch	auto dial/ auto answer		Bell 103, 212A, CCITT V.22 bis compatible
1200	300, 1200	FSK, PSK	full duplex	asynch	auto dial/ auto answer		Bell 103, 212A compatible
COMPUTER COMMUNICATIONS SPECIALISTS INC. 6683 Jimmy Carter Blvd., Norcross, GA 30071, (404) 441-3114							
Audiomodem Audiomodem II	1200	FSK	half duplex	asynch	auto dial/ auto answer		Bell 202 compatible, verbal response to inputs from touch-tone phone or hand-held terminal
CONCORD DATA SYSTEMS 397 Williams St., Marlborough, MA 01752, (617) 460-0808							
224 Autodial	1200, 2400	DPSK, QAM	full duplex	asynch, synch	auto dial/ auto answer	450(Q1)	Bell 212, CCITT V.22, V.22 bis compatible
224 Series II	300, 1200, 2400	FSK, DPSK, QAM	full duplex	asynch, synch	auto dial/ auto answer	695(Q1)	Bell 103, 212, CCITT V.22, V.22 bis compatible; MNP error correction
V.32 Trellis	4800, 9600	QAM	full duplex	asynch, synch	auto dial/ auto answer	3,495(Q1)	CCITT V.32 compatible
CTS FABRI-TEK INC. (DATACOMM PRODUCTS DIV.) 6900 Shady Oak Rd., Eden Prairie, MN 55344, (612) 941-9100							
2424ADH	110, 300, 600, 1200, 2400	FSK, DPSK, QAM	full duplex	asynch, synch	auto dial/ auto answer	395(Q1)	Bell 103, 113, 212A, CCITT V.22 bis, V.22 AIB, Hayes compatible
2424AMH	110, 300, 600, 1200, 2400	FSK, DPSK, QAM	full duplex	asynch, synch	auto dial/ auto answer	495(Q1)	Bell 103, 113, 212A, CCITT V.22 bis, V.22 AIB; Hayes compatible
Half-Pak #24	110, 300, 600, 1200, 2400	FSK, DPSK, QAM	full duplex	asynch, synch	auto dial/ auto answer	395(Q1)	Bell 103, 113, 212A, CCITT V.22 bis, V.22 AIB compatible, plugs into IBM PC/AT/XT, Portable
DATA RACE INC. 12758 Cimarron Path, San Antonio, TX 78249, (512) 692-3909							
RACE I & II	1200-19.2K	FSK, PSK	full duplex	asynch	auto dial/ auto answer	1,495/1,695(Q1)	Bell 103 compatible
RACE I & II AF	1200-19.2K	FSK, PSK	full duplex	asynch	auto dial/ auto answer	1,645/1,845(Q1)	Bell 103, 212A compatible
RACE-BMX	1200-19.2K	PSK	half duplex	asynch	auto dial/ auto answer	1,195(Q1)	
DATAGRAM CORP. 11 Main St., East Greenwich, RI 02818, (800) 235-5030							
DCE-224	300, 1200, 2400	FSK, PSK, QAM	half, full duplex	asynch, synch	auto dial/ auto answer	695(Q1)	Bell 103, 202, 212A, 224, CCITT V.21, V.22, V.22 bis, V.23 compatible, plugs into IBM PC
DCE-9600	4800, 7200, 9600	QAM	full duplex	synch		1,495(Q1)	CCITT V.29 compatible
DCE-14400T	4800, 7200, 9600, 14.4K	QAM	full duplex	synch		4,995(Q1)	CCITT V.29 compatible
DATALINK READY INC. (ARK ELECTRONIC PRODUCTS) P.O. Box 2169, Melbourne, FL 32902-2169, (305) 676-0500							
DLR9.6/208B	4800, 9600	DPSK, QAM	half duplex	synch	auto dial/ auto answer	2,160(Q1); 1,620(Q100)	Bell 208B compatible, rackmount
DLR12,000 DIAL	9600, 12K	QAM	half duplex	synch	auto dial/ auto answer	2,900(Q1); 2,175(Q100)	rackmount
24K Plus	1200, 2400	DPSK	half duplex	synch	auto dial/ auto answer	545-595(Q1); 409-446(Q100)	Bell 103, 212A compatible, plugs into IBM PC or rackmount
DECATEK INC. 4754C N. Royal Atlanta Dr., Tucker, GA 30084, (404) 493-7273							
ZIPmodem/MF	9600	QAM	half duplex	synch	auto dial/ auto answer	1,995(Q1)	CCITT V.27, V.29 compatible
ZIPmodem/PC	9600	QAM	half duplex	synch	auto dial/ auto answer	2,995(Q1)	CCITT V.27, V.29 compatible; plugs into IBM PC/AT/XT
DIGITAL COMMMUNICATIONS ASSOCIATES INC. (DCA) 1000 Alderman Dr., Alpharetta, GA 30201-4199, (404) 442-4000							
DCA 932	9600	QAM	full duplex	synch		2,695(Q1)	CCITT V.29 compatible, multipoint

Company Model	Data rate (bps)	Modulation method	Transmission mode	Synchronization	Calling mode	Price $ (quantity)	Notes, features
DCA 940	14.4K	QAM	full duplex	synch		4,995(Q1)	CCITT V.29 compatible, built-in multiplexer
IRMA's FASTLINK	18K	FSK, DPSK, DAMQAM	half, full duplex	asynch	auto dial/ auto answer	1,995-2,395(Q1)	Bell 103, 212A, CCITT V.22, V.22 bis compatible; plugs into IBM PC or standalone; includes CROSSTALK software
DOWTY INFORMATION SYSTEMS (DIV. OF DOWTY RFL INDUSTRIES INC.) Powerville Rd., Boonton, NJ 07005-0239, (201) 334-3100							
Quattro	2400	FSK, DPSK, QAM	half, full duplex	asynch, synch	auto dial/ auto answer	695(Q1)	Bell 103, 202S, 212A, CCITT V.21, V.22, V.22 bis, V.23 compatible; plugs into IBM PC
ELECTRONIC VAULTS INC. 12347-E Sunrise Valley Dr., Reston, VA 22091, (703) 620-3900							
upta 96/I	4800, 7200, 9600	FSK, DPSK		asynch	auto dial/ auto answer	895(Q1)	CCITT V.29 compatible; plugs into IBM PC or compatible, error detection/correction
upta 96/S	4800, 7200, 9600	FSK, DPSK		asynch	auto dial/ auto answer	995(Q1)	CCITT V.29 compatible, standalone, error detection/correction
EVEREX SYSTEMS INC. 48431 Milmont Dr., Fremont, CA 94538, (415) 498-1111							
Evercom II EV-920	300, 1200	FSK, DPSK	full duplex	asynch	auto dial/ auto answer	249(Q1)	Bell 212A compatible; plugs into IBM PC/AT/XT; includes Bitcom software
Evercom 24 EV-940	300, 1200, 2400	FSK, DPSK, QAM	full duplex	asynch	auto dial/ auto answer	289(Q1)	Bell 212A, CCITT V.22 bis compatible; plugs into IBM PC/AT/XT; includes Bitcom software
FASTCOMM DATA CORP. 12347-E Sunrise Valley Dr., Reston, VA 22091, (703) 620-3900, (800) 521-2496							
FASTCOMM 2400	300, 1200, 2400	FSK, DPSK		asynch	auto dial/ auto answer	599-619(Q1); 389-402(Q100)	Bell 103, 212A, CCITT V.22 bis, Hayes compatible; plugs into IBM PC
FASTCOMM 2496	300, 1200, 2400, 4800, 7200, 9600	FSK, DPSK		asynch	auto dial/ auto answer	979-999(Q1); 636-649(Q100)	Bell 103, 212A, CCITT V.22 bis, V.29 compatible; plugs into IBM PC
FASTCOMM 9600	4800, 7200, 9600	QAM		asynch	auto dial/ auto answer	899-919(Q1); 584-597(Q100)	CCITT V.29 compatible, plugs into IBM PC, error detection/correction
FUJITSU AMERICA INC. 3055 Orchard Dr., San Jose, CA 95134, (408) 946-8777							
M1921L	9600	QAM	full duplex	asynch	manual orig./ manual answer		CCITT V.29 compatible
M1923L	9600	QAM	full duplex	synch	manual orig./ manual answer		CCITT V.29 compatible
M1926L	14.4K	QAM	full duplex	synch	manual orig./ manual answer		CCITT V.29 compatible
GAMMALINK 2452 Embarcadero Way, Palo Alto, CA 94303, (415) 856-7421							
GammaComm	4800, 7200, 9600	QAM	half duplex	synch	auto dial/ auto answer	1,395(Q1); 1,046(Q100)	CCITT V.27, V.29 compatible; plugs into IBM PC/AT/XT
GammaFax	2400, 4800, 7200, 9600	QAM	half duplex	synch	auto dial/ auto answer	995(Q1); 746(Q100)	CCITT Group III Facsimilie compatible, plugs into IBM PC/AT/XT; PC-FAX dial-up product
GammaModem	4800, 7200, 9600	QAM	half duplex	synch	auto dial/ auto answer	1,495(Q1); 1,121(Q100)	CCITT V.27, V.29 compatible; standalone
GANDALF DATA INC. 1020 S. Noel Ave., Wheeling, IL 60090, (312) 459-6630							
ACCESS Series 12S	300, 1200	FSK, DPSK	full duplex	asynch, synch	auto dial/ auto answer	495(Q1)	Bell 103, 113, 212A compatible
ACCESS Series 24S	300, 1200, 2400	FSK, DPSK, QAM	full duplex	asynch, synch	auto dial/ auto answer	595(Q1)	Bell 103, 212A, CCITT V.22, V.22 bis compatible
SAM 201	2400	DPSK	half, full duplex	asynch, synch	auto dial/ auto answer	725(Q1)	Bell 201C, CCITT V.26 compatible
GENERAL DATACOMM INDUSTRIES INC. Rt. 63, Middlebury, CT 06762, (203) 574-1118							
DC 208B/A	4800	DPSK	half, full duplex	synch	auto dial/ auto answer	1,545(Q1)	Bell 208 compatible
Multiport 9600	9600	QAM	full duplex	aysnch, synch	auto dial/ auto answer	2,495(Q1)	CCITT V.29 compatible, integral 4-channel multiplexer
Multiport 14400	14.4K	QAM	full duplex	asynch, synch	auto dial/ auto answer	5,490(Q1)	CCITT V.29 compatible, integral 6-channel multiplexer
HAYES MICROCOMPUTER PRODUCTS INC. P.O. Box 105203, Atlanta, GA 30348, (404) 449-8791							
Smartmodem 1200	300, 1200	PSK	half, full duplex	asynch	auto answer	599(Q1)	Bell 103, 212A, CCITT V.22 compatible
Smartmodem	300, 1200,	FSK, DPSK,	half, full	asynch,	auto answer	899(Q1)	Bell, CCITT V.22, V.22 bis compatible

Company / Model	Data rate (bps)	Modulation method	Transmission mode	Synchronization	Calling mode	Price $ (quantity)	Notes, features
2400	2400	QAM	duplex	synch			
Smartmodem 2400B	300, 1200, 2400	FSK, DPSK, QAM	half, full duplex	asynch, synch	auto answer	739(Q1)	Bell, CCITT V.22, V.22 bis compatible; plugs into IBM PC or compatible
IDEASSOCIATES INC. 29 Dunham Rd., Billerica, MA 01821, (617) 663-6878							
IDEAcomm 1200	300, 1200	DPSK	half, full duplex	asynch	auto dial/ auto answer	495(Q1)	Bell 103, 212 compatible; plugs into IBM PC/AT/XT; includes IDEAcomm software
IDEAcomm 2400	300, 1200, 2400	QAM	half, full duplex	asynch	auto dial/ auto answer	695(Q1)	Bell 103, 212, CCITT V.22 bis compatible; plugs into IBM PC/AT/XT; includes IDEAcomm software
INCOMM DATA SYSTEMS 115 N. Wolf Rd., Wheeling, IL 60090, (312) 459-8881							
Rainbow 2400 PC	300, 600, 1200, 2400	FSK, QAM, QDPSK	full duplex	asynch	auto dial/ auto answer		Bell 103, 212, CCITT V.22, V.22 bis compatible; plugs into IBM PC/AT/XT or compatible; includes Quick Link software
Turbo 2400	300, 600, 1200, 2400	FSK, DPSK, QAM	full duplex	asynch, synch	auto dial/ auto answer		Bell 103, 212, CCITT V.22, V.22 bis compatible; includes Quick Link software
Turbo 4800	300, 600, 1200, 2400, 4800	FSK, DPSK, QAM	full duplex	asynch	auto dial/ auto answer		Bell 103, 212, CCITT V.22, V.22 bis compatible
INFINET INC. 40 High St., North Andover, MA 01845, (617) 681-0600							
224 Dial Modem	300, 1200, 2400	FSK, DPSK, QAM	full duplex	asynch, synch	auto dial/ auto answer	795(Q1); 715(Q100)	Bell 103, 212A, CCITT V.22, V.22 bis compatible; MNP error correction
IDM 144	9600, 12K, 14.4K	QAM, TCM	full duplex	synch	auto dial/ auto answer	6,100(Q1); 5,400(Q100)	CCITT V.33 compatible, private line, error correction
INMAC (DATACOM DIV.) 2350 Zanker Rd., San Jose, CA 95131, (408) 435-1700							
Clear Signal 2400	300, 1200, 2400	QAM	half, full duplex	asynch, synch	auto dial/ auto answer	459(Q1)	Bell 103, 212A, Hayes compatible
Clear Signal 4800	2400, 4800	QAM	half, full duplex	synch	manual orig./ manual answer	1,095(Q1)	CCITT V.27 compatible
Clear Signal 9600	4800, 7200, 9600	QAM	full duplex	synch	manual orig./ manual answer	1,495(Q1)	CCITT V.29 compatible
LEADING EDGE HARDWARE PRODUCTS INC. 225 Turnpike St., Canton, MA 02021, (800) 343-6833							
Model "L"	1200	FSK, PSK, QAM	half, full duplex	asynch	auto dial/ auto answer	149(Q1)	Bell 103, 212A compatible; plugs into IBM PC or compatible; includes Bitcom software
Model "L"	2400	FSK, PSK, QAM	half, full duplex	asynch	auto dial/ auto answer	289(Q1)	Bell 103, 212A compatible; plugs into IBM PC/AT/XT or compatible; includes Bitcom software
MICOM SYSTEMS INC. 4100 Los Angeles Ave., Simi Valley, CA 93062, (805) 583-8600							
M3124EH-S1	300, 1200, 2400	FSK, DPSK, QAM	full duplex	asynch, synch	auto dial/ auto answer	549(Q1); 439(Q100)	Bell 103, 212A, CCITT V.22, V.22 bis compatible; MNP error correction
MULTI-TECH SYSTEMS INC. 82 Second Ave. S.E., New Brighton, MN 55112, (612) 631-3550, (800) 328-9717							
MT212AH2	300, 1200	FSK, PSK, DPSK	half, full duplex	asynch	auto dial/ auto answer	399(Q1)	Bell, CCITT, Hayes compatible
MT224EC	300, 1200, 2400	FSK, PSK, DPSK, QAM	half, full duplex	asynch	auto dial/ auto answer	699(Q1)	Bell, CCITT, Hayes compatible; plugs into IBM PC/AT or compatible; MNP error correction
MT224EH	300, 1200, 2400	FSK, PSK, DPSK, QAM	half, full duplex	asynch, synch	auto dial/ auto answer	749(Q1)	Bell, CCITT, Hayes compatible; MNP error correction
NCR COMTEN INC. 2700 Snelling Ave. North, St. Paul, MN 55113, (612) 638-7944							
7164	4800	QAM	full duplex	synch		2,995(Q1)	IBM 3864 compatible
7165	9600	QAM	full duplex	synch		3,995(Q1)	IBM 3865, CCITT V.29 compatible
7166	14.4K	TCM	full duplex	synch		3,995(Q1)	CCITT V.33 compatible
NOVATION INC. 20409 Prairie St., Chatsworth, CA 91311, (818) 996-5060							
1200XE	300, 1200	FSK, PSK	half, full duplex	asynch	auto dial/ auto answer	299(Q1); 249(Q100)	Bell 103, 212 compatible
1200XE/HC		FSK, PSK	half, full duplex	asynch	auto dial/ auto answer	199(Q1); 179(Q100)	Bell 103, 212 compatible; plugs into IBM PC
P2400	300, 1200, 2400	FSK, PSK, DPSK	half, full duplex	asynch, synch	auto dial/ auto answer	795(Q1); 495(Q100)	Bell 103, 212, 224, CCITT V.22 bis compatible; MNP error correction
PARADYNE CORP. 8550 Ulmerton Rd., Largo, FL 33540 (813) 530-2292							
FDX 2400 Plus	2400		full duplex	asynch, synch	auto dial/ auto answer	595(Q1); 565(Q100)	Bell 103, 113, 212A, CCITT V.22 bis compatible; plugs into IBM PC; MNP error correction

Company Model	Data rate (bps)	Modulation method	Transmission mode	Synchronization	Calling mode	Price $ (quantity)	Notes, features
HDX 9600/208B	4800, 9600	QAM	half duplex	synch	auto dial/ auto answer	1,995(Q1); 1,495(Q100)	Bell 208B compatible
208A/B	4800	DPSK	half duplex	synch	auto dial/ auto answer	1,295(Q1); 1,095(Q100)	Bell 208A/B compatible, plugs into IBM PC
PENRIL DATACOMM 207 Perry Parkway, Gaithersburg, MD 20877-2197, (301) 921-8600							
Datalink 2400	300, 1200, 2400	FSK, DPSK, QAM	half, full duplex	synch	auto dial/ auto answer	695(Q1)	Bell 103, 212A, CCITT V.22 bis compatible
Datalink 4800	2400, 4800	DPSK	half, full duplex	synch	auto dial/ auto answer	1,395(Q1)	Bell 208A/B, CCITT V.27 bis/ter compatible
Datalink 9600	2400, 4800, 7200, 9600	QAM	half, full duplex	synch	auto dial/ auto answer	1,795(Q1)	CCITT V.27 bis/ter, V.29 compatible
PRENTICE CORP. 266 Caspian Dr., Sunnyvale, CA 94088, (408) 734-9810							
P-208A/B	4800	DPSK	half, full duplex	synch	manual orig./ auto answer	1,295-1,395(Q1)	Bell 208A/B compatible, standalone or rackmount
P-2424	300, 1200, 2400	FSK, PSK, QAM	half duplex	asynch, synch	auto dial/ auto answer	595-695(Q1)	Bell 103, 212A, CCITT V.22 bis, Hayes compatible; standalone or rackmount
P-9600A/B	4800, 7200, 9600	QAM	half, full duplex	synch	manual orig./ auto answer	2,050-2,150(Q1)	CCITT V.29 compatible, standalone or rackmount
QUADRAM CORP. One Quad Way, Norcross, GA 30093, (404) 923-6666							
Quadmodem II	110, 300, 1200, 2400	PSK	half, full duplex	asynch	auto dial/ auto answer	425-695(Q1)	Hayes compatible, plugs into IBM PC or compatible, includes CROSSTALK XVI software
RACAL-MILGO 1601 N. Harrison Parkway, Sunrise, FL 33323, (305) 476-5609							
9600VP	9600	QAM	half duplex	asynch, synch	auto dial/ auto answer	1,495(Q1); 1,271(Q100)	Bell 103, 212, CCITT V.29 compatible; MNP error correction
RM-1822D	18K	FSK, PSK, DPSK, QAM (multicarrier)	half duplex	asynch	auto dial/ auto answer	2,395(Q1); 2,036(Q100)	Bell 103, 212A, CCITT V.22, V.22 bis compatible; minimal fallback
RM-9632	4800, 9600	QAM, TCM	full duplex	synch	auto dial/ auto answer	3,500(Q1); 2,975(Q100)	CCITT V.32 compatible
RACAL-VADIC 1525 McCarthy Blvd., Milpitas, CA 95035, (408) 946-2227							
2400VP	300, 1200, 2400	FSK, DPSK, QAM	full duplex	asynch, synch	auto dial/ auto answer	595(Q1); 488(Q50)	Bell 103, 212, CCITT V.22 bis compatible; MNP error correction
4850PA	2400, 4800	DPSK	half duplex	synch	auto dial/ auto answer	1,295(Q1); 1,100(Q50)	Bell 208B, CCITT V.27 ter compatible
9600VP	300, 1200, 9600	FSK, DPSK, QAM	half, full duplex	asynch, synch	auto dial/ auto answer	1,495(Q1); 1,270(Q50)	Bell 103, 212, Vadic compatible; MNP error correction
TEK-COM CORP. 120 Charcot Ave., San Jose, CA 95131, (408) 435-9515							
TC212AD	300, 1200	FSK, DPSK	half, full duplex	asynch	auto dial/ auto answer	359(Q1)	Bell 103A, 212A, Hayes compatible
TC2400 PC1	300, 1200, 2400	FSK, PSK, QAM	half, full duplex	asynch	auto dial/ auto answer	499(Q1); 374(Q100)	Bell 103A, 212A, CCITT V.22 bis compatible; plugs into IBM PC or compatible
TC2400 SA	300, 1200, 2400	FSK, PSK, QAM	half, full duplex	asynch, synch	auto dial/ auto answer	550(Q1); 412(Q100)	Bell 103A, 212A, CCITT V.22 bis, Hayes compatible
TELENETICS CORP. 895 E. Yorba Linda Blvd., Suite H, Placentia, CA 92670, (714) 524-5770							
24a	300, 1200, 2400	FSK, PSK, DPSK, QAM	full duplex	asynch	auto dial/ auto answer	495(Q1); 347(Q100)	Bell 212A, CCITT V.22 bis compatible
24i	300, 1200, 2400	FSK, PSK, DPSK, QAM	full duplex	asynch	auto dial/ auto answer	495(Q1); 347(Q100)	Bell 212A, CCITT V.22 bis compatible; plugs into IBM PC or compatible
24s	300, 1200, 2400	FSK, PSK, DPSK, QAM	full duplex	asynch, synch	auto dial/ auto answer	695(Q1); 487(Q100)	Bell 212A, CCITT V.22 bis compatible
TOUCHBASE SYSTEMS INC. 16 Green Acre Lane, Northport, NY 11768, (516) 261-0423							
WorldLink 1200	300, 1200	FSK, PSK	full duplex	asynch	auto dial/ auto answer	199(Q1)	Bell 103, 212A, CCITT V.21, V.22, Hayes compatible
TRANSEND CORP. 884 Portola Rd., Portola Valley, CA 94025, (415) 851-3402							
PCM 1200	300, 1200	DPSK	half, full duplex	asynch	auto dial/ auto answer	159(Q1); 140(Q100)	Bell 212A compatible, plugs into IBM PC
TRI-DATA 505 E. Middlefield Rd., Mountain View, CA 94043, (415) 969-3700							
OZ Guardian 533	110, 300, 1200	FSK, PSK	half, full duplex	asynch	auto dial/ auto answer	750(Q1)	Bell 103, 212A compatible

Company Model	Data rate (bps)	Modulation method	Transmission mode	Synchronization	Calling mode	Price $ (quantity)	Notes, features
TYMNET (MCDONNELL DOUGLAS NETWORK SYSTEMS CO.) 2710 Orchard Parkway, San Jose, CA 95134, (408) 942-5254							
932	1200, 2400	DPSK, QAM	full duplex	asynch, synch	auto dial/ auto answer	495(Q1); 455(Q100)	Bell 212A, CCITT V.22 bis compatible
933	1200, 2400	DPSK, QAM	full duplex	asynch	auto dial/ auto answer	795(Q1); 652(Q100)	Bell 212A, CCITT V.22 bis compatible; X.PC error correction
934	1200, 2400	DPSK, QAM	full duplex	asynch	auto dial/ auto answer	1,295(Q1); 1,115(Q100)	Bell 212A, CCITT V.22 bis compatible; X.PC error correction, supports up to 3 terminals or PCs over same dial-up line
UNIVERSAL DATA SYSTEMS 5000 Bradford Dr., Huntsville, AL 35805, (205) 721-8000							
208A/B	4800	DPSK	half, full duplex	synch	manual orig./ auto answer	1,295(Q1)	Bell 208A/B compatible
9600A/B	4800, 7200, 9600	QAM	half, full duplex	synch	manual orig./ auto answer	1,995(Q1)	Bell 208A/B, CCITT V.29 compatible; diagnostics
V.33	9600, 12K, 14.4K	QAM, TCM	full duplex	synch	manual orig./ auto answer	2,995(Q1)	CCITT V.29, V.33 compatible
US ROBOTICS INC. 8100 N. McCormick Blvd., Skokie, IL 60076, (312) 982-5001							
Courier 2400e	300, 1200, 2400	FSK, DPSK, QAM	half, full duplex	asynch	auto dial/ auto answer	699(Q1)	Bell 103, 212A, CCITT V.22 bis compatible; MNP error correction
Courier HST	300, 1200, 2400, 9600	FSK, DPSK, QAM, TCM	half, full duplex	asynch	auto dial/ auto answer	995(Q1)	Bell 103, 212A, CCITT V.22 bis compatible
VARmodem 2400	300, 1200, 2400	FSK, DPSK, QAM	half, full duplex	asynch	auto dial/ auto answer	499(Q1)	Bell 103, 212A, CCITT V.22 bis compatible; plugs into IBM PC bus
VEN-TEL INC. 2342 Walsh Ave., Santa Clara, CA 95051, (408) 727-5721							
2400 Plus	300, 1200, 2400	FSK, DPSK, QAM	half, full duplex	asynch	auto dial/ auto answer	695(Q1)	Bell 103, 113, 212A, CCITT V.22, V.22 bis compatible
Half Card	300, 1200	FSK, DPSK	half, full duplex	asynch	auto dial/ auto answer	549(Q1)	Bell 103, 212A compatible; plugs into IBM PC/AT/XT or compatible; includes CROSSTALK XVI software
Half Card 24	300, 1200, 2400	FSK, DPSK, QAM	half, full duplex	asynch	auto dial/ auto answer	695(Q1)	Bell 103, 113, 212A, CCITT V.22, V.22 bis compatible; plugs into IBM PC/AT/XT or compatible; includes CROSSTALK XVI software
VISIONARY ELECTRONICS INC. 141 Parker Ave., San Francisco, CA 94118, (415) 751-8811							
Visionary 1200XT	300, 1200	FSK, PSK, DPSK	half, full duplex	asynch	auto dial/ auto answer	495(Q1); 223(Q100)	Bell 212A, CCITT V.21, V.22, Hayes compatible
WESTERN DATACOM 5083 Market St., Youngstown, OH 44512, (216) 788-6583							
424 Error Free	300, 1200, 2400	FSK, DPSK, QAM	full duplex	asynch, synch	auto dial/ auto answer	645(Q1); 419(Q100)	Bell 103, 113, 212, CCITT V.22 bis, Vadic compatible; MNP error correction
MESA424	300, 1200, 2400	FSK, DPSK, QAM	full duplex	asynch	auto dial/ auto answer	995(Q1); 646(Q100)	Bell 103, 113, 212, CCITT V.22 bis compatible
WorldCom 200	300, 1200	FSK, DPSK	half, full duplex	asynch	auto dial/ auto answer	495(Q1); 321(Q100)	Bell 103, 113, 202, CCITT V.21, V.23, Videotex compatible

Bibliography

"Acoustic Coupling for Data Transmission," Thomas J. McShane, *Digital Design*, June 1980. Description of various problems inherent to acoustic couplers.

"Advances in Lightwave Systems Research," Tingye Li, *AT&T Technical Journal*, January 1987. Latest in fiber technology.

All About Microcomputer Modems, Datapro, July 1986. Tutorial on modems and results of reader surveys. Datapro conducts frequent surveys of various telecommunications equipment.

"Analyzers Keep Pace With Communications Protocol Development," John H. Mayer, *Computer Design*, March 1, 1987. Survey of protocol analyzers.

"Asynchronous Communications: Shopping for Software," M. David Stone, *PC Magazine*, October 28, 1986. Review of 34 communication programs.

"Automatic Testing of Telecommunications Equipment," Richard S. Napier and Billy J. Henderson, *Test & Measurement World*, April 1987. Short review of automatic test methods.

The Basic Book of Data Communications, third edition, Codex Corporation. Simple introduction to modems.

"Beyond the Hayes Standard," M. David Stone, *PC Magazine*, November 25, 1986. Discussion of the Hayes standard and its extensions.

"Comparison Tests Streamline Complex Dial-Up Modem Measurements," John H. Humphrey and Gary S. Smock, *Electronic Design*, May 1987. Comparisons of signal-to-noise sensitivity of various modems.

"Corporate Communications," Frank J. Derfler, Jr., *PC Magazine*, September 3, 1985. Review of business communications software.

Data Communications, Networks, and Distributed Processing, Uyless D. Black, Reston Publishing, 1986. Good introductory course.

"Data Communication over the Telephone Network," *CCITT*, Volume VIII, Facsimile VIII.1, 1985. Bible of modem standards.

Data Communications Testing, Members of Hewlett-Packard Technical Staff. Excellent handout during in-house seminars.

Data Modem Selection and Evaluation Guide, Vess V. Vilips, Artech Press, 1972. Early description of modem applications.

Digital Communications, Kamilo Feher et al, Prentice Hall, 1981. Theoretical background of data communication.

"Evaluate Transmission-Cable Merits With Eye-Pattern Tests," Paul G. Schreier, *EDN*, October 1978. Review of "eye" pattern tests.

"Going for Speed," Bill Musgrave, *Datamation*, February 1987. Review of high speed modems.

"Hayes Faces Fight with IBM and AT&T," Dana Blankenhorn, *Data Communications*, February 1986. Comparison of Hayes HSI suggested standard with other synchronous standards.

"Low Cost Modem IC Plugs Into Power Lines," Dan L. Hariton and Paul F. Patterson, *Electronic Design*, October 2, 1986. Signetics modem chip set for transmission over power lines.

"Low-Cost Techniques Determine Group Delay," Dave Badger, *Microwaves & RF*, January 1985. Review of delay distortion measuring methods.

"Modems Accelerate Capabilities," Jesse Victor, *Mini-Micro Systems*, March 1987. Review of high speed modems.

"Modems Demystified," David Schwaderer, *PC Tech Journal*, July 1984. Excellent review of modem principles.

Modem Design Handbook, Exar Corporation. Review of design principles of Exar modem chips.

"Modems, British Standards," editors, *Electronics & Wireless World*, December 1985. Review of European developments.

"Modems," J.R. Davey, *Proceedings of IEEE*, November 1972. Classic paper about modems.

Micros and Modems, Telecommunication with Personal Computers, Jack M. Nilles, Reston Publishing, 1983. Review of data communication with references to modems.

"OSI 7 Levels of Standardization," Eric Hindin and John Helliwell, *PC-Week*, May 12, 1987. Good description of the OSI model.

PC Magazine, May 12, 1987. Special issue on data communications. Survey of modems, describing individual features.

"PC Security Modems," Howard Marks, *PC Magazine*, February 24, 1987. Review of securitty modems.

PC-Week, "Connectivity inserts." Contributions to *PC-Week* magazine dealing with latest developments in data communication and modem technology.

R2424DS Designer's Guide, Members of Rockwell Technical Staff, January 1985. Descripton of the 2400 bps modem chip set.

"RS-Type Communications Standards," L. Dennis Page, *Personal Engineering & Instrumentation News*, April 1987. Review of serial interface standards.

Science and Engineering Programs for the IBM PC, Cass R. Lewart, Prentice-Hall Inc., 1983. Programs include BER computations for various modulation methods.

The Small Computer Connection, Neil L. Shapiro, McGraw-Hill, 1984. Survey of bulletin boards.

Technical Aspects of Data Communication, John E. McNamara, Digital Press, 1982. Introductory course in data communication.

"Two-Chip Modem Suits High-Speed LAN Systems," Prasanna M. Shah, *EDN*, March 31, 1987. Description of the NE5080/81 chip set.

Understanding Data Communications, staff members of Texas Instruments, Howard W. Sams & Co., 1986, part of Radio Shack Library. Excellent introduction.

"Understanding PSK Demodulation Techniques," J. Mark Steber, *Microwaves & RF*, March and April 1984. Excellent theoretical description of PSK-based modulation techniques.

"V.22 Bis Defended," Dale Walsh, *Data Communications*, February 1986. Review of CCITT standards, in particular 2400 bps modems.

"23 Modems," Stephen Satchell, *Byte* Magazine, December 1986. Evaluation of 23 modems and their ability to handle impairments.

Index

acoustic modems, 220-222
Accunet, 34
adaptive equalizer, 165-166
American Standard Code for Information Interchange (ASCII), 10
amplitude modulation (AM), 52-53
analog-to-digital conversion, 1, 156
answering mode, 13
antistream timer, 192
application layer, 23
asynchronous operation, 10, 68
asynchronous transmission, 48
AT&T, 2, 16, 29, 32
AT commands, 119-120
AT command structure, 120-124
AT result codes, 123
attenuation, 10
attenuation tester, 252-254
auto dial, 109
automatic answer, 110
automatic speed select, 110
bandwidth, 8
battery options, 40
basic communications commands, 137-139
basic software features, 134-135
baud, 45-46, 48-49
baud rate device, 157
Baudot, Emil, 49
Bell standards, 181-187
Bell 103A modem, 55
Bell 212A modem, 55-56
Binary Synchronous Communication protocol, 70
bit error rate, 63-65
bit error rate test (BERT) set, 260-261
Black Box Corporation, 90
break-out boxes, 245-248
Byte Information Exchange (BIX), 141

call progress tone detector, 168
call progress tone recognition, 111

call variations, 36-40
Canoga Perkins Corporation, 214
carrier detect level, 192
carrier signal, 1
carrier system, 2
Carterphone decision, 2
CCITT, 176
CCITT standards, 176-177, 181, 187-191
channel capacity, 47
channel bank, 2
Channel Service Unit, 34-35
cheater cable, 107
chip design, 155-156
Class 5 office, 15-16
clock calendar, 112
Codex Corporation, 210, 225
commercial bulletin board session, 141-144
commercial modem options, 191-193
commercial modem features, 176-177
commercial modem software, 194
Common Carriers, 2-3
complete modem, 168-171
COM1/2/3/4 capability, 111
command and script files, 139-141
command-driven programs, 135-137
communications software, 133-134
compromise equalizer, 165
compromise fixed equalizer, 38
constellation diagrams, 54-56
converter (asynchronous to synchronous), 161
current standard weaknesses, 131-132

D/A converter 165
data access arrangement devices, 2-3
data buffer, 113
data communications equipment (DCE), 79
data compression, 152
data input control, 160
data link layer, 22, 24
data service unit, 34-35
data signaling rate, 48
data terminal equipment (DTE), 79
data/voice capability, 113
decision tree, 69
definition, 1
delay distortion, 10
delay distortion measurements, 254-255
demon dialer, 112
demodulator, 13
deregulation, 2-3
dial backup option, 193
dialing mode, 72
differential phase modulation, 57-58
Digital Equipment Corporation, 71
digital information transmission, 12-15
digital switched service, 29
digital-to-analog conversion, 1, 156
DIP switch settings, 106
direct access arrangement (DAA) circuit, 101
direct connect, 109

distortion equalizers, 37-38
echo, 18-19
echo suppressor disabler, 193
echo suppressors, 19-20
electrical noise, 10
electronic mail, 144-147
Emulex Corporation, 203
encoder, 163
energy spectrum, 51
error checking, 147-148
error correction, 114
escape code, 72
external modems, 99-105
  block diagram of, 102
eye patterns, 41-43

facsimile modems, 203-206
fallback option, 192
Federal Communications Commission (FCC), 2-3
  approval, 115
  requirements, 116-117
far-end echo, 18-19
fiber optic links, 29
fiber optics, 211
file transfer speed, 152-153
Fourier, 7
four-wire transmission, 8-9
frequency division multiplex system, 13-14, 52
frequency modulation (FM), 53-54
frequency shift keying, 53-54
front panel indicators, 111
full-duplex, 11-12, 19, 46, 59. 109

Gaussian error function, 63

half-duplex, 11-12, 19
handshake mode, 129
Hayes compatibility, 109
Hayes Corporation, 71, 119
Hayes modes of operation, 128-131
Hayes synchronous interface, (HSI), 71, 97
Humphrey, John H. 31
hybrids, 18-19
hybrid service, 27

impedance, 18
impulse noise, 256-257
indicator lights, 233-236
information services, 115-116
initial settings, 105-106
integrated analog device, 158-159
intelligent operation, 98-99
interface connections, 92-93
interface converters, 90
interface protocol, 75
internal modems, 99-105
  block diagram of, 101
internal switches, 115
International Standards Organization (ISO), 20

Kermit protocol, 151

Large Scale Integration, 3
leased line pricing, 32
leased voice grade lines, 29
Lighting Sponge, 209
limited distance modems, 207-214
  using AC power, 214-216
line conditioning, 31
line equalization, 35-36
line loading, 17

local area network, 21
local command mode, 129
local loop, 17
loopback tests, 237-238
Lotus Express, 145-147

menu-driven programs, 135-137
Microcom Network Protocol
(MNP), 150
modem, 13
modem address, 193
modem card size, 114
modem building blocks, 159-168
modem features, optional, 108-115
modem incompatibilities, 106-108
modem standards for PCs, 98-99
modulation method, 62
modulator, 13, 163-164
multiplexers, 224-227
multi-point network, 33

National Semiconductor
Corporation, 54
near-end echo, 18
network layer, 22, 24
noise measurements, 256-257
noise sensitivity testing, 243-244
non RS-232-C interfaces, 87-89
null modem, 81-85
NYNEX, 34
Nyquist, Harry, 45

Ohm's Law, 252
Omnicon Information Service,
25
on-line command mode, 129,
131

Open Systems Interconnect
(OSI) model, 20-21
application of, 23-25
current status of, 25
layers, 21-23
operating mode transitions, 130
originate/answer mode, 110
originating mode, 13
oscilloscope, 41

PAR meter, 258
parallel interface, 75
parity bit, 10
PCjr serial interface, 80
phase jitter, 10
phase jitter measurements, 258
physical layer, 21
point-to-point network, 32
presentation layer, 23
private lines, 27-29
proprietary high-speed modems,
202-203
protocol analyzer, 248-250
decision tree of, 249
protocols, 1, 10
Public Telephone Network, 15-16, 31, 36-37, 39, 59

quadratic amplitude modulation
(QAM), 47, 54, 58-59

RAM chip, 101
Rockwell International
Corporation, 156-157
ROM chip, 99
RJ11C telephone jacks, 111
RS2424DS, 156-157
basic building blocks
of, 158
RS-232-C connector, 77-78

RS-232-C serial interface, 75-82
RS-232-C signal levels, 81
RS-232-C testing, 244

sample rate device, 157
scrambler, 161-162
security modems, 223-243
self-adjustive adaptive equalizer, 38
self-test features, 236-243
serial interface, 75-76
serial interface specifications, 91
session layer, 22-23
Shannon, Claude, 46
signal processor, 157-158
signal quality option, 193
signaling options, 40
Signetics Corporation, 210, 214
simplex, 11-12, 59
smart modems, 124
Smock, Gary S., 31
specialized testers, 258-259
specific fixed equalizer, 38
S-Registers, 119, 124-128
stacking, 2, 13
steady noise, 256-257
stop bits, 10
switched capacitor design, 159
switched connection, 27-29
switched wideband digital service, 33-35
Switchway, 34
synchronous operation, 10
synchronous transmission, 67
synchronous transmission protocols, 70-72

Telebit Corporation, 202
Tele-Quality Associates, 31
telephone number storage, 112
terminal emulation, 135
testing capabilities, 112
testing methods, 231-232
tone dialer, 166-167
touch-tone decoder, 113
Trailblazer, 202-204
transmission distortion parameters, 36
transmission impairments, 10-11
transmission measuring sets, 251, 259
transmission medium, 8
transmission parameters, 31
transmission speed, 48-49
transmission speed/cost, 178-181
transmitter, 12-13
transmit level, 192
transport layer, 22, 24
trellis modulation, 59, 62, 190
two-wire transmission, 8-9
Tymnet, 141

universal asynchronous receiver and transmitter (UART), 85, 99, 102

Van Geer, John, 221
Very Large Scale Integration, 155
Via Net Loss method, 18
Viturbi decoder, 59
voice band, 7-8
voice-band channel, 45-47
voice-band circuit attenuation, 38
voice-band circuit envelope delay, 39
voice-band commercial modems, 194-202

high-speed modems, 200-202
low-speed modems, 195-197
medium-speed modems, 197-200
voice-band transmission facilities, 29-33
volume control speaker, 115

Wheatstone bridge, 18
wideband analog lines, 29
wideband modems, 217-219
wire/carrier option, 191

XMODEM protocol, 148-149
X.PC protocol, 149

YMODEM protocol, 150

WITHDRAWAL